Follow the Trail
Win the West

Richard S. Miner

Copyright © 2024, Richard S. Miner

ALL RIGHTS RESERVED.
No part of this publication may be reproduced, stored in a
retrieval system or transmitted in any form or by any
means whatsoever, whether electronic, mechanical,
magnetic recording, or photocopying, without the
prior written approval of the Copyright holder
or Publisher, excepting brief quotations
for inclusion in book reviews.

Published by:

Janaway Publishing, Inc.
Santa Maria, California 93454
www.janawaygenealogy.com

2024

ISBN: 978-1-59641-485-3

Front Cover Photo Credit: Kevin Lance

Made in the United States of America

Contents

Chapter One: HOME
 Found Ghost in the Attic 1
Chapter Two: FIELDS
 Mistress Mary quite contrary 5
Chapter Three: PAINTED POST
 Watch Out for that Felloe* 11
 Land of the Post 19
 Delivering the Goods – Take it easy 24
 Home – Happy Trails 29
Chapter Four: MILITIA
 Off to Lundy's Lane 33
 Decisions – Return 39
Chapter Five: OFF TO KENTUCKY
 Where? 47
 The Cumberland Gap – Allen Reaches Maturity 52
 A Revelation – In the Dark of Night 56
 Kentucky – Home away from Home 60
 Baptized Licking – Locust – What? 65
 Time to Leave – I'll Become a… 68
 Louisville – A New Life? 72
Chapter Six: "FREE" OHIO
 Lindale 77
 Cincinnati Docks – Down to the Docks 83
 Cincinnati Hills – Up to the Hills 85
 Lindale – A new Home 89
Chapter Seven: SOPHINA
 Life Moves On 95
 Courting – Western Style 99
Chapter Eight: CHANGING TIMES
 Pro-Slave Backlash 105
 Organize? – How 111
Chapter Nine: CINCINNATI SLAVERY
 Timorous Cautionists or Not 121
 Anti-Slavery Societies – Immediate Emancipation 131
 A Balm in Gilead – Lindale Baptists Heal Themselves 135
 Indiana Tour – Ripley, Believe it 146
Chapter Ten: SOCIETY BUSINESS
 The Mundane 151
Chapter Eleven: INDIANA
 An Ally 155
 Indiana Plans – Jeffersonville Meeting 161
 Risky Business – Ride through the Night 163

Chapter Twelve: ON THEIR WAY
- New Friends 167
- Indianapolis – Dreams 171
- Otter Creek, Indiana – A New Life 177
- Madison, Indiana – A Young Man's Dream 183

Chapter Thirteen: FARM LIFE
- Community Effort 189

Chapter Fourteen: NEIL'S CREEK ANTI-SLAVERY SOCIETY
- Developments 195

Chapter Fifteen: WISCONSIN?
- Why? 203
- News from Wisconsin – Moving On 205
- Wisconsin Politics – What's Happening? 209

Chapter Sixteen: GETTING INVOLVED
- Support 213
- Racine – Anti-Slavery Society Meeting 217
- Time to Meet – Plans 225
- Private Lives, Public Lives – Sad Days 229

Chapter Seventeen: DIFFERENT OPPORTUNITIES, DIFFERENT PLACES
- California Ho – Gold – Yes. Ice? 235
- Kansas? 238
- Moving On – Epic Journey to Walla Walla, WA 245

Chapter Eighteen: COMING TOGETHER?
- Mitchell, Iowa 253
- Mitchell Reunion 2 – Not to Be 258

Chapter Nineteen: MARYSVILLE? MITCHELL? 263
- Off to Marysville – Separate Ways 267
- Long Way to Go – Through Better or Worse 274
- Easy Ways? – Well... 277

Chapter Twenty: WELCOME TO SAN FRANCISCO
- The Emperor 283

Chapter Twenty-One: MARYSVILLE
- Long Awaited Family Reunion, sort of 287

Chapter Twenty-Two: HOME
- Marysville, Mitchell, Mattole? 293
- Too Long Delayed – Mitchell Reunion 298
- Welcome Home – Mr. Adventure 301

Chapter Twenty-Three: AND THEN...
- Again 309
- On to the Mattole River – The Marysville Settlers 313
- On to the Mattole Valley – Via the Mattole River 318

Epilogue: Someday Dreams Come True 326
Afterword: Source Notes 329
Illustrations 353
About the Author 354

Introduction

Follow the Trail, Win the West follows a single character whose life story illustrates the real history of western expansion. Attempting to trace that history led me to study legal and financial issues, local, state, and federal government maneuvering, politics, and racial conflicts. There's no doubt that it is a complex story and no doubt that I found it all much more intriguing than cowboy, John Wayne, or mountain men legends. It's my hope that readers will enjoy the complexity and become as intrigued as I have. If so, they may see relevant parallels in our age of division with this previous age, the age that finally led to the US Civil War.

Searching out all the details led me to many fine local librarians and historians. Meeting and communicating with them became a favorite activity. Small towns like Painted Post, NY, Mitchell, IA, Eureka, CA and others all have people dedicated to preserving their local history, and all I had to do was express my interest and they helped and then helped some more. I go into some detail about their efforts, and I attempt to express my appreciation in the Afterword, subtitled Source Notes. In the age of the Web, I do not use traditional source notations and instead concentrate on praising the really helpful people and sources. Finally, I want to express heartfelt thanks to my persevering editor, a true professional and careful reader, Carol Van Mater-Miner. Without her help, dear readers, you would have had good reason to say, often, something like "What?"

Chapter One

Home

Found Ghost in the Attic

Thump! Bill and I, startled, awoke suddenly. We knew that noise; it was the ladder up to the attic, in the closet in the corner of our bedroom, hitting the floor. Something had let it down clumsily. We saw the shadow, a man. We gasped or made some other noise; the shadow responded, "Shut Up!" Who was this? Not Dad: he did not say things like that. As far as we knew the whole WWII generation never said things like that. If "we" did, Mom washed our mouths out with soap. We shut up; ghosts might say things like that. Except for that thump and "shut up", it made little noise; did it glide? It went up the ladder to the attic and we heard nothing for what seemed like a long time. Then our bedroom door creaked shut. The thing had managed to exit the attic, climb down that ladder, and leave our bedroom without us noticing, a ghost for sure.

We didn't move for quite some time. Bill, four years older and braver, finally crept out of bed, opened the door an inch or two, and furtively searched the hallway. He looked all the way down past the bathroom to our sister's bedroom door. Nothing. No wait. Something on the floor. He was about to open the door further and even gave a thought to sneaking out to see more, when Dad came out of the master bedroom around the corner from our sister's. He picked up what we later assumed the ghost had dropped; sheets of papers, it seemed to Bill, at least they bent like paper—old, crumpled paper.

In the morning, in the rational light of day, as they say, we still had no rational thoughts about our nighttime visitor. Well, not 'no rational thoughts', only rational thoughts that did us no good. We did come up with questions about ghosts like how can they pick up papers, lower ladders, or open doors when they are ethereal, essentially without substance? We were too young, perhaps, to use words like ethereal, but not too young to think about gliding shadows able to move things. Maybe that's why he dropped the papers; not good at holding on to anything. One thought did help. Maybe the papers were ethereal too, without substance, an illusion. Forget the doors and the ladder, we wanted to know about those papers. That's what we wanted to find, and Dad had picked them up, one substantial being picking up something that must have been substantial. Where were they? We knew that answer instinctively; no rational thought was needed.

There were other mysteries in our young lives. Dad's bureau was one and a central one at that. We did not dare open or, at times, even approach such a sacred object; Dad would be offended. Dare I say the gods would be offended? Those papers were in that bureau; we knew it. If we were going to find out anything about them, we needed to risk invading Dad's sacred privacy. Scary thoughts worthy of following a scary night. We'd need to talk about this, and, if we decided to take the risk, we had to plan carefully.

Several days later, after a number of other exciting thoughts intervened, like jumping off the porch roof conveniently accessed through a window in our bedroom, (would I need my cape?), we decided we would take the ultimate leap and invade Dad's bureau. Of course, we planned to do this when Dad was at work leaving only Mom to, yes, distract. Bill would invade the bureau while I distracted Mom. That seemed right; he'd at least seen the papers we were now sure existed, and he was, as mentioned, older and braver. Besides I had a somewhat conniving mind, perfect for distracting Mom. My plan, yes, I hereby confess, it was my plan, seemed simple enough. I'd just casually mention to Mom that I wanted to ride my bike up Meadowbrook Road, you know, casually like a conniving 10-year-old. Up the road was allowed. And, the bike was inconveniently (or conveniently for connivers) in the front of the garage, inaccessible until the car was moved.

Mom would need to concentrate on finishing up whatever she was doing, find the keys, get the car out of the garage, and then take down the bike hung high up on the ceiling by a dad who knew a thing or two about kids. She'd then have to wait to put the car back, after I wandered as lazily as possible out of the garage with the bike. The car did have to go back right away; we were nothing if not an orderly family. The genius of the plan rested in the number of ways I could get in the way and delay long enough for Bill to rifle the bureau and find those papers. If I did my part well enough, he might even have time to read some before putting them back precisely as he had found them. That orderly thing applied most rigidly to whatever Dad kept in the bureau.

I must say I played my part masterfully. I started off by hiding the keys far from the stairs leading up to the master bedroom in the third or fourth place she would be likely to look. I got underfoot as effectively as the dog while she finished up the kitchen work. I blocked her way to the door and pretended to play tag. She always liked that and ran after me for quite a while. Good fortune was on my side, too. The car door was locked, and that lock never worked right. Must have been a good 3 or 4 minutes just opening the door. And of course, I got in the way and took my time getting out of the way, before she could back out. I insisted on "helping" her get the bike down; you can guess how that went. No rush getting the bike out of the garage; and I, artfully playing stupid, put down the bike stand with the bike squarely in front of the car. Mom is not easily miffed, but I guess I overplayed this last act. Not happy, she was.

Meanwhile I ached to know how brother Bill was doing. Delay, delay; I had at least to pretend to ride up Meadowbrook Road a bit. The play I'd started had to go on despite my rabid curiosity. And, when I finally got back, the bike had to go back where it belonged, Mom needed to move the car.... would the charade never end? Yes—but actor to the end I sauntered up the stairs; running would be too obvious.

Bill had found the papers almost immediately. They were right on top, in the top drawer, the first place he looked. Downhill from there, though. The papers really were very old and yellow, smudged, too. Reading any of it took too much time, despite my best efforts to give him all the time he should have needed. Also, what he did manage to decipher sounded odd to his modern ear, as old and out of date as the yellowed pages. It was written in script, very fancy script, but not particularly easy to read script—script that looked like the writer was somewhere along, but not far enough along, a very long learning curve.

Bill did glean at least a few ideas. The beginning was written by a young boy, maybe even about my age. There was a farm, animals, a field, a stream—just the sort of place Bill and I, suburban youth, knew next to nothing about. He could have been reading a book or, yes, a diary. That's it, we decided we had, or Dad had, a long, lost diary. But whose diary? Where was the farm? And, though we probably knew even less about the word "salacious" than we knew about "ethereal", if we read further, would we find any of that stuff? Afterall, a ghost had gone to a lot of trouble to get it back, it had to be something good. Many years would pass, my father and mother would pass, before we found out.

Chapter Two

Fields

Mistress Mary quite contrary, -how does your garden grow?

Worms crawly creatures smell hay new mown fish worms wandering down to the stream Mary there no Mary nobody no body not in the stream fish circling over by the rocks under the oak float down the stream meet the creatures all over me hello spider hello creepy. Plunk, looking at it bite will you now strike miss wait mosquitoes strike miss strike miss strike got it pull it in got it fish slime show Dad later gut it fire Mom later dinner horn....

soldiers, bedroom red and blue line them up topple them fire away topple them canons topple them flags take them where are they Oxen smell harness leather smells watch feet dung smells barn hay dried where is

"Allen, wake up. 'Take a break' does not mean to nap the rest of the morning."

"Dad, what? I, I, Uh, where?"

"Your mom could use some help. Keep up with your wood splitting for the winter, that Franklin stove is a hungry beast. While you're at it, split some for the fire pit. Your mom's going to cook up the fish you caught earlier this morning; she put them in the cold cellar. You'll need to gut and scale them."

Allen wondered about what to do first, but did not ask his dad, Allen Miner, Sr., wanting to appear fully conscious by now. Actually, he knew once he thought about it, wood first then fish. Right. For the fire pit she'll like some apple wood, left from the dead apple tree, for its smoke flavor and maybe Red-bud and oak to heat up that Franklin Stove monster come winter. Easy enough, he'd enjoy it. Gut, scale, fillet all the fish, easy enough, too, even though there were six; but not as much fun as preparing the wood.

The dream tumbled through his mind as he walked up toward the woodshed. He'd fished and taken the catch to his mom, but after that had only dreams of fishing. That part was straight out of his life. The creepy-crawlies too. He loved mornings when his dad suggested that he catch some fish instead of the more mundane tasks. The stream, the eddies, the pools under the banks where perch waited for him. He'd fish, yes, but he would think about things, too, think about what might be out in the woods beyond the stream. Where the trail through the woods might go, and who or what might be lurking along the trail? He didn't really know, and he wasn't supposed to go far enough away from home to find out. But he'd heard stories, and he could guess. Bears, panthers, and Senecas for sure. Dangers, yes, he knew were there, waiting should he be fool enough to disobey the rules and explore. Mary though, he didn't know a Mary, where did that come from? He did have toy soldiers, and he did play with them. No Mary, though, except in the bible. Dreams, strange.

Get busy, there's much to do before that mid-day dinner horn called the family in. He set about splitting the wood, first placing each log carefully on the large splitting log just right, so he could see the weakest grain line he wanted to strike. He was good at this. The accuracy of his swings pleased him, especially if the first swing split the log all the way through and as a bonus left the two halves still standing ready to be split again. He could entertain himself this way for hours. Then the stacking, that was fun, too. Finding the perfectly equal sized pieces to crisscross at each end of the stacks, filling in the middle with the lumpy logs, saving the worst for the top where they wouldn't destabilize the pile. Finishing the pile, that was a fine moment. He'd then count the piles ready for winter; 1, 2, 3, 4, 5, 6, already, and it was only June. He'd have his dozen if he could only keep up this pace until September.

Preparing the fish went well, too, considering. He split the bellies down the middle with the fish knife Dad had started allowing him to use a couple of years ago, figuring then, at age seven, that he was old enough to handle it carefully. Heads and tails stayed on because Mom liked them that way. Why? He'd never asked. Scaling, that was the worst part. Couldn't leave any on, and, if he were going to cut himself, holding on to that slimy tail and trying to scrape, well, he'd nicked himself before doing this carelessly.

Dinner was exceptional. His mom, Dad, his two younger brothers, and sister, they all enjoyed it. The fish had been cooked perfectly, seasoned with rosemary and thyme from the vegetable garden, grilled, along with the very first summer squash, over the open fire he'd carefully laid. All topped off with Mom's biscuits, baked a couple of days ago.

All that remained were the usual afternoon and evening chores. Chickens, sheep, and pigs to be fed. The oxen, that's what really took the time. Dad liked them under cover at night, and rounding them up, such big and surly beasts, wasn't easy. He had a favorite stick he'd carefully selected and whittled for the task. Somehow, he'd found time to sharpen the fish knife and to spend several hours shaving off the bark and shaping it. He'd even split one end into several strands, so it was almost whip-like. Once the oxen were under cover, there was water to haul for all the animals, lots for those oxen.

Dad had mentioned that he intended to make a run into town in a couple of days, and Allen knew that meant the leather harness for the oxen needed to be in prime shape and that the wagon should be set to go. He got to work on the leather first; it needed a couple of days, at least, to dry after cleaning and oiling. He soaked the old cloth rag he kept for the purpose and rubbed Mom's soap on it. Then he unbuckled all the harness straps and cleaned off every bit of dirt he could find. He let the straps dry out some, while he checked the wagon. Then he wiped down the straps with flax seed oil and layed them out to dry further.

Later that evening, after supper, Dad went to bed almost immediately and Allen followed a bit later after he mused about his day again. He still had trouble getting Mary out of his head, and once he fell asleep, thoughts about her revolved around in his dreams.

He awoke and dressed around 5:00 am, then laid the breakfast fire, before going out to weed the vegetable garden, as he did often during the summer. Weeding was work best done in the relative cool of the morning. Work, yes, but sometimes he managed to take some joy in the task by turning it into a game. The game began after hoeing, once he got to hand picking weeds close to crops. He'd classify the weeds by paying special attention to root types. There were the "deep roots", the "multi-roots", and the "stringy creepers", as he called them. For the "deep roots" the game was to see just how long a root he could extract; 10 points for the whole root, various lesser amounts depending on how thick where the break occurred. "Multi-roots" were difficult to score, but generally he just made up a number depending on how many of the tiny strands he figured he'd gotten compared to the number he figured he'd left behind. Sometimes he even dug down to see just how many strands he'd missed. Then, he gave himself extra points for taking portions of that remainder. "Stringy creepers", well, they usually had long roots and they sprouted any number of side creepers. So, how many side creepers could he locate and dispatch and again how long were the roots of each one extracted? Not an easy calculation, but where's the fun if it's too easy? *

About an hour later, Mom appeared and blew that awfully loud horn, calling the family in for breakfast. She'd cooked pancakes over the pit fire he'd laid for her earlier. She used her favorite iron skillet, propped up on a three-legged iron support Dad made years ago. They'd use some of the precious syrup from the maple tree, gathered in the late winter, boiled down, and preserved in the cold cellar. Yes, he did, he admitted it, sneak down there on hot days when no one was looking. But taste that syrup? He didn't dare; everyone in the family knew just how much was left.

Breakfast was a good time. Allen, his brothers, John and Jonathan, his sister, Esther, his mom, Dorothy, and his dad, all sat and relaxed and even talked some. Dad had freshened up by sprinkling water over his head at the well, and even Allen, Jr. had gone to the well to clean up a bit, necessary after weeding. They couldn't sit together often during the day; they worked, and when they worked, they didn't sit or talk. They ate well while they talked, knowing there would be no further break until the afternoon dinner horn would actually sound welcoming.

Dad had his plans to discuss; he intended to leave for Addison in a couple of days he said. He'd be gone for as much as a week or maybe more, meaning even more work for Allen and his brothers, both in preparation and once he was gone. His dad would be hauling what they had all produced to sell over the past year. Allen and his brothers had helped their dad make oak barrels from white oak staves cut to size and then aged for up to two years. Mom had knitted mittens and shawls with some help from young Esther. The wagon was open to whatever weather might occur, so the mittens and shawls were secured in a wooden box to protect them. The barrels needed no such protection, though they did need to be firmly secured. The Miners hoped that these handmade items along with their two cash crops, bags of wool and flax seeds, would bring in whatever money they might need to see them through the year.

If Dad could ever be said to be excited, his voice sounded just a bit that way this morning. Allen knew his dad would visit friends in Addison, that he would stop at the local supply store, purchase whatever not too subtle hints from the family suggested they needed or would like, and not at all incidentally catch up with the latest news from others who visited that store for the same reasons. Addison was the best place to get a newspaper and hear the latest news. He'd bring that paper home for nightly readings to the family. Allen was excited. News was an uncommon delight. Of course, sometimes, especially in the summer of 1813 with the war so active, 'delight' wasn't really the right word. Still, having recently turned nine in April, Allen was becoming anxious to hear about whatever was going on beyond the limits of his home.

*See the diary entry below for the deep root, the multi-root, and the stringy-creeper calculations. It is not clear in the diary what time frame the numbers represent—maybe weekly averages or maybe just best and worst days.

Chapter Three

Painted Post

Watch Out for that Felloe*

Several days later, Allen's dad decided he would leave in that wagon pulled by those unruly oxen, oxen guided by the newly cleaned and dried leather harnesses, which he much appreciated. They would feel good in his work roughened hands. He had a long way to go, some 30 miles or so, over the usual muddy trails from their home in Greenwood to reach Addison or, for reasons Allen didn't fully understand, what his dad preferred to call Painted Post. Allen, Sr. knew the way well. He would follow trails along the rivers, the Canisteo and Tuscarora, trails he knew would be even worse than normal because of the recent rains. Hauling the barrels and other goods he'd be selling in Painted Post meant the trip would take at least two days, probably three, if he didn't get stuck somewhere along the way.

*A felloe is a wooden part inside the metal rim of a wagon wheel. The outer ends of the spokes insert into the felloe.

Dad left right after breakfast, after carefully securing the wooden box full of those knitted items for sale, or perhaps barter, and throwing in some fresh hay and feed for the oxen. Though the trails were as bad as he had expected—muddy in some spots and just water filled ruts in others—he made decent time well into the afternoon. He'd allowed himself 3 days to travel to Painted Post, with a stop about halfway at the Nicholas Brotzman homestead. He'd met Nicholas years back, a year or so after they both first arrived in what had been a nearly unsettled part of Steuben County, former Seneca territory. Their meeting had been a fortunate coincidence. They crossed paths only because both chose the same day to return from trips to Painted Post, and now a trip to Painted Post always meant stopping to see Nicholas, both coming from and going to.

The morning went well, and he was feeling good about the trip. The recent late June/early July rains had left the moistened leaves of the trees shining. The sun caught a large spider web just right so that it sparkled like diamonds strung in mid-air. The morning was cool, clean, and dry as it often is after a storm clears the air. If he'd been of the whistling sort, he might have spent most of the day whistling a happy tune. Sure, the wagon slipped sideways a few times, but that was to be expected, given the general conditions caused by the recent rains.

The oxen plodded along right on through the afternoon despite the slips; they seemed to know how to compensate. His cargo shifted a bit, too, but he didn't think the shifting serious enough to stop and re-adjust the load. That was his first mistake. His second? He trusted the oxen a bit too much. At a bend, the beasts were presented with a choice of ruts—one headed up on the higher side and one headed down on the lower side. Trust them to take the lazy choice, down not up, and, as it turned out, a dumb not smart one. Smarts were supposed to be Allen Sr.'s business. His third mistake? Having been lolled into a good mood, he didn't think ahead.

The wagon slipped, again, but this time kept on slipping, pulling the oxen with it. Down it went, smashing into a large boulder on the way, then over a slight ledge; slight but just enough to tip the wagon over and spill all the contents, including Allen Sr., out into the brambles. The oxen struggled to their knees but couldn't get footing. Fortunately, neither Allen nor the oxen broke anything, but the wagon, well, nothing entirely good comes of such events. One wheel was twisted, seemingly damaged beyond repair. At the very least, he'd need an anvil and woodworking tools to fix it.

As he surveyed the damage, Allen Sr., always a rational man, realized (after what for him passed as a curse or two) that he was lucky to be alive let alone unbroken. He had scrapes on his left arm, the side he'd fallen on, and a gash on his right leg just below the knee where he had struck a rock as he rolled. And, the oxen were unhurt, except for a few scrapes and scratches. They did need to be freed, though. First things first; free the oxen. He untangled their now muddy and twisted leather harness, so carefully cleaned and oiled by his son, and removed their yoke. The oxen struggled to their feet and climbed out of the brambles back to the trail, looking as relieved as dumb beasts of their sort can be imagined looking. He'd take them with him as he sought help. Leaving them there, prey to bears or panthers or maybe even a Seneca or two not yet captured and dragged off to the reservation, would not do.

Fortunately, he was not more than a mile from the Brotzman's homestead, not far from willing help and just the place to fix the wheel. That leather harness was now about to suffer further abuse. He needed to use it to retrieve the broken wheel from the brambles. First, he climbed back into the brambles and tied the harness to the wheel, easy enough, but not at all easy to convince, threaten, whip, and cajole those oxen back into the brambles just far enough to attach the other end of the harness to them. He did it but getting those oxen in place took the better part of an hour, raising Allen's concern that darkness might overtake them as they made their way to help and safety.

Certainly, he regretted having to leave everything behind. The wagon, the barrels and the other cash goods represented something a bit too close to his family's survival over the winter for him to be at all comfortable. He couldn't even take his wife's work along. Of course, they were independent and resourceful homesteaders, but, but.... He suppressed these thoughts enough to think his way along the trail dragging the wheel and leading the oxen with darkness coming on faster than he had hoped. A sprained ankle at this point would cost him dearly; the gash on his leg was bad enough. He did not relish the thought of having to heave himself up on the back of one his beasts and leave them to pick the way along the so-called trail. He'd done that and now he was paying for being complacent enough to trust them.

What worried him more now, as the sun slid down below one of the western hills, was finding the side trail to Brotzman's place. He'd had trouble before finding it in the light of day. He felt he was close. He began checking his memory for clues, perhaps special trees near the turn-off, a red bud or sugar maple or an oak with an odd branch off to the side, perfect for a swing, yes, that's it, he remembered thinking he wished he had one for his children. It should be, there it is, that oak.

OK, now where is that trail? He halted the oxen and left them tied to a sapling. Then he began to carefully scan the right side of the main trail. All he needed to find was the break in the underbrush. As thick as the underbrush was, any break would be that side trail. Finally, he found it or thought he had; he headed down a way, just to be sure. He looked for the stone marker that Brotzman had for some reason not placed on the main trail but a ways in. Was Nickolas still fearing Senecas? No, he would know that Senecas would know all about his whereabouts. Probably, he was just cautious about any wandering folk who didn't know his little trick and therefore probably didn't know him. Caution is good, except when a friend is stumbling in the near dark looking for help. There, there it is; stumbling is good only if you stumble into the right pile of rocks.

Relieved, Allen returned to the main trail and stuck a branch next to the side trail to make it easier to find again and then retrieved the oxen. Feeling better now, he thought about leaving the stick where it was, just to thwart his friend, but he thought better of it; he was about to ask for lots of help. As he approached the house, he felt better—still-worn, scratched, and hurting, but better. As luck would have it, (and he had been lucky) Nickolas was standing at the door as he approached. They greeted warmly and took care of the oxen before going on inside. His friend had enough sense to save questions about the damaged wheel and lack of a wagon until they were more comfortable inside. Of course, he could guess. Allen somewhat suddenly realized that they were alone. Where was his friend's wife, Julia Anne, and the rest of the Brotzman family? He, too, waited to ask.

Once inside the cabin, Allen felt relieved and almost good. Nicholas made him feel even better when he mentioned that he had just tapped a well-aged barrel of cider, offering just what Allen needed most, a relaxing brew. Nicholas was one of the few among Allen's friends who had his own cider press, and Nicholas had perfected (better than anyone else Allen knew) the art of pressing, fermenting, storing, and aging cider. Sitting with his friend, fine cider flowing, sore muscles relaxing, well, talk soon flowed too. Nicholas began.

"Well, a busted wheel, two oxen, one worn friend—got to be a story."

Allen took his time responding, there was no need to sound too much the fool. "You know, with the rain the trails are about as bad as I've ever seen them. Kept slipping, you know. But I seemed to be making good time until the fool oxen took the wrong set of ruts on a curve. Down we went, finally tipping over a ledge, just the right ledge for spilling everything, but leaving us not too banged up."

"So, my friend, you got the busted wheel and made it here."

"Well, it wasn't quite that easy. First, I had to free the oxen; they needed untangling from the twisted harness, and they needed to work some to even stand up in the mud. Then the wheel, well I needed the oxen to go back into what I figure they considered troublesome territory, back into the brambles, so I could attach that wheel to the harness to get them to pull it out from under the wagon. Took quite some time, and it was getting dark."

"Dark, yes, that would make finding my place interesting."

"Interesting isn't exactly what I was thinking at the time," Allen replied, a bit more abruptly than he might have intended. "Somewhere between difficult and impossible crossed my mind. Then I saw that oak with the limb angled out perfectly for a swing. Wish I had one like it for my young'uns. Remembered that it wasn't far from the cleverly hidden entrance to your trail."

"Yes, well, you know, can't be too cautious out here alone. No knowing who might be on the prowl out there."

"Speaking of being alone, where's your family?"

"Oh, they're spending a couple of days visiting at my neighbor's place; lucky you didn't arrive yesterday when I was using up most of the afternoon and evening transporting them there."

Luck again, Allen thought, but said nothing about it. Instead, he picked up on the mention of the missing family and said, "Well I suspect you'll find your way back more easily than I did when you pick them up, unless fate provides you with a tale of your own to tell. At least you left that pile of rocks a ways in to help me. Felt much better when I stumbled over that."

"And here you are in need of something to eat, I'd guess, and some sleep, and some help come morning."

"All true, I'm afraid, all too true."

"But first, let's have another glass of that cider. Oh, let me tell you about the best of hard cider apples. There's a strange one that adds such flavor; it's yellow with black spots. The other looks like any red apple but it, too, is of a variety that works with cider. Now something to eat. Fortunately, my thoughtful wife made up several meals for me; she knows what a lousy cook I am. Won't let me in the kitchen except to build the fire. And, to make cider; She likes it, too."

And so, they ate, had another cider, and then Nicholas showed Allen where he could sleep before heading to bed himself. The next morning Allen was at least rested but fearing the loss of those left-behind possessions, he was anxious to get going on repairs. Breakfast could wait. Fortunately, Nicholas understood and pitched in enthusiastically. Three of the fourteen spokes were broken, the felloe cracked, and the rim bent. The anvil Nickolas had would suffice for rim repair. They hefted the good side of the wheel up on a table, so the bent side could lay on the anvil. The trick was to bend the rim back into place without further damaging the cracked felloe. It took time and not quite gentle persuasion, but Nicholas managed to hammer it back in place.

The spokes needed precise shaping so the angle from hub to felloe would be right. Both ends are needed to fit into their appropriate slots. Seasoned oak logs from the woodpile provided material, long enough, but the shaping, well, that was difficult. They had an ax to work with, not the most precise of instruments, but rough-cut spokes would do the job. They could chisel the ends once they had the length and shape right. Lathe work could wait until Allen got to Painted Post. That felloe, though, they'd have to think about that. Besides, breakfast was by now calling both too loudly to be ignored.

Nicholas proved he was not the best of cooks by whipping up some overcooked eggs and then adding some burnt toast. He just threw it outside to the dog, and they sat down with a ramekin of butter, bread, and some venison jerky. They ate more sparingly than they might have wished while they talked about repairing the felloe. They both agreed that two of the replaced spokes could be inserted into the cracked felloe and the third into the adjoining still whole felloe. They thought that, since the cracked felloe was not completely broken, they might be able to take advantage of the crack by bending it slightly but carefully to properly insert it back into place next to the adjoining felloes. What puzzled them most was the considerable pressure that the two spokes would exert on the weakened felloe, especially with a heavily loaded wagon. Maybe, they thought, they could find a piece of scrap metal to breach the crack. They agreed that would be the best they could do until Allen could get a replacement wheel in Painted Post. They'd have to look around and find whatever metal object might serve the purpose temporarily.

After breakfast, the work went pretty much as planned. Shaping the spokes and chiseling the ends took time, as expected, but they got the job done. The new spokes looked awful, but it seemed like they would function. Fitting the spokes into the felloes went well. The cracked felloe slipped into place without further damage more easily than they had anticipated. Sometimes that happens. Not often but sometimes. Looking around for a scrap of metal the right size to breach the crack in the damaged felloe, well, sometimes the opposite happens. After an hour or so of searching they found an old iron skillet that they figured would have to do. The handle was just long enough, so all they had to do was saw it off. Ruined a saw doing that, and did a bit of damage to their mood, but eventually they hacked and whacked it off and then bolted it into place.

Finally, Allen began to breath a bit more easily. Nicholas had promised to help get the oxen and wheel back to the wagon and to help with the wagon repair. They took with them a long metal bar, figuring they would need a lever to lift the wagon sufficiently to get the wheel back on. Off they went with the oxen dragging the wheel and the metal bar. When they reached the wagon, Allen felt a flood of relief, all was still there as he had left it. The project would take time, but both felt good about getting to it. They cleared the area of the barrels that were in their way, levered the wagon up, just enough to attach the wheel, and then used the oxen and the much-abused leather straps to pull it back onto the trail. Loading the wagon seemed like a breeze compared to the rest of the project, and after hitching up the oxen properly they headed down the trail without incident. Once they reached the path that led to the Brotzman homestead, Allen thanked his friend, as long-time friends thank each other; and then, anxious to be on his way to Painted Post, he headed on down the ruts that led that way, as Nicholas made his way down the side trail to his place and back to his unfinished chores.

Land of the Post

Normally levelheaded, Allen Sr. managed with some effort to contain his relief as he made his way to Painted Post. He asked himself several times how that jury-rigged wheel could hold together with so much weight on it. Maybe he should get off the wagon and walk. Finally, no longer trusting to luck, he did just that, leading the oxen this time saying to himself, "I'm not going to make that mistake again."

First, he planned to stop off at William Hill's residence, a log cabin, much like others in the area. This one, though, had an attached barn with all the right equipment for repairing or replacing the limping wagon wheel. "Someday," William often said to anyone who would still listen after several years of hearing the same story, "I'll build a proper wagon shop in town." Most folks knew the story and most thought they would be stopping in at William's barn for wagon repairs many years into the future. Certainly, Allen knew exactly where to go; as a yearly visitor to Painted Post and to various haunts within the town where stories of this sort were told over and over, he could hardly avoid knowing.

Hearing the approach of Allen's rickety wagon, William came out of the barn to greet what he rightly assumed was new business. He spotted the slight lean toward the makeshift wheel and approached with what seemed to Allen like a bit too much of a smile. Looking more closely, he greeted Allen with what was intended as praise, "Now that's quite a piece of work."

Allen, not at all sure praise was intended and struggling a bit to be diplomatic, replied, "Desperate situations often require creative solutions, and I guess 'creative' is the best word I can come up with to describe our efforts."

He then gave William a brief rendition of the accident, his efforts to reach the Brotzman homestead, and the help he'd received with the repair efforts. He managed to leave out just how desperate he had felt about the possible loss of the wagon and goods; for some not immediately clear reason, he didn't want to appear too desperate in front of William. Did his reticence have something to do with what he expected William to charge? Maybe, he thought. His sense of dignity? Maybe.

William was willing to drop a long-term project he had just started and get to work on this more immediately necessary and lucrative one. He had, at least, developed the business instincts he needed if he ever did build that shop in town. And, of course, Allen was ready and even anxious, though he made a strategic effort to hide any anxiety. No sense in giving a possible reason to inflate the price. They went back and forth for some time over whether to repair the old wheel or to just create a new one. Allen went for repair and won out in the end. William joked about hanging the old one up in his barn as a curiosity but gave in eventually. He had a lathe to form proper spokes and felloes and a forge to shape and repair the rim. The work would take time, so they agreed that the oxen could stay in the stalls located at the back of the barn while William completed repairs and Allen went into town.

Once again Allen needed to leave his valued work behind, but at least this time he was leaving it in safe hands. William estimated he'd have everything done in a couple of days giving Allen time to visit and to seek out buyers for the barrels and his wife's handiwork. Allen agreed that once he sold as much as possible, he'd be back and pay for the work. He'd half hoped that William would barter, but William had sheep and therefore wool, as well as a competent wife, so there was no chance to try to barter using the shawls or mittens. The barrels would fetch a better price in town.

The potential buyers there knew his reputation for quality work from his previous sales.

The walk into town wouldn't be too difficult, he thought, even though the gash below his right knee was smarting a bit more than he could have wished. He should do something about that, he guessed. But, first, he wanted to seek out his friends Reuben and Lemuel Searle, particularly Lemuel. No one knew what was going on around town like Lemuel, and besides Allen enjoyed his company. If there were new stories floating around, he'd know them, and he'd describe them in just the sort of detail Allen found entertaining. All that stood in his way was the Conhocton River. Crossing it required dealing with the local boat man and, more troubling, cost money or some equivalent. Perhaps the boatman would accept some shawls or mittens as payment. At least he could carry them easily enough.

The walk went about as he'd expected with no problems, and the road seemed a bit easier to navigate on foot alone than with those oxen. Even negotiations with the boat man went well; he took a shawl for the trip across and even back, anytime Allen was ready to return.

Arriving mid-afternoon, Allen was fortunate to find both Lemuel and his wife, Elizabeth, home and happy to see him. They were trying out Elizabeth's fresh baked bread and strawberry jam, so they added a chair and serving for Allen. Allen could hardly avoid thinking there really was nothing like a comfortable farm home, something tasty to eat, and good friends. Add in the conversation that began almost at once, and Allen was relaxed and beaming.

"So, Allen," Lemuel began, "what brings you to Addison this fine summer day? And, on foot with no oxen, no wagon, no barrels to sell, and a limp, just to mention a few oddities."

Allen hesitated but replied, hoping he could keep the story short and get on to local news. "It's a long story, but simply put the oxen and goods to sell, including barrels, are at Hill's place while he repairs a broken wagon wheel. Just easy to carry woolen goods with me, currently. I'll bore you both with details about the broken wheel at some point, but I'm betting there are more interesting tales to tell about what's happening here around town."

Lemuel well understood how starved for news his friend always was when he managed to reach what for him might seem like civilization, so he didn't object to the change of subject. Besides, as a prominent man of Addison with Constable and other town titles part of his nearly 60 years of life, Lemuel was used to talking about the history and the news of the town and enjoyed it in fact.

"Did I ever tell you the story of Asahel Stiles' mother and the big black dog?" Lemuel asked. He had, but Allen wasn't about to interrupt his friend. "Well, you know, she's old and close to blind, but reported she'd seen a big black dog in the middle of the frozen Canisteo River. Others, of better sight, checked that out and found that the dog had transformed itself into a bear. Magic happens in these parts, I suppose. Anyway, Sam Rice got himself a club and decided to attack the bear. Bet you can imagine how that went. Sam beat a hasty but slippery retreat, bear nipping at his heels. Stiles came to the rescue, smashing the bear over the head with a hoe. I'm not sure who was crazier, Sam or Asahel, but that hoe was heavy enough to fell the bear, so in some sense I guess Asahel knew what he was doing, or he was just plain lucky. One dead bear—dressed soon after."

Allen couldn't help adding, "I'm thinking just plain lucky."

Lemuel nodded agreement and then went on to add some more recent news. "You should get a copy of the Buffalo Gazette for war news. We've captured a major British fort, Fort George on Lake Ontario, and there's talk of action at the British outpost of Lundy's Lane in Canada north of Buffalo. I read a copy at the Post Office, but you might want to get the most recent edition and take it on home for a full read when you've got some free evenings."

"I do like a paper to read at home; my wife and children enjoy it too. I'll get up to the Post Office and see if they still have a copy. But first, I'll need to find someone to buy the barrels I brought with me. Any ideas? I figure you of all people know what's selling around here and who's buying."

"Right," Lemuel replied. "For those fine barrels you make, I'd check out Will Wombough. His new sawmill is thriving, and he's added a distillery to his enterprises. Bargain with the man; Lord knows he doesn't need to squeeze you on price; richest man around. Course he's smart, too; he'll figure you aren't about to go to the trouble of taking those barrels back home. You might think about getting specific price information from George Goodhue first; he's the best potential competition. Been around awhile too, and curious about everything that sells, as he is, he'll know the going price for barrels. Trust him."

After accepting the Searle's gracious invitation to spend the night, he enjoyed a fine supper and an oh so welcome good night's sleep. Allen left after breakfast with a little less of a limp. He'd gratefully accepted the offer of one of Lemuel's daughters (like his wife, also named Elizabeth) to clean and dress the wound. Now he needed to consider what he could do to get his wagon full of goods to market. It troubled him, as it always did when he made these trips, that he would need to go all the way up to the Bath bridge to get the wagon across the Conhocton, a good two days lost that he'd rather spend in Painted Post. It troubled him enough that this time he thought harder than usual about finding another way. He knew that the number of rafts used to transport boards from the mills to markets to the south had increased; no reason he couldn't bargain for one of those to use for a much shorter trip into Painted Post. Once he got the barrels and other items across, he'd ask Will to take the wagon and oxen back to his place and ask Lemuel for help in getting his goods to market. It is good to have friends.

Allen walked around Painted Post, stopped to talk with those with time to listen, and eventually ended up taking Lemuel's advice talking with George Goodhue before Will Wombough. George suggested a better price for the barrels than he had expected, and George had thoughts about who might want the wool and woolen goods, too. With that information in hand, he went on to Will

Wombough's new distillery. Will was there entertaining several locals; so, much jolly conversation took place before Allen had a chance to get down to business.

Will seemed interested in the barrels, though he tried not to show it. Allen felt he had done well in the end, nearly talking Will up to the price George had suggested. Of course, he needed to tell that broken wagon wheel story once again as he had at George's, hoping he'd not have to tell it endlessly. Allen was capable of hope, even when hope defied reality, as it did in this case. He preferred to talk about his home life, his wife and family. Fortunately, his friends were kind enough to ask about them, so he got his chances.

Delivering the Goods - Take it easy

Allen's plan for hiring a raft to cross the river went well, initially. After an uneventful walk back to William Hill's wagon shop/home, William helped him load the newly repaired wagon and harness the oxen. He went with Allen to the Conhocton riverbank, a good way upstream from where he wanted to end up on the Painted Post side. William even waited to help load the barrels and other goods onto a raft they finally managed to hail. They had timed their arrival for near evening, knowing that raftsmen would want to stop at Painted Post to enjoy whatever pleasures they might find there and to spend the night. William had picked their spot well; they waited near an eddy that was close to shore, which slowed any raft, easing communication and making a landing possible even for a raft, clumsy as they were.

The raft pilot, one healthy specimen of backwoods manhood, seemed to find the request as amusing as it was unusual. Two of the oarsmen looked less than pleased, even threatening, or maybe it was just their massive size and the effort expended wrestling the oars for the landing. But the pilot was the boss, and he was willing; one shawl for his wife did it, a bargain again. The barrels were loaded and secured quickly with help from all, including the oarsmen, who were cheered, perhaps, by the knowledge that they would be stopping at Painted Post for sure. William waved a quick goodbye and headed home with the empty wagon and oxen. Allen would pick them up later, on his own way home.

They eased out of the eddy until the current caught them. "Caught them", that's a bit tame for what happened; caught them by surprise, despite the pilot's knowledge and expertise, and spun them around 180 degrees. The barrels so carefully secured, or so they thought, swung around slamming against Allen and one of the oarsmen, knocking the massive oarsman down and sending Allen into the stream along with three barrels still tied to the raft. Allen, a competent swimmer, managed to grab onto one of the barrels and hold on. Lucky again; one of those barrels could have whacked him in the head in that nasty current and knocked him unconscious. Instead, the one he grabbed was quickly pulled to the side of the raft by the felled but quickly recovered oarsman while the other oarsman and the pilot struggled, with every bit of the considerable strength they possessed, to gain control and to head the raft around again. Fortunately, such Conhocton currents fall as suddenly as they rise; the raft righted, the barrels steadied and were secured. They all managed to breath more easily, calmed by what seemed like a magically transformed river.

By the time they approached Painted Post, after carefully guiding the raft across the river, they were all recovered and in a good enough mood to joke about the still soaked Allen. "Serves you right for not taking the bridge." "Going to have to explain that garb to the ladies." "Now make up a good story—throw in a bit of heroics—something about a drowned rat." Allen took it with what approached laughter for him, despite knowing he would need to tell this tale, too. Lemuel, in his laconic style would insist, as he had when Allen showed up on his earlier visit with a limp, no oxen, no wagon and nothing except woolens to sell. Lemuel, waiting on shore as planned, didn't fail to note his friend's newest condition.

"Well, looks like you have another story to tell. This time at least you have barrels to sell, though a couple look somewhat battered. And we knew you would have no way to transport them, that's why

I'm here; but look at those clothes, they almost tell a story by themselves. Details, my friend, that's what I need. We'll fill it all in and make a good story of it, once we get you and the barrels ashore."

Given how anxious the oarsmen were to get on to the pleasures of Painted Post, such as they were, unloading the barrels and other goods from the raft and reloading them onto Lemuel's wagon took very little time. Off they went their separate ways, oarsmen off to we-know-not-where but could guess were we so inclined, Lemuel with Allen and the goods to his home for a quieter night. Morning would be the time to sell, this evening was the time to make up a proper story.

With the promise of a quiet evening and a good meal, along with amused but kindly friends surrounding him, Allen finally felt he could relax. They had found some dry clothes that sort of fit, making his appearance better but still somewhat comical, as they all found ways to note. "That shirt," Lemuel remarked, "puffy as it is, reminds me of styles left behind; Shakespeare would love it." Daughter Elizabeth chimed in pretending sympathy, "I think he looks quite distinguished; one could imagine him an Earl." Lemuel's wife Elizabeth tried to hold back but failed. "Now that would take a heavy dose of imagination." Allen beamed and took it all in easily, now completely relaxed and enjoying his friends.

Rounding out the story took the rest of the evening—a good natured and absorbing task. The young Elizabeth wanted to add a water snake somehow; she'd seen one a couple of days prior. She decided the snake, nearly 6 feet long and thick as her arm, her upper arm no less, attacked Allen just as the oarsman began pulling him in. Lemuel, caught up with the notion, wanted to have Allen let go of the barrel to wrestle with the snake. A mighty struggle followed, of course. They allowed that extra details could be added at whim during any particular story telling. Basically, they agreed that the snake wrapped itself around Allen, and Allen, conveniently provided with a knife he managed to reach despite any improbability that might entail, hacked away at the creature until badly wounded it let go and slithered away. Several variations of the battle followed: each a bit more exciting. An underwater version with Allen nearly drowning got rejected, but still they did allow that he had great difficulty staying above the surface.

As the story grew, they had Allen detached from the barrel, quickly floating away from the raft, wounded so that swimming was difficult. Allen, himself, threw in the wounded part; figuring, if a listener asked to see the wounds, he could just plead modesty or something. Lemuel's wife enhanced the fantasy by suggesting that one of the oarsmen heroically jumped into the water to help Allen. Someone suggested the oarsman thought enough to grab a long rope attached to the raft so a fellow oarsman could pull them both back once he reached Allen. Crediting an oarsman with bravery and quick thinking got a good share of the ensuing debate, but in the end, they allowed it. Now they had a wet Allen and a wet oarsman, but they just ended up figuring no listener would care despite the earlier oarsman joke about Allen's damp garb. They had it, a much better story, thanks in great part to Elizabeth's snake. All acknowledged her excellent contribution, including the none too modest young lady herself.

The next morning after breakfast, armed with the better story and carting the barrels and cash crops, Allen and Lemuel headed for Will Wombough's distillery. They took their time, even stopped by Martin Young's homestead to try out that new story. Martin didn't quite fall for the snake part. Six feet and as thick as an arm; he doubted Allen could fight off such a creature or even that such a creature existed. They ended up admitting a "slight" exaggeration but stuck with the rest of snake story.

The time passed pleasantly; Martin was a good friend with local news. He had lots to say about the most recent war activities, mostly from what he'd heard others relate after they had read the latest Buffalo Gazette. Allen mentioned that he had wanted to take a copy home, but Martin didn't have one. Both Martin and Lemuel agreed that he'd be able to find one if he kept asking as he traveled through Painted Post. Martin did mention a couple of battles fought against British regulars near Niagara, NY, with casualties on both sides including the death of a US army officer and the wounding of several New York volunteers.

After leaving Martin, Allen and Lemuel headed on to Wombough's distillery, arriving a little late for lunch. They weren't too late, though, to mingle with the half dozen or so men hanging out near the distillery. The distillery tended to be a popular spot, and Will encouraged folks to seek it out by providing tables, chairs, and occasionally even a taste or two of whatever product might be available, knowing small sips might well lead to big sales. Discussion ranged from local happenings to local politics and on to the war. Several had read the Niagara article and wondered if their local militia might be pulled into whatever response might be devised. Unfortunately, no one had a copy of the paper.

Allen had just asked about a copy before talk was interrupted as Wombough himself appeared. A man of business he went immediately over to the wagon to look at the barrels he had promised to purchase sight unseen. He was pleased with the quality of the wood working; the white oak staves cleanly shaped and joined, the trussed metal hoops perfectly hammered tightly into place. Better than he had expected, in fact, even though he was aware of Allen's reputation for fine craftsmanship. He was so pleased that when he picked up on the talk of the paper, he promised Allen his own copy, the one he'd just finished reading the previous evening. Smiles all around, a sip or two, and the deal was done—finally actual money in Allen's hands.

Allen, anxious to be on his way home as soon as possible, decided to push on to William Hill's place to pick up the wagon with its newly repaired wheel and pay Hill what he owed for work on the wheel and for care of the oxen, now that he could. Lemuel drove him to the riverbank, first stopping at a new general store, small but stocked with items Allen needed to take home. He selected a Barlow knife for his eldest son, Allen, sling shots for his two younger sons, embroidery needles for his wife, a fancy, red ribbon for his young daughter, and a goodly quantity of salt they had trouble getting locally. The store owner, willing to barter, took the wool and flax seed as partial payment, saving most of Allen's newly acquired money for William Hill and whatever else he might need to purchase over the next year. Definitely on a roll now, he met up almost immediately with the boatman who had taken him across the river initially and had promised a return trip. Hearty thanks to friend Lemuel, a quick trip across the river, payment and thanks to William, and Allen was on his way home with his oxen and nearly empty wagon.

Home - Happy Trails

Allen wanted to stop in and visit the Brotzman's, as usual, but not in the dark. He did not want to stumble around trying to find the side trail to their place this time. Instead, he spent the night in his wagon by the side of the trail, leaving the oxen yoked but nearby in a meadow to graze. He fed them oats early next morning and arrived at the Brotzman's well before mid-day. This time Nicholas, his wife Julia, and their seven children greeted him with the happy chaos such greetings involve, a spirit boosting change from his last fraught visit with Nicholas alone.

Dinner preparations were just underway, and adding one more to a large family meal was no problem. While Julia, with help from older children, prepared the meal, Allen and Nicholas took care of the oxen and worked together doing outdoor chores. At dinner Allen regaled the family with tales of his adventures, choosing to tell the actual story of his river crossing on the raft to these long-time friends rather than the snake enhanced tale, though he did add that they had worked up the more elaborate version with masterly help from the young Elizabeth Searle. He let them know that the barrels Nicholas had helped save were easily sold and that the woolen goods were bartered to good effect. He saved the more general news for last, reading from the newspaper he had gotten from Wombough. Nicholas expressed some concern about the war and possible militia involvement; he and his eldest son might be called to serve. Allen shared his concern, thinking of his own eldest son, even though Allen Jr. was only nine. Who knew how long this second British war would last?

Though Allen Sr. certainly enjoyed the company, he wanted to get home soon, and that desire pushed him to move on. His family might worry, he thought, given the unexpected length of his absence. Besides, honest with himself, he knew the main reason; he just wanted to get back home to his family. So, he ended the visit as soon as he felt he could do so gracefully. He even came up with an admirable transition; "Julia," he said, "I have something out in the wagon I'd like to show you." They all went out to see. Then Allen took out the last shawl he'd been saving for them and presented it to Julia thanking them all for their hospitality and Nicholas for all his help. Julia was delighted and extended her thanks to his wife.

Parting from the Brotzman's left him with the long road home ahead. He got down from the wagon and led the oxen, anticipating the spot where the ruts took a low road or high road depending on which the lead ox chose. This time he would be the leader, not them. As they approached the scene of their previous disaster, though, he couldn't help feeling that even the oxen knew which set of ruts to take. They seemed to be hugging the high side on their own. Should he credit them with the power to think or did they have a memory? He'd file those questions away for some other day. Meanwhile home seemed so much closer now.

When he arrived, toward evening, the scene was just as he wished; wife, sons, and daughter smiling their greetings as well as heartily expressing them. As he looked around, he could see that the family had taken good care of their place, even though he had not been there to help. His son, Allen, quickly took the reins from him to take care of the oxen and wagon. The father and son exchanged a quick glance, both remembering the original condition of those reins as they noted the current condition. The son thought, "another couple of days ahead working them back into shape, but Dad's home, so all's good." His dad was now free to seek a more comfortable seat inside—home for sure. The other children brought him treats to eat and babbled away energetically, encouraging him to tell his stories immediately. Mercifully, his wife calmed everyone, giving him a chance to relax.

The stories of his adventures came later, when Allen, Jr. joined them and during a much-appreciated supper. He told them about the mistake the oxen made, the wagon wheel disaster, and even mentioned the oak with the perfect limb for a swing that gave him the clue he needed to find the trail to the Brotzman's place. He spent a good deal of time on the disaster that befell him during the river-crossing, adding in the snake version made up by Elizabeth. They all much preferred it to what actually happened, giving Elizabeth a hearty round of giggling credit. He got a bit serious when he thought to tell his family about all the kindly help he had received from his friends along the way.

After supper he broke out the gifts; the Barlow knife for Allen, the sling shots for his John and Jonathan, the embroidery needles for his Dorothy, and the ribbon for Esther. He asked Allen to teach his brothers, John first and then Jonathan, how to handle a knife with care, so that when they were old enough, they would be ready to handle their own knives safely. He did not talk about his injuries; though later, of course, his wife Dorothy would pry those details from him.

He saved his somewhat crumbled copy of the Buffalo Gazette for last. "Here's what I know will interest you all; it certainly did me. It's the June 1813 Gazette, the latest I could get in Painted Post."

His son, Allen, interrupted. "Wait, you call Addison 'Painted Post'. Why?"

"Now that's a good story. Actually, there are several stories. Anyway, as far as I can tell a Seneca chief had the original post erected and painted to commemorate victory over a rival tribe. Not clear what happened to that post, but the name stuck. Gruesome accounts mention enemy blood as paint. But, back to the Gazette."

He then read from it at length, especially an article about what was going on around Niagara, NY. His voice grew serious as he read.

> "On Saturday the mounted men under Maj. Chapin passed down to Queenston. On Sunday Me. E. Sloot, of this town, crossed at Black Rock, and with Ab. Ranson, late of this village, proceeded to Queenston: when they passed the foot of Lundy's Lane, (a place principally settled by the rangers who fought Butler in the revolutionary war,) they were fired upon by a small party of the enemy concealed, and Ransom was made prisoner. Sloot making his escape to Queenston."

Allen Jr., caught up in the action, interrupted asking, "What happened to our men after the battle?"

Allen Sr. answered quite simply, "We don't know much; here's all we have so far, gathered, the paper says, from a couple of our men who escaped."

> "The battle continued for some time, when the enemy out-flanked and surrounded our men and have very probably captured them. We know not the loss in killed but hope we may obtain some correct account this day. We learn that Joel Thorp of this town was killed in the beginning of the action."

"Wait", Allen Sr. said, "I may have jumped ahead to a different engagement. Anyway, I'd say we are not doing well up there. Wouldn't be surprised if we end up sending considerable reinforcements. Maybe even our militia. Guess we'll hear something either way at the next militia muster, or as I prefer to think of it, get together. I'll be sure to take this Gazette along. Always lots of news and talk at musters and a bit of fun, too. Since all us men folk are required to sign up, I'll see lots of men I don't normally." He mentioned the talk and fun partly because it was true but also to lighten the mood after noting several looks of concern.

Chapter Four

Militia

Off to Lundy's Lane

Allen Sr.'s conjecture, after reading the newspaper article on the Queenston battle about the need for significant reinforcements soon, perhaps including his own militia, proved largely correct. At the next militia muster in August 1813, as usual a joyous meeting with old friends mixed with no small amount of drinking and revelry, he received the unpleasant piece of news he had guessed he might. Reinforcements were needed, and eventually his militia would be heading to Niagara to reinforce the regulars and militias already there. It did come as a slight surprise, though, that they would be heading out next year, in the dead of winter. Winter travel takes lots of forethought. On the way home from the muster he began preliminary planning. The local militia members would need a sleigh and team of horses, snow being almost guaranteed; his wagon and oxen just wouldn't be of any use.

They might have hoped to meet up with other NY militias headed their way along the main route; but if not, all they knew was that they were to join the 55th regiment under Lieutenant Colonel Clark Allen when they reached Niagara.

Once home he began to consider the so-called main route more carefully. He'd heard at the muster from those closer to the route that it was mostly just trails formed by Senecas; following them would be no easy task. He'd heard that some of the terrain was swampy, so for those sections they might need to stick to the hills wherever possible, winding their way through what were reportedly heavy stands of primeval forests. He'd heard that these trees were often of immense size and completely covered the intervening hills and valleys.

Other concerns began to tumble into Allen Sr.'s mind as he considered the winter departure. He had no idea how long he would be away. Would he need to develop a plan for spring planting in case he wasn't home to direct it himself? Would he need to accelerate smoking and salting extra meat and store extra vegetables to provide for his family through the winter and even spring if he was away that long? Would he need to provide at least some smoked meat and vegetables for himself as he traveled?

Then, another thought jumped in from nowhere. Wouldn't the experience of such an undertaking as a militia march to the front be good for his eldest son, Allen? Yes, he was only nine years old, but he had shown himself so capable, taking care of so much of what needed doing over the last few years. He seemed ready for adventure. The younger sons could handle chores—even the oxen and planting with a little further instruction. They'd been out there with him often; basically, they knew what to do, and if they had questions, Dorothy knew everything that they needed to learn. She'd reminded him, after all, about what he needed to do more times than he would care to admit. Would she agree to let their son go? Convincing her took a couple of days, but she did agree, though somewhat hesitantly. After getting her OK, he got busy preparing; and, as the summer turned to fall and eventually to early winter, he became quite confident that those left behind would be fine.

Subsequent militia get togethers confirmed a January departure date. Also, he had further reason to believe that young Allen would be ready for his adventure. In early November, during the first snowstorm of the season, he took Allen out hunting with him for extra venison, trudging along together through the snow. He even let Allen take the shot that brought down a sizable buck; one shot, right between the back and belly just behind the front legs, perfect, in fact. That was a hard shot with the wind somewhat gusty and with snow obscuring vision, making range and elevation even more difficult to calculate. This youngster pleased his father often these days. He thought, "I'll have him dress, salt, and smoke this one by himself. Even better, let's start now with dressing for the trek back home." Then aloud he said, "So, son, your kill, now what?"

Young Allen quickly and somewhat proudly drew his new Barlow from his pants pocket and then looked up for approval as he went right for the glands in the hind legs. After removing the glands with care, he proceeded to gut, removing the entrails—the bladder, bowel, intestines, stomach—again carefully to avoid contaminating the body cavity. His father, ever so slightly, nodded approval as his son worked away. The carcass, now considerably lighter, was easier to drag home through the snow. Except for the heart and liver, they left the entrails behind for buzzards or whatever creature got there first.

Once home Allen skinned the hide carefully. His father had warned him how easily hair from the hide could spoil the flavor of the meat. Then, under his father's supervision, he divided the meat into convenient portions, some larger for smoking, some smaller for salting. The salting would take up to a month. First, Allen rubbed salt into the meat, covered it with more salt, and then shelved it in the cold cellar. Each morning, he had to add more salt to the meat, just another chore for young Allen. Once it was no longer damp, he would bag it, place it back on the shelf, and leave it to age.

The smoking took place in a smoke room provided with its own smoke pit, separated from the living quarters, located just behind the kitchen. Allen kept that smoking fire going for up to a month, adding oak or apple for the flavor they all liked, not hickory which they considered too strong. A couple more successful hunts and careful management of all that went into preservation would provide what the family needed with enough left over to take some along on their upcoming trip to Niagara.

Allen, Sr. and six other militia men who lived relatively nearby had discussed some plan details at a late November muster. The only militia member with a sleigh large enough to handle all the men, young Allen, and their supplies was Uriah Stephens. He also had four strong horses. He lived north of the others; so, first Uriah would head south, alone, to pick up the Miners, Edward Williamson, and Andrew McMullin before heading north again to pick up a couple of members living in that direction and then further north toward the Seneca trails that lead to Niagara. December passed quickly, celebrating Christmas seemed charged with more emotion than usual, and soon the time came for the much-anticipated trek to Niagara.

On the assigned day, in early January of 1814, Uriah arrived at the Miners', after picking up the two others as planned, and then headed North. Allen and his son's parting with their family was short and sweet but tinged with concern, concealed, yes, but not without effort. Allen Miner, Sr., Uriah, Edward, and Andrew sat up front where they could talk with young Allen toward the back out of hearing. Uriah began the conversation, "Wondering if any of you have traveled up this way this time of year. Sure can be spectacular, especially once we reach the Bennetts Creek road."

Allen had been thinking that he wanted his son to learn to drive a sleigh, so he could help along the way to Niagara. He took the opening the mention of Bennetts Creek provided, and suggested tentatively, "maybe that would be a good place to allow my son to practice driving."

Uriah agreed. "That would be a good place. The road's smoother and driving the sleigh easier."

By the time they reached Bennetts Creek, they had picked up two more militia men. Uriah, Allen, Sr., and the other passengers had much to talk about and began almost immediately, but not before Uriah shouted back to the young Allen, "about time you made your way up front and took these reins."

"Coming." Was it a dream – a 9-year-old, driving a sleigh, with militia men and gear through a valley of unusual beauty, enhanced by the newly fallen snow? Add in the ice-covered trees glistening in the afternoon sun, and one can imagine young Allen's delight.

They reached the Stephens' homestead well before dark, as planned. The Stephens family, along with several neighboring families, had prepared a meal fit for a grand farewell. Food on the trip might be sparse, but the sendoff was splendid—venison freshly prepared, potatoes from the cellars, the summer season's stored vegetables, and pies from apples that had been carefully stored. The hard cider flowed freely; and, not at all surprisingly, the decision to camp right there for the night was unanimous.

Young Allen stayed up a bit later than might have been wise, quite a bit later, having met more young folks his age among the Stephens and their neighbors than he had ever met before. They swapped stories, fishing tales, even talked about girls when the girls weren't around. When his new friends found out that Allen was going all the way to Niagara with the militia, he became the envy of the group and when the girls found out, well, that brought forth feelings he was scarcely capable of understanding.

Morning brought more food, eggs and corn bread aplenty, along with good cheer and amply satisfied appetites. They all knew they wouldn't be eating this well again, or enjoying their families again, for a long time; how long they didn't know. Not just a few thought, maybe never. Those were not the thoughts of young Allen, however, especially after Uriah asked him to drive the sleigh again. He would be heading off to war with the militia, and he would be managing the team of horses upon leaving as his new young friends looked on, even the girls. And so, he did it with all the elan a nine-year-old can manage, waving and shouting back to his new friends, "I'll be back, let you all know how it went."

Allen drove north as directed and, as intended, stopped at the Moore homestead to pick up the last of their members, James and John Moore, as well as the Moore's smaller sleigh and horses that they used to carry supplies and equipment. The men were glad to let young Allen drive, more time for them to talk and joke amongst themselves. Allen driving and the men enjoying each other's company became the pattern, even when they reached the so-called main route of Seneca trails. They had hoped to meet up with and join other militia detachments headed their way but that did not happen. So, that night and on following nights, they camped alone. They were lucky the first night; Allen Sr. bagged a couple of rabbits and a quail to supplement the sparse diet they had anticipated. They made short work of creating a fire and of dressing and spit roasting them. They built the fire up to warm themselves, talked on and on until one by one they fell asleep. They did alternate guard duty. A few renegade Senecas still roamed the hills and trails, and panthers, bears, and other creatures of the wild might be interested if they smelled what was left of the meal.

So, it went for several days and nights. Sometimes they were lucky to supplement their meals with game of various sorts, sometimes not. The trail did from time-to-time dip into swamp filled valleys, which during warmer weather would have made for damp or even downright wet and difficult traveling but not in January with the ground and water well frozen. None-the-less they traveled across these sections with care, sending out several men ahead of the sleighs to look for weak spots in the ice. Once, they found a spot that they considered weak enough to cause real concern, and it took them most of a day to clear a way around it. Even the cleared path looked weak, so they ended up taking the horses over first. Then they tied one end of a long rope to the larger sleigh and the other end to the horses now on solid enough ground to pull it across. They repeated the operation with the smaller sleigh. After that experience, they did a lot more walking to lighten the load. No sense in taking chances.

Decisions - Return

Finally, in early February, they reached the main Niagara, NY encampment, having met another contingent on the last day of their trip. Supplies were no longer a problem; large encampments like the one gathering at Niagara had its own supply line from nearby centers and Buffalo, networks any such troop gathering requires. The militia men, including the new arrivals, would be there training and hanging out along with the regular troops until needed, if ever. Camp life was every bit as routine as their farm chores, but given the camaraderie, not without good feelings when they got a break.

Once Brigadier General Scott arrived in March, those breaks didn't come often. Under Scott's regular army regimen, known for extreme toughness, drills began at 4 AM and lasted 11 hours a day. Allen, Jr. joined in on the exercises occasionally, though there was no requirement for him to do so, and an hour or two was enough for a nine-year-old. There was plenty for him to do to fill the other hours of the day. With the help of several officers, he continued his studies, concentrating on US history. He aided the chef by retrieving food from storage and helping with preparation chores. He saw to the needs of horses and other animals, ran errands for officers, and generally tried hard to be useful.

For militia members whatever good feelings they were still able to generate, despite 11 hours of drilling, were diminished further by general camp conditions; lousy food, tainted water, cold, and a serious lack of alcohol, a lack that even the hospital experienced when a slug or two was needed for medicinal purposes. Still, in the afternoon after drilling was complete, there was time to talk, and the militia men had one issue to discuss when they weren't talking about their families, their adventures, and their own future. They wrestled back and forth over what ought to be the limits of New York state militia participation in the war against the British if the state itself was not threatened. Uriah Stephens spoke up quite forcefully.

"Look, we're New York's militia, charged with the solemn responsibility of protecting New York. Crossing into Canada and invading a foreign county is simply no business of ours. If those British Army Regulars, Canadian militiamen, or even their Indian allies, crossed the border into New York state, well, then we'd be more than ready. As the New York militia we protect our own, defend our homeland."

Elias Sloat, who had already seen action in Canada as a New York Militiaman, spoke up with a definite edge to his voice. "Don't tell me we shouldn't strike back at Canada. I've already done so. They attacked us here in Buffalo. Destroyed the place. We remember the battle of Black Rock back in December. We were defeated, damned embarrassing, and we intend to show them just what New York militiamen can do when we retaliate. Yes, we'll destroy their homes just like they did ours."

Allen and his son heard his passion and saw many militiamen show vigorous signs of agreement though members of their small group were not among them. Allen, Sr. spoke up as calmly as he could manage, attempting to mitigate his opposition to Elias and his many supporters.

"Right, it's hard to forget what they did. But doing the same to them, wouldn't that in some sense justify it? We are more than ready to defend New York if they come here again. Our passion will match anyone's in defense of New York against invasion, but we are not ready to invade another country. Some of us agree with the New England militias who also refused after similar Canadian invasions."

Uriah Stephens realized that this conversation couldn't go much further. Besides, he had more immediate matters on his mind, so he brought the conversation to a halt by pointing to the serious condition of two members of the Allen/Stephens contingent.

"Look, right now we have problems here. Our friends, James Moore Jr. and his brother John, are not well. James seems to have the measles, but the doctors can't figure out what's wrong with John. And they both seem to be getting worse as time passes. James is past the rash stage, but for some reason he's still not recovering. Both need to get back to their families where they can get decent care. We all know they won't get anything like decent care here, certainly not in what they call a hospital."

Allen, Sr. added, "Besides, it's nearly April. If Uriah's sleigh is used, James and John need to be transported before those icy streams melt and snow disappears entirely. So, who should take the sleigh back and return the two sick men to their families? Much as I hate to say it, makes me nervous, but the answer is all too obvious. My son knows the way, knows how to manage the sleigh, and as a nine-year-old and even when he turns ten in a couple of weeks, he's not obligated to remain with the militia. Despite my own serious misgivings, I've got to say that my son can handle it and he's available. At least he'll have two grown men with him, sick though they are."

On this issue all agreed. They got right to work scrounging the camp for any spare food and blankets for the trip that they could find. That took a couple days, given the scarcity of both, but they were successful. After gaining permission to return the sick men to their home, all was ready, and young Allen left with both sick men wrapped up well against the cold. He was elated to be trusted with such a critical responsibility and nervous, too, though he hid both emotions well enough. Off they went, four horses, the sleigh, and two sick men: a grand moment for him, a nervous yet proud one for his father.

All went quite well enough for a good number of days; it was perfect weather for the sleigh, the horses, and Allen, not so fine for his passengers. James, especially, was suffering more severely from chills and fever. Allen worried but didn't understand. He thought what most people thought; the measles rash was gone, it was time for improvement, not decline. Seeing the decline, though, he decided to slow down and even stop a bit more often, despite worrying about the possibility that sleigh travel would become more difficult, if the April weather turned warmer, melting the ice and snow.

Then, what Allen and John thought of as the worst, did happen, and Allen had to make decisions no one his age should have to make. Early in the morning both Allen and John began to realize that James was not just getting worse, he was dying. Allen began to understand that James would not make it home; John probably understood, too, but it was his brother and he refused to allow himself to admit the possibility. But just before that noon James removed all doubt; he died, held tightly in his brother's arms. John covered him, laying him down on the sleigh, and tried hard to hold himself together. Allen could not find any way to comfort the grieving man over twice his age, so he just remained silent. Eventually after unsuccessfully offering John lunch, he decided to act in a manner that would indicate the need to move on. He fed the horses, checked the reigns, and stowed the lunch he hoped John would eat later. That was all he could think to do, and all he needed to do. John understood and climbed into the sleigh without saying a word.

Death should have been enough to handle for one day, but the day and the need to act under stress was not over. Within an hour Allen saw, up ahead on the trail, what appeared to be another body. Then, as they approached, the body moved and even attempted to stand before stumbling and falling. It was a young boy, even younger than Allen, a boy who clearly needed help. But it wasn't just any young boy, his dress indicated quite clearly that he was a Seneca native boy. To help him came naturally to Allen; the boy was a human and needed help. But questions came almost as immediately. What was he doing here alone? Where were his elders? Was there a party of Senecas who left him here or who lost him or what? Seneca had always meant danger to Allen, right up there with bears and panthers in his imagination and his training.

What if he and John stumbled across the Seneca warriors (weren't they all warriors) who abandoned him? Allen decided to help despite his misgivings. Grabbing a blanket, he signaled to the boy that he should wrap himself in it, and then indicated the sleigh and helped the boy in. John said nothing. Allen acted on his own, and John was too sick and heartbroken to care.

After supper their new traveling companion seemed to improve. Apparently, part of his problem, if not all, had been hunger. Next morning, he ate all he was offered and seemed like he could eat more. He got out of the sleigh, walked around, but did not in the least act like he wanted to bolt or sneak off. When it was time to move on, he got back in the sleigh, ready to go. Allen and John both wondered what they were going to do with him. He didn't speak English, they didn't speak Seneca, and asking with gestures proved futile. Drop him off at a Seneca reservation? They had no idea where one was, and they were far too anxious to get to their own homes. It didn't take long for them to resolve to take him to the Moore's homestead and figure out the next steps once there with help from clear minded relatives and friends.

It was a good plan, but not what happened. Shortly after resolving what to do, the plan vanished, like many good plans. About 100 yards ahead of them sprang into sight half a dozen of those Seneca warriors Allen so feared, renegades from the reservations, no doubt. Now what? Again, Allen acted; John could hardly move by now, so there was no alternative. Fight trained Seneca warriors? Not a chance. Turning the sleigh and running? Impossible. No, the only chance was the one Allen took; he signaled to the boy to get out of the wagon and walked with him right up to those warriors, making his peaceful intentions as plain as possible.

Allen, in that critical moment trusted human nature above fear; the Seneca, the stuff of his nightmares, were human with sons like this Seneca boy he had helped. That revelation proved the best of his young life. The Seneca boy didn't just walk with Allen, he ran ahead to greet his elders and made clear to them that Allen was a friend. By the time Allen reached them the story of his aid to one of their own had been excitedly told and the fierce, Seneca warriors transformed right before Allen's eyes into accepting, even perhaps friendly, people.

Friendly enough, in fact, to help Allen with the next danger he faced. The trip across a potentially dangerous, icy stream lay just ahead. He had done some thinking about this problem. He would have to leave the wagon, check the ice and, if safe, then proceed. That would take time, and the thought of determining whether the ice was safe troubled him. And this time he would be hard put to get all the weight out of the sleigh before going on. He could lighten the sleigh some by carrying supplies across weak spots separately, but with one dead man and another scarcely capable of moving, either they must remain in the sleigh or be dragged across the thin ice one by one.

Instead, the Senecas guided the sleigh across the ice, and, when they sensed the first weak spot, they helped Allen cautiously guide the horses and sleigh around it. They did hesitate when Allen indicated the two sick passengers might go first. They knew about sick white men and the risk of getting too close; they left John and his dead brother in the sleigh. They repeated their aid through several more spots until, after scouting ahead, they knew all would go well. What's the sign for thanks? Allen didn't know, but he gave them the best friendly wave and smile he could manage and proceeded on his way, solid ground beneath them once more.

By comparison the rest of the near month-long trip was all downhill, well, up and down hill but not difficult or dangerous, and quite manageable by a young man who had matured considerably. They reached the Moore homestead without further incident. Allen helped John out of the sleigh as members of his family rushed out. There was no avoiding the shock they experienced when they saw the wrapped body there. All John or Allen could say was 'James didn't make it'. John took the lead this time; it was his family, his horrible news to convey. James Jr. was dead, mourning would follow, shock was what the family felt immediately. Allen still held

John up, and Allen alone helped him into the house. The others, in shock, straggled in, and, only after a few moments, managed to refocus sufficiently to concentrate on John, who so clearly needed them. Two family members even managed to think of the horses and sleigh, returning outside to handle both.

John was washed up with warm compresses, dressed for bed, and quite simply mothered. A doctor was called, but after examining John, he had no more idea what was wrong than had previous doctors in Niagara. Recommended treatment was simple—bed, rest, and easy to digest food. Allen remained for several days, worried about John and helping as best he could. John did recover slowly, and once that recovery became clear, Allen became anxious to be on his own way home. He left on foot, leaving Uriah's sleigh in the care of the Moore family. Home was just a 10-mile trek through the still gorgeous, snow-covered Bennetts Creek valley.

Chapter Five

~~~~~

Off to Kentucky

Where?

Home at last, tired but relieved and greeted warmly by his family, Allen settled into the home routine easily. Given that his dad was still with the militia in Niagara, he resumed responsibility, as eldest son, for chores around the farm that typically would fall to his father. He had his younger brothers, especially John but Jonathan, too, to help with chores and the early May planting. Jonathan was relieved; he had some time again to just be a kid. Their mom did all she always did as well as provide advice and help when needed. She felt relief as she and Allen sat after supper and shared plans for the next day.

Not until December of 1814 would the war on the Canadian border seem to be under control. The British retreated into Canada for good, and what remained of the New York militia in Niagara was able to return home. Allen's father, though, was released early, partly to check on the Moore family and partly in recognition of his son's contribution to the cause. He took an excellent riding horse left behind by the Moore brothers, and he was given saddle bags for food, enough for the two-week ride back to the Moore's. He got home in early October, well before winter would have required a sleigh again. Still, that meant Allen, Jr. and the rest of his family had gone through a whole growing season and harvest without him.

John Moore's family had informed Allen Sr. by mail that Allen Jr. and their son, John, had made it back to the Moore's safely but that James Jr. had died on the way. Allen Sr.'s family sent him letters, too, but none went into any detail about young Allen's adventures. He had to wait to hear about that incredible series of events until his October return. On his way home Allen stopped at the Moore's to offer condolences, to drop off the horse, and to mention how much he appreciated hearing that his son had made it safely to their place. He expressed his relief after seeing just how successfully John had recovered. The Moore's let him know that young Allen had tales to tell once he got home, but they refused to ruin his stories by giving any details in advance. Allen, Sr. was anxious to get home anyway, but now curiosity added to that urgency. He left the next morning, walking along the same Bennetts Creek route as his son, still beautiful but without the added sparkle of the snow that his son had so enjoyed.

Home at last, pleased and relieved to see all in order despite his long absence, he waited for young Allen to tell the stories of his own return home, figuring his son would be unable to hold back from the telling. He was wrong. Instead, Allen asked about his father's militia encampment and his return. So, the father went first with his relatively boring story, in comparison to his son's. Camp life had been routine. There were the discussions about whether NY militia should cross the Canadian border to retaliate for the damage done to Buffalo in December 1813 or stay in NY to protect the home front. Allen already knew about those debates, but the rest of the family showed real interest.

The trip home had been easy. Riding a horse to the Moore's instead of driving a sleigh across occasionally treacherous terrain made it almost routine. He mentioned his stop at the Moore's, and though Allen, Jr. and the rest of the family had heard news from the Moore family recently, his wife, Dorothy, pressed him for the latest update. His news that John Moore had fully recovered cheered them all.

Allen's father took that moment of good cheer to transition from his story to his son's. He felt some relief in taking the opportunity. His son, also glad for the transition, changed the mood quite abruptly, though, by starting with just how ill both John and James Jr. became, despite efforts to keep them warm and fed. He mentioned how puzzled he had been when James's rash disappeared and yet he got worse, not better. The family had heard that James had a rash and that it had been attributed to measles, but not even Dorothy had any idea that after the rash disappeared measles might transform into a disease as serious as pneumonia and become deadly, as in James's case.

Young Allen became particularly intense when he began telling the Seneca adventure. "James dead and John so sick that he could barely move. Then, what do I see? A small body, dead too? Then it moved, tried to get up, but fell. I saw it was a young Seneca boy, a boy in trouble. A boy in trouble, that's what I saw. Had to help. I helped and John said nothing. I got the boy into the wagon and fed him. He recovered quickly."

"Quite right," his dad responded, "to help one in need, so right despite where you might imagine it could lead."

"Oh, I did lots of that imagining. What would we do with him? Drop him somewhere? A reservation? 'Course we didn't know of any reservations; couldn't get to one anyway. We just took him with us. Maybe when we got to the Moore's someone would have an idea. Turned out that was only a little problem. Suddenly, up ahead, a group of Seneca warriors. Now what? Turn and run, attack, come on, not a chance. I knew that in seconds. So, I just got the boy out of the back and approached the warriors with him. It worked; the boy helped us. 'Course we didn't know what he said, but it worked. They didn't kill us."

His dad couldn't help but express his pride and admiration. "Had to be a quick call and you did it despite your well known and quite justified fear of Seneca warriors. Close call, but the right one it seems."

Dorothy nodded her agreement. "Right and very brave. And, as I said before when you told us about it, 'I'm proud of you.'"

"Oh Dad, you don't know how right. I'd worried about how I could get through those swampy areas with what might be thin ice. Hard to lighten the wagon with a corpse and a man too sick to move in it. How would I get the wagon and horses across? Those warriors? They figured out that I'd need help before I even asked. Ask? Couldn't ask. Might have tried pointing or stamping my feet, I guess, but didn't need to. They led the way and did everything needed. Checked the ice and got the wagon and horses across. Wondered why they didn't take the body and John first. Left them in the wagon. Guess they knew something about white men and their diseases."

Dad was all smiles and admiration, as was the rest of the family. How right his son had been to show compassion to a young Seneca boy despite his well-known fear of Senecas and of his immediate fears of what might happen as a result of picking one up. Even more pleasing, when his son met his ultimate nightmare, he acted as quickly and decisively as anyone could possibly wish. And those fear inducing warriors, what incredibly humane reactions they displayed. One could hardly hope for a better story or a better son, and his dad, mom, brothers and even Esther were quick with words or at least clear signs of admiration. Allen, awash in praise slept well that night, after recording it all, especially the praise, in his diary.

Nothing in the next five years or so came close to the excitement of the returns of father and son or the telling of their adventures. Life on the farm went along as easily as such lives could. Allen Sr.

made his annual trips to Painted Post, but relative to his earlier trip, not memorable. Young Allen and his brothers became so capable at running the farm that their father was able to relax some, though he continued to work at building barrels. And young Allen had a chance to read more. As he approached 15, he became particularly intrigued by what he read about the country's founding fathers and the US constitution. His father, when young, had a similar interest and managed to secure a copy of the Federalist and of the constitution itself. He was pleased to see how avidly his eldest son dug into both.

His son's interest, though, widened to include stories of the new frontier. He developed some vague plans about his own future. His thoughts went so far that he began to stash money away, by working a bit at a neighboring farm, and building his own barrels for sale. His father agreed that profit from half the barrels his son made would go to the family, as his contribution to their finances, and half to Allen's savings.

Not quite suddenly, those vague plans began to take shape in Allen's maturing mind. He had uncles, the Miners in Kentucky, whom he could visit, and on the way, he could see more of the world. So, one day he mentioned the possibility of visiting his uncles to his parents. Reactions were mostly what he expected them to be; resistance at first, transitioning more quickly than he could have hoped into acquiescence, despite the added pressure of maintaining the farm that losing him would put back on his father and on his younger brothers. Then he took the first concrete step by spending a good deal of his savings on a horse and saddle. Not too surprisingly, recalling the Battle of Lundy's Lane, he named his horse Lundy. He really was going to do this. Allen, Sr. simply agreed, as did Dorothy, after adding that he should at least wait until he was 16. Allen, Jr. smiled warmly while thinking to himself, "Once I reach 16, I will be on my own, entirely responsible for what I do, starting with my visit to Kentucky."

So, at the end of the first week of April 1820, he was ready and raring to go. His father had helped him figure out the best route after talking with William Wombough on his most recent trip to Painted Post. William had traveled South to Philadelphia over what passed for trails years earlier; he knew the routes better than almost anyone else. Young Allen, himself, knew only that he wanted to take the Wilderness Road through the Cumberland Gap, the route of the first pioneers to the West. William knew of a trail heading west from Philadelphia that he thought joined the Wilderness Road, but he had not traveled on it and didn't recall its name. His best advice was to keep heading South in Pennsylvania until he hit that trail then ask someone local whether to head east or west on it to reach the Wilderness Trail.

Allen, Jr. figured he'd start out taking the same road along the Canisteo River that his father took on trips to Painted Post. But, from there he'd figure on heading south into Pennsylvania. His father had mentioned a creek that seemed to have origins to the south and that fed into the Canisteo, and next to the creek there was what seemed to be a path of sorts. Allen figured if anyone could follow a path of sorts he could, even if it turned out to be no more than an old Indian trail; he'd had practice.

Allen left at the end of April; the final preparations took some time. The uncles had to be informed and agree to a visit, and given the communication delays, he was lucky to leave as soon as he did. Farewells were tinged with both excitement and trepidation. Yes, it was a brand-new life he would begin. But there were dangers in travel as both Allen and his family knew only too well. Besides, a new life meant just that; would his new life ever bring him back home again? No one mentioned the possibility that they might never see each other again, but there was that worrisome tickler in the back of his mind and certainly in the minds of his parents.

The Cumberland Gap-Allen Reaches Maturity

Allen couldn't have picked a better time to depart. For an April morning, the Canisteo trail was remarkably dry and easy to navigate. On horseback, he had no problems, unlike his father had with those oxen and a wagon full of goods.

Not even finding the stream flowing into the Canisteo River from the South proved as difficult as he thought it might, and he soon discovered there was a trail of sorts, as he had hoped there would be. It looked just about as well defined as the Seneca trail from Niagara that he had managed to navigate, and he had no sleigh or sick passengers this time. He could even imagine that he felt freedom flowing into his life like the stream, a stream he later learned was named the Tioga. That first evening he tied Lundy to a tree near a grassy patch before picking at some left-over lunch and then settling in for the night without even bothering to start a fire for warmth; it was that good a day and night.

After a sparse breakfast of bread and preserves, eaten slowly as Lundy grazed, he headed out along the trail. All too soon he began to discover that the trail was a bit less defined as he progressed, eventually badly defined to the point where he was just following the stream for long stretches. With a trail that had vanished and a stream that might well lead nowhere, his concern began to mount. Then on turning a bend, he saw up ahead another human being, a young man close to his own age. "Good", he thought, "bet he knows what lies ahead." The young man, blond and blue eyed, seemed almost as pleased to see Allen. There were not too many folks his age, or any age for that matter, to meet and talk to in these parts. They sat down together on the banks of what Allen's new acquaintance identified as the Tioga.

Allen had learned, from years of observing his father in various conversations, not to jump to a point immediately. Instead, he introduced himself and the young man responded with his own name, Ernst. Allen then asked an obvious question, "Just wondering what brought you along such a deserted trail."

"Well, I live close by, just a short way down the stream."

An invitation to lunch quickly followed, not a bad start to a conversation. Allen followed up by asking what his family was like and what they did in what appeared to be such a deserted area. He learned that the family consisted of just three; his new friend, Ernst, and his mother, Agathe, and father, Arndt. They farmed, as Allen would have guessed, and carted farm produce to market. The market comment opened the conversation in the direction Allen had hoped. He asked where the market was, hoping it might be in the direction he wanted to go; it could hardly be in the direction he had come given that the trail he had followed could not handle a wagon. Ernst deferred the question, mentioning that his father would be the one to ask. Allen had to wait.

Of course, Ernst wanted to know what Allen was doing on such a deserted trail, too. Allen obliged, saying he was on his way from his home in central New York to Kentucky to visit relatives. He added that he didn't really know more about the route than that he wanted to find the Wilderness Road so he could go through the Cumberland gap on his way. Ernst, who hadn't been more than ten miles from where they sat in his life, was fascinated. His parents were as strict as they come, which explained his ten-mile limit. He asked, suddenly excited, "How did you get your parents to allow such an adventure?"

Allen answered by mentioning his own parents' initial resistance but then added, "They knew from my past experiences that I would manage well enough."

Ernst bit, "What past experiences?"

Allen had his tales to tell; driving the sleigh to Niagara, the militia encampment and his responsibilities there, his sick and eventually dying passenger on the way home, the Seneca encounter, the treacherous path through the marsh. It was a long tale and Ernst enjoyed every bit of it. Allen ended, not exactly modestly, by saying, "I guess my parents figured if I could survive that ride home six years ago, I would survive this trip, now that I've grown."

Ernst stored it all away; he would use it someday to make his own break from what he had felt and now had even more reason to see as a confined existence. Talk ended, or at least trailed off, after Allen's tale, so they decided to head for Ernst's place. Ernst did mention that his parents would find Allen's current and past adventures interesting. He even said, "You know my parents will want to hear all about you; you'll have to tell this all over again."

They enjoyed walking together with Lundy trailing behind. They even stopped a couple of times to skip stones in the creek and to watch a buck who eyed them with similar interest. The buck led to talk of other creatures—bears, panthers, and even that giant snake Elizabeth had invented to enliven Allen's father's tales of his trip to Painted Post. Ernst couldn't top that one but told one about his own father's encounter with a bear, a large one he single-handedly beat off with nothing more than an ax for self-defense.

Eventually they arrived at Ernst's place, the Schneider homestead. It certainly looked familiar to Allen; the cabin was not too different from the one he had just left with a home garden like the one he had managed for years, a barn and several horses (he didn't see any oxen), and oddly, most surprising, containers for flowers and herbs on the front porch, just like the ones his father had built years ago for his mother. He had thought of those containers as a uniquely charming gift, and he hadn't seen them at any of the other homesteads he had visited. Just for a moment missing home welled up inside; he put those feelings away as quickly as he could and concentrated on Ernst's parents as he was introduced to them.

Ernst's father, Arndt, was a tall, broad-shouldered man bordering on stout, taller than Allen and certainly beefier; he towered over his wife, Agathe, who was diminutive with dark, slightly silver tinged hair; she seemed almost to disappear by his side. Disappear, that is, until the talk began. Then she took over with that air that made readily clear who ran the home. She ushered them all inside and sat them down around the table, quickly setting a place for Allen while allowing her son and husband to find their accustomed places. Ernst and Allen had timed their arrival well; lunch was ready, and the boss had made clear that they were to wash up and prepare to eat before the food got cold. What a treat for Allen; warm food with no fire to start and no cooking to do.

During dessert, a pumpkin pie no less, Allen finally saw a chance to introduce the questions Ernst had suggested that his father could handle best; what sort of routes lay to the south, and would they lead to the Wilderness Road? But getting to the question took some time. Allen began by discussing barrel making which led to selling them and then, after Allen mentioned Painted Post and his father's adventures, led to asking where Arndt sold his farm produce. Allen was disappointed to learn that the trail Arndt used did not get much better and that it headed east/west, as did the Tiago River, to a small town named Wellsboro. When Allen mentioned the Cumberland Gap, Arndt had little information other than to suggest what Allen already knew; he needed to head south by whatever paths he could find and then pick up the East/West road to find the intersection with the Wilderness Road. At least Arndt provided a name for the road; he called it the Great Wagon Road.

Ernst fidgeted a bit through most of the discussion; he still wanted to make sure Allen got around to telling his Niagara adventures. So, finally, he just interrupted the talk of Allen's current travels to mention that Allen had traveled by himself before. As Allen's tale unfolded, Ernst was quite pleased to see his father's astonishment. Maybe there was hope that his father would loosen up a little; at least Ernst felt his new friend made quite an impression. Allen, even though he'd gained little new information, was ready to go soon after lunch. He left as soon as he could gracefully, thanking all for their hospitality and for the information Arndt had provided.

A Revelation - In the Dark of Night

"Head South", was about all Allen had to go on. Trails tended to head east and west; heading south required North Star navigation at times, even a few detours east or west when no south trail existed. Quite a few days into the journey Allen came across another cabin and was invited to stay for lunch. People in such sparsely settled areas not only welcomed strangers, they genuinely enjoyed them. He learned a bit more, too. He found out that continuing to head south would take him straight into an impassable mountain ridge. He would need to take an easterly detour through a gap in the mountains and then follow the Great Valley Road as it turned south to reach the Wilderness Road.

The plan began to take shape and the road improved once he reached the Great Valley Road. Better, but longer; he was on it for several hundred miles. He spent days of eating whatever he could hunt or forage, seeking out pastures for Lundy, and sleeping when and wherever possible—before he reached what appeared to be the Wilderness Road. He waited until other travelers came along who could confirm that, yes, it was the Wilderness Road, and yes, it would take him through the Cumberland Gap on the way to Kentucky.

The valley portion of the trip was down-right pleasant; he met other travelers along the way and even purchased some fresh food from those transporting goods down to Roanoke. He gave some thought to traveling a bit further south to see Roanoke but decided, anxious to see the gap as he was, that he'd just push on.

The Wilderness Road turned out to be much improved from what he had read about it. It was not just the rugged horse and foot accessible, only minimally improved Native American trail he had expected; wagons were using it. If he hadn't been so travel weary, he might have wished for something more in tune with his imaginings of the pioneer days, but he was weary and ready to get on to Kentucky. Besides, he was running short on both food and money.

Just a few miles short of the gap itself, late in the afternoon of a cloudy day, he managed to bag a rabbit. He thought he would take a good, long break, start a fire, and cook himself a decent meal, then settle in for the night. He found just the right spot with grass for Lundy and a place to tie him up, accessible but off the trail just far enough so he could still see it but not be bothered by noise and dust from any other travelers who might pass by. There was even a slight indentation one might be tempted to call a pond where rainwater had collected. Water and food and isolation, all was good.

He finished cooking up the rabbit and nearly finished eating, just as the clouds darkened and what had been mist turned into a drizzle. He covered Lundy with a horse blanket and then constructed a temporary shelter for himself, using the over-sized poncho he had brought along with such inclement nights in mind, propping it up with branches he collected. Not an ideal evening awaited him, but he was reasonably comfortable; he'd certainly faced worse. He even nodded off sooner than he had intended.

Real sleep, though, that was not to be. Suddenly he awoke, startled by a sharp sound, the crack of a whip he realized, and an inhuman scream. He stared, trying to see through the drizzle and the darkened evening, and managed to make out a line of walking figures, figures that had been walking but now seemed suspended, a tableau against the rocky cliffs rising up on the other side of the trail.

That whip was being applied without mercy to a fallen figure. Was the one being beaten smaller than others in the line? Was it a man, a boy, a woman? He couldn't really see clearly enough to tell. Nothing was clear, except that all those in the line were evenly spaced as if linked together. Chained together? Yes, had to be. He'd heard slaves were taken west for sale this way but had never seen anything like it. Back home he'd seen a couple of Black men who worked in William Wombough's brewery; Allen had thought they might be slaves. He'd never seen them in chains and never heard that they were beaten. He didn't think much about it back then, but this was different; this was ghastly.

Finally, the tableau moved on again, the beaten figure limping badly, helped along as much as possible by the figures directly behind and in front of him. The whole horror show seemed to pass far too slowly down the path before being swallowed up by the darkening skies. That image lingered in his mind for hours. Allen tried to get rid of it; he just could not let it go. But he was tired, and he needed to sleep; he intended to make significant progress on his way to his relatives the next day.

Sleep of sorts did come eventually, but what he had seen lingered in dreamscape. Images twisted and turned. The beaten figure became a boy then an old, hunched man, then something demon-like. Blood flowed from the wounds, lots of blood all over. Lightning flashed like whip cracks. The hillside collapsed and buried the man with that whip. Chains broke and figures danced for joy before the whole horror scene came rushing back. Dreams like this one do mean that sleep occurred, but they do not mean it was a restful sleep. In the morning Allen awoke feeling as if he had been dragged along with the slaves, hurting from the rough ground and far from rested.

By the time he packed up it was a lot later than he had intended; he'd lost the early start he'd wanted but at least the rain had passed with the night. He threw off the dream and the images, ate what was left of the rabbit, and got on his way. This trail was better than many he had been on, and Lundy made reasonably good time despite the puddles left over from the rain. He thought he might even skip lunch to make up for the late start. Then the horror show returned. The line of slaves was right there up ahead of him, this time in the clear light of day. He would need to pass by them up close; they were holding to the middle of the trail, so he would need to pick one side or the other. Actually, the choice was easy; he did not want to be caught between the mountain and the slaves, so he picked the lower side. He'd wait a bit until that side of the trail opened up enough so that he would be able to get off the trail if necessary.

As he followed along as slowly as the slave chain, he had plenty of time to note all he had missed about the slaves the previous evening, particularly when they snaked left or right with the winding trail. The whipped figure was an old man bent and still limping, and clearly in danger of falling again or maybe even giving up altogether. The motivation to drive himself on must have been strong in that old man. "Family, maybe", Allen thought, "what other good could possibly lie ahead for him?" And that blood he thought he had dreamed up turned out to be quite real. The chains dug into the ankles of every one of the slaves, and they were all bleeding from the chafing. The old man's struggles, yes heroic struggles Allen thought, and the blood from the chains revealed so clearly just how inhumane this slave driver, walking along so calmly, was. How inhumane slavery really was. That blood, even from a slave owner's perspective, was just plain stupid; that slave driver was damaging the future slave owner's property.

Finally, the break in the trail he was looking for came, and he took it as quickly as he could. He couldn't help a quick glance at the old man, but when he reached the slave driver, he didn't allow even a hint of acknowledgment. Clear of the horror show he broke into a trot for a bit. He wanted to distance himself as quickly as possible. He was on his way; he was heading for his Kentucky relatives; something sane and comfortable lay ahead, he thought.

Kentucky - Home away from Home

The directions from the gap to Allen's Kentucky relatives was clear enough. Communications from his Uncle Tom prior to his leaving home contained quite precise instructions from Harrodsburg, just off the Wilderness trail, to Shelbyville and then to their homestead on Guist Creek. He'd just head north on the Wilderness trail, essentially following the Kentucky River, and then head west on the road to Shelbyville. The weather was nearly perfect, partly sunny but with patchy clouds that protected Allen and Lundy from the sun's heat most of the time. The somewhat hilly terrain provided scenic variety but no problems. Travelers he met along the way let him know when he reached the Shelbyville road. All went well, and he arrived just before evening, after several days on it.

Uncle Thomas Miner, Aunt Mary, and Cousin Peter welcomed him with open arms. Peter cared for Lundy while Allen washed up, and then Mary sat them all down for supper. Thomas reminded

Allen to some extent of his father, the same dark hair and ample beard, rough cut. He was somewhat taller and slimmer than his dad. Aunt Mary did not look at all like his mother; she was very slim and tall, just a bit shorter than her husband. Peter was a couple of years older than Allen, and he had certainly taken on his parents' slim shape and height. Allen, who had never felt short back home, did feel short here.

Allen's adventure stories filled the evening, but the Cumberland Gap images, currently so prominent in his mind, were left out; he did not mention the slaves chained and bleeding, heading for Kentucky. Allen's father had let him know that these Kentucky relatives owned slaves. Allen hoped that their slaves had gotten here in some more humane way than being driven by a brutal slave driver like the one he had witnessed, or that they were born here. He hoped they were well treated. He didn't know what more to hope; he knew so little about slave life. He was sure, though, that he wasn't going to mention a subject so new to him while he was being treated so warmly by his slave-owning relatives. After all, he intended a long stay. There would be plenty of time for such uncomfortable topics to come up under less awkward circumstances, if they came up at all. Aunt Mary, realizing how tired he must be, ended the story telling by suggesting that he might want to get to bed after such a long day and asked Peter to show him where he could sleep.

The next morning, after breakfast, Peter offered to show Allen around the farm and Allen gladly accepted. They were young and healthy, so a good walk suited them both. Uncle Thomas was pleased to have a friend for his son around; after a few chores he encouraged them to just enjoy the morning. They took some fishing gear with them and headed off to a small stream near a far corner of the farm. There was nothing quite like sitting down by a stream with lines cast out as a way to get to know each other.

Peter started the conversation, "This place has been fine for me so far, no real complaints, but I feel the need to start my own life sometime soon. Come to think of it, you are doing just that right now."

Allen took that thought up. "You're right, that's just what I'm doing. Had to leave the comforts of home to figure out what I want to do next. Got to tell you, though, I've sure left home a long way off. Glad that you folks down here gave me a reason to leave and a place to stay that made some sense to my parents."

Peter responded. "Yes, I've been looking into a place nearby, though. Dad may still need some help here. Don't want to go too far."

"Awkward," Allen thought to himself, "just the one son, with no other brothers to help like the ones I have. 'Course they have the slaves." He left those thoughts unspoken, just pulled in his line and cast it out again. Fishing helps a conversation in many ways.

Peter just sat gazing out at the stream and fishing for quite a while before saying that his father did have other sources of help with the place. "Of course, my dad does have the five slaves to help, and they do much of what needs to be done anyway. Can't run such a large place with just two people in the fields. You'll probably see them out there working away with Dad when we go back. Come to think of it, would be good if we at least caught one fish so we can say we did something, too."

Allen smiled. "Not much happening on my line, yours either, far as I can tell."

Peter chided. "Well, aren't you the impatient one. Set yourself back and relax. Not often we'll get a whole morning to waste. Enjoy, we'll just take the heat if we end up with nothing."

Allen felt quite able to laugh this time. It was good talking with someone new and roughly his age, and good that slavery had come up without his having to mention it. He felt comfortable enough sitting next to that stream just smiling and laughing with his new friend to ask, as offhandedly as possible, "Where do they live, the slaves, I mean?"

Peter surprised Allen by just as offhandedly offering to show him. "We can pass by their place on the way back. It's not too far from our place."

And, so they did, without a fish to show for the time they'd spent; a productive time though, if the new bond is a measure of productivity. The slave quarters lay in a slight hollow out of sight of the main house, though near as Peter had said. There were two small shacks, one for a family of five: the mother, Priscilla, the father, George, two daughters, Amanda and Luan, and a son, Jim, all field hands. The other even smaller shack was for an old man living alone named Tom. He was too old to contribute much to the work anymore, but important to the well-being of the others, as Peter explained. "The old man keeps them content. Sings songs and plays some sort of stringed instrument they brought along when they arrived years ago. Content slaves are good slaves."

Just then the old man appeared. He came out of his cabin to sit in a chair just in front and to the side of the door. "And there he is, not in any shape to work the fields as you can see." Peter said, pointing him out. Allen was tempted to wave in the old man's direction; but, taking his cue from Peter, didn't. Instead, he followed Peter on toward the main house. Thoughts of the old man he had seen beaten on his trip through the Cumberland Gap came to mind. Both old men looked about the same age—one beaten bloody, one sitting contentedly, it seemed, and relaxed.

The days passed quite enjoyably for Allen and Peter, working hard together as they both had been brought up to do, enjoying talking and joking as close friends, in a way neither had much of a chance to do before with anyone in their separate lives. The family routines continued with Allen as just one more to share. Allen had never worked alongside slaves before, but even that new experience became more and more normal for him. It was still quite far from feeling as normal as it was for his cousin, though.

Only one event broke the pattern. After a few weeks, Allen felt comfortable enough to consider making his way down to the slave quarters on his own. While sitting on the main house porch, he had heard, on several evenings, instrumental music and voices coming up from the hollow. The sound carried but it was too distant to hear clearly. He wanted to hear the music more distinctly; he wanted to know what they were singing about. Did the music in any way help to make them "content" as Peter had mentioned? He thought about inviting Peter along, but then thought, no, he wanted to be alone; he wanted to think about what he heard without being influenced by Peter's thoughts.

The right evening eventually came along. He heard the music, and his relatives were all inside; he was free to wander on down to the slave quarters by himself. He headed out but stopped short. Instead, he just leaned up against a tree, close enough to hear clearly but far enough away, and hidden, so he could listen and observe without interrupting them. He'd learned enough from working in the fields next to slaves with Peter to know that the appearance of the slave owner, or any White person for that matter, changed a slave's behavior.

What he saw seemed strange, certainly stranger than anything he had imagined while sitting and listening on the porch. The old man sat in his chair with what looked like a short, primitive longbow, though it was way too short for shooting arrows effectively. One hand held a stick of some sort while the other held the bow that was braced against the ground. The bow was short enough so he could reach the higher end with his mouth. So strange; he had the string at the high end actually in his mouth. He seemed to open and close his mouth while strumming the string. Tones magically changed depending, as far as Allen could make out, on how far he opened his mouth. The music seemed joyful, and the two young daughters, Amanda and Luan, were dancing to it, but Allen could not make out a word of what they were singing. The language was just plain alien, the dance, with lots of slapping and clapping, was like nothing Allen had ever seen.

Then the dancing and the music stopped. It seemed as if the mood had suddenly changed. All either sat down or stood quietly, and a haunting melody emerged without the musical bow. This time the words were in English. Allen struggled to hear and tried hard to remember what he heard, but all he remembered was:

"Oh, my home, when shall I see my home?
When shall I see my native land?
I will never forget my home!
My father at home, my mother at home
When shall I see my native land?
I will never forget my home!"

Home: these slaves missed something they called home. Where was home for them? Clearly not here. He missed home too, but not with the kind of pathos this song expressed so movingly. The thought lingered; the feeling lingered. Allen left his hiding place behind the tree and headed back. He knew he would not mention what he had seen and heard, but he wouldn't forget it either. In fact, as he approached the main house, he realized that he wanted to know more. What more? He didn't know, but he did know he'd have to find out.

Baptized Licking-Locust - What?

A couple of weeks later, Peter invited Allen to look at the land he was thinking of buying for that future he envisioned. Thomas, by now, knew the day was approaching when his son would want to shape a life of his own, so he did not object to this exploratory outing or to any other trips that might be required. He and Peter talked openly about a new life, and he promised to back him financially, within reason, whatever he decided to do. Allen, too, would leave at some point. Thomas realized he would have to run his farm soon enough without help from Peter and Allen; starting with short absences seemed a reasonable way to ease into the coming transition.

The land Peter had in mind was less than 10 miles to the southeast of home along Tick Creek, as he explained to Allen. Walking suited them both, so they set out, early, on foot. They talked about their futures, noticed a few farms along the way, and reached their destination just in time for the supper they had packed the previous night. Again, they sat by a creek together, but without fishing gear this time.

Allen couldn't help noticing that the creek and general layout looked remarkably like Peter's current home. Of course, there was no main house or slave dwellings, but there were indications that the land had been a farm of sorts at one time. There was a Kieffer pear tree and other indications of an old orchard along with a clear area with the remains of what might have been a foundation for a house.

Allen took this all in at a glance or two before Peter asked the obvious question. "So, what do you think of the place? It's 100 acres including that forested area over there."

Allen replied, "I'd say it has the makings of a good future, but one with a lot of hard work ahead."

Peter simply nodded agreement and then added, "On the way back let's take a little detour. I'll show you Clay, the local settlement. It's not much, but good to have something nearby for supplies. At least there's a grocer of sorts, and they will have a sawmill soon, or so I've been told."

So, after spending the night on mats they'd brought, they went on to Clay and truly Clay was not much. They passed by a Baptist church, Bethel Baptist, and just as they were about to leave it behind, they met a man who introduced himself as John Clynes. Peter was pleased to think he might be able to learn more about Clay from someone who might know the area, so he considered the meeting fortunate. Allen found the conversation that followed very interesting, if for somewhat different reasons than his cousin.

John spoke first. "Don't see many strangers out here, mostly local folk. Are you just passing through?"

Peter answered, "Well, the reason my cousin Allen and I are down here now is that I'm considering becoming a local. Thinking about buying those 100 acres for sale down by the creek. Name's Peter Miner, glad to meet someone from the area."

"We could use some young folk taking up residence here, and that old farm, though it needs lots of work, should yield good crops. You'll need help though, a slave or two to start, I'd say, and they aren't cheap or plentiful around here, that I can tell you."

Peter responded, "All in good time, got to make some decisions for sure, at least there's a Baptist church here, I see."

John hesitated then went on for more than a bit. "That particular Baptist church is not my kind of place. In fact, it's a curse—not a blessing at all. Those that attend, and there aren't many, are poor folk mostly, and they follow a pastor who objects to owning slaves. Plenty of us would like to see him run out of town. And the name they call themselves, it will give you a good laugh; it's the Baptized Licking-Locust Association. An association of scoundrels; actual locusts would be better to have around, I think. Like to give some of them a good licking. Let them try to run my place without slaves."

Allen smiled at the name and John's play on it. Peter simply agreed. "Can't run 100 acres or so without slaves. Can't be done."

After a few more pleasantries, Allen and Peter thanked John for his willingness to talk with them, and then they left for home. The trip to Clay had been in the direction of home, so it was a short walk back, without much if any conversation. Both looked forward to something in the way of a meal when they arrived. Allen spent some time during the walk wondering about slaves and slavery but said nothing. He thought he might be interested in returning to the church, alone, so he could hear what someone from the church had to say on the subject without anyone in his new family or someone like John finding out that he was curious. Showing interest in front of Peter and his family would clearly not be comfortable. And he certainly didn't want rumors by John or anyone else spreading around the county that he was some sort of sympathizer. He was sympathetic but not ready to aggravate his Kentucky relatives or to endure the level of hostility he imagined he might, if he became widely known as someone who was anti-slavery.

Time to Leave - I'll Become a....

Allen became just plain restless. The Kentucky experience had been both enlightening and pleasant; he had been challenged by the trip through the gap, he liked his relatives, and he felt liberated by his independent life away from home. But it was a visit, after all, not the whole new life he had set out to discover. What that new life might be still remained unclear; no that's too gentle, it remained completely mysterious. He wanted to experience more.

What he did know was that he had precious little left in the way of the funds he'd had when he began searching for this new life, and that he had nothing like the fatherly financial backing Peter had to continue looking for it. So, first things first. How could he make some money? All he could think of, in terms of what might both interest him and earn money, was his reading of the constitution, the founders, and by an easy extension, the law. Lawyers made money; all he had to do was figure out how to become one.

Fortunately, Uncle Thomas had some solid ideas about how Allen could proceed. He had several friends in Louisville, and he had done enough in the way of business with one in particular to be comfortable writing a letter of recommendation introducing his nephew. It was time for Allen to move on, and Allen knew it, Thomas knew it, and even Peter, somewhat reluctantly, realized it. Louisville wasn't that far away, they all reasoned. They'd see each other again. Welcome is one part of life, goodbye is another part of life, just as "see you when you can stop back again" is yet another part of life or not, often just a wish, really.

So, Allen headed off to Louisville in late August on Lundy, packing what he owned along with that letter introducing him to Uncle Thomas' friend and business associate Henry Duncan, the father of William Garnett Duncan. William was a lawyer slightly older than Allen who had recently graduated from Yale law school. Uncle Thomas had kept in touch with Henry Duncan sufficiently to know the son was back from Yale. He figured who would be better to teach Allen than William—young, newly graduated, up on whatever were the most recent laws of the land. He sent a letter to let the Louisville folks know his nephew would be coming to see them, hoping the stagecoach with the message would get it there before Allen arrived. He'd given Allen a copy just in case the mail failed to deliver it in time.

First, though, before going on to Louisville, Allen took a slight detour. He still wanted to stop back, alone, at the Bethel Baptist church in Clay to satisfy his curiosity by talking to the pastor, or at least a church member, about their stand on slavery. Peter and his family had been quite clear about what they thought; so clear that Allen didn't even want to let them know he was curious about what slaves thought or felt. Certainly, he didn't want to let them know he was so curious that he would go out of his way to seek out the opinions of Baptized Locust-Lickers.

When he arrived at the church, he noticed one person about to enter. He dismounted, called out to him, and found himself within minutes in exactly the conversation he had sought. He'd lucked out, though he didn't know, at the time, how lucky he was.

After a brief introduction, really just an exchange of names and 'where you from' small talk, Allen couldn't help asking, somewhat bluntly for him, what his new acquaintance thought about an organization he had heard called the Licking-Locust Association. He could hardly have picked a better person to ask; he'd just met an original member and prime mover in the "Baptized Licking-Locust Association, Friends of Humanity", George Waller. Waller, a traveling pastor, just happened to be entering the church on one of his rounds in support of what had recently become the "Kentucky Abolition Society".

George answered Allen quite politely. "The full name is the Baptized Licking-Locust Association, Friends of Humanity. It's somewhat clumsy, I guess; it refers to a local river and creek, good for baptizing. Got to say even I've heard the name ridiculed, and I laugh myself sometimes, too, at the jokes. But it's not a joke. It started as an anti-slavery association of local churches, mainly in Kentucky. It evolved into the Kentucky Abolition Society. That says what it stands for quite clearly, I think. Of course, nothing is simple. There's a branch called the American Colonization Society. I'd guess that's more than you wanted to know."

Allen was intrigued and let George know that he wanted to know even more by saying, "Actually what you're telling me is exactly what I want to know. To tell you the truth, I'm here because I heard the name ridiculed and wanted to hear about it from your side. Please, if you are willing, tell me more. What's the American Colonization Society?"

George responded, "They believe that the best solution for slaves is to return them to Africa. They think attempts to integrate them into this country just won't work. We simply won't be able to get along with them."

The thoughts Allen had been going over again and again in his own mind, based on his recent experiences with slaves along the Cumberland trail and at his relatives' homestead, poured out, released by talking to a kindred spirit and no longer pent up by concerns about what his Kentucky, slave owning relatives might feel.

"Look, I've seen some slaves recently, and they seemed incredible to me, so full of human emotions that I felt strongly connected to them, emotions so strong that I admired them. Coming through the Cumberland Gap I saw chained slaves bleeding where the chains rubbed their ankles raw. I saw an old man beaten without mercy and then others, chained to him and wounded themselves, help him carry on. At my cousin's place I listened to slaves sing and dance, sing along with another old man playing something that looked like a longbow, and then all of them mournfully remembering their home more passionately than anything I have ever felt about what I've left behind. I wanted to embrace them, not send them away to Africa."

George was moved. "You have put into words what many of us feel. As White men we can't just ignore common humanity because we need the Blacks to run our farms or, in some cases, our plantations. There has got to be a better way."

Allen responded, "As far as I can tell, no alternatives have ever occurred to the slave owners I've met down here. They simply say that running a farm of 100 acres or so is impossible without slaves, end of discussion."

George considered and then added, "There are slave owners and even those who own plantations who manumit or free their slaves. Usually, though, they do it in their wills. Course that just leaves the problem of supporting their 'way of life' to those left behind. It's not a solution likely to lead to full emancipation."

"Right", Allen agreed, and then remembered an earlier question he had. "You had mentioned that churches belonging to the association were mainly from Kentucky. Does that mean it is more widespread?"

George replied, "Not the Baptized Licking-Locust Association. Outside of Kentucky there's just Claremont, Ohio, right across the river from the Pendleton association. More generally, though, I believe that anti-slavery movements of all sorts are widespread and gaining support."

Allen took up a thought he'd had several times at mention of the Ohio River, "In all the time I've spent down here, I haven't even seen the river. I'm really on my way to Louisville where I hope to study law; guess I'll be sure to see it there."

George suggested, "Be sure to go down to the port in Louisville. It's a very busy place. Everything that is shipped down the Ohio River must be unloaded and ported around the falls before going south to the Mississippi. Lots of money's made in Louisville doing just that. There is some talk of a canal around the falls but that's mostly talk so far, except for an attempt on the Indiana side. And law you say? You might think some about helping the anti-slavery movement, if you do end up a lawyer. We need lawyers. In fact, since I'm often in Louisville, you might consider looking me up once you've become a lawyer, or any time. Just check with the local Baptist church; they'll know how to contact me."

Allen thanked him for the advice and the invitation; they parted company, both the better for their conversation. Allen had much new information to digest on the ride to Louisville. Was his new life taking shape? Maybe, he thought, but first practical matters. He needed to get in touch with William Duncan and start studying law before he planned much further.

Louisville - A New Life?

Uncle Thomas had provided directions for finding the Duncan family, and the advance letter of introduction he had sent did precede Allen's arrival, despite the usual postal delays. The family greeted him warmly and, anticipating that he had no immediate accommodations, offered a place to stay. Thomas had mentioned that his nephew had stories to tell beyond what most his age would have, so a good portion of the first evening was spent retelling some once again. Allen included his War of 1812 adventures and his attempts to find the Cumberland trail but left out anything that he thought might seem controversial. William had a few stories of his own, mostly about Yale and trips back and forth; but, as usual, nothing matched Allen's. What William did have was knowledge of the law, and he readily agreed to take Allen on as a pupil. They agreed that, once Allen was established in his own practice, he would provide 10% of his profits from his first year to William as compensation for the training.

The next morning, after breakfast, Allen scanned a couple sections of Kentucky law from information William had on the subject and looked at related cases from William's texts. He mentioned that he had not yet seen the Ohio River and that he had been told the falls and portage around the falls were especially interesting. William agreed that they should visit the area after lunch, and added, "Lots of legal wrangling surrounding what is and isn't happening down there."

I've thought about getting involved in some of the issues as one of my first legal cases. Might make an interesting addition to your studies, if you'd like to follow along as I figure out what to do myself."

Allen jumped at that invitation. "Sounds like an opportunity not to be passed up. Thanks for the thought, and yes, I'd like to follow along." And so, Allen was not only going to study the law, but he would be doing so, it seemed, in the traditional Western manner; following a lawyer as he sought business and maybe on through real legal activity. Not many lawyers out West went to law school as William had. Instead, they learned as Allen did, bit by bit, from a local lawyer and by participating as an aide in that lawyer's legal activities. No degree was needed in the newly developing West to practice law, just ability.

The Louisville waterfront was busy despite the continuing 1819 financial panic that slowed economic activity but, as William and Allen discovered, increased legal wrangling. It was late summer when the river was at its lowest and the falls most visible. As Allen noticed, "falls" was a misnomer. What he saw were rapids with small descents, where water rushed around rocks, not "falls" but certainly not a safe place for boats of any size, let alone steamboats or even flat boats.

William explained that there were actually three named chutes through the falls—the Indian chute on the Indiana side, the aptly named Middle chute, and the Kentucky chute. During the late winter and early spring, when water in the river rose, flat boats could make their way down river usually through the less rocky Indian chute, and even steamboats could be pulled up-river, mostly through the Kentucky chute. He added that the one on the Kentucky side, full of rocks jutting through the surface, was the worst one to navigate, even given the rising waters of late winter and spring, but that since the current was considerably less rapid through it, than through the other two, steamship captains headed up-river against the current were forced to use it.

After hearing all this detail from William, Allen responded, "Pulling a steamship up-river? How's that work?"

William answered, "There are some who make a business of it. They secure a rope around a capstan on the steamboat, take the other end upstream and secure it around a tree. Then hefty members of the crew grab the spokes sticking out of the capstan and turn it, like a winch, pulling the rope in and the steamboat upriver. It's called warping."

"Sounds risky; those steamboats are heavy."

"Risky, and likely to lead to lawsuits, I suspect, probably mostly against the warping folks, though I doubt they have the means to pay much. But the big business down here is still portage, despite talk of canals, and, you know, where there are competing business owners, there are legal issues."

Allen focused on William's mention of a canal, remembering that the Baptist, George Waller, had said something about a canal on the Indiana side. "Heard they were building a canal on the Indiana side, are they?"

William knew about that effort. "Well, they started building one over there. Then the economic disaster hit. They stopped work and wrangled over what had been advanced just to get started. Now those favoring a canal here on the Kentucky side, keeping Louisville as the major port, and those who started the one on the Indiana side and would like Jeffersonville to get the port business, are wrangling over who actually gets to build a canal. Many lawsuits, land ownership disputes, and plenty of politics. I'm going to be looking into it all for sure."

Allen nodded, "Sounds promising."

After a little more looking around the Louisville port and more talk about what they saw, William and Allen returned home. For the next several months, Allen studied law under William. They followed the legal wrangling over the canal and over various disagreements between steamboat builders over innovations. It took time for William to break into any of the cases, but finally he took a small part in land disputes related to the Kentucky-side canal. William even got to do some preliminary work under James Guthrie, the lawyer leading the case. Guthrie proved a difficult man to work for, but a man who never gave up and usually succeeded in the end, as in this case. The canal would be built by the Louisville and Portland Canal Company on the Kentucky side, the cheaper and more sensible approach, driven by Guthrie's excellent legal acumen and at times aided by William's input and even, early on in the case, by a word or two from Allen.

While aiding William's legal efforts, Allen had time to do a bit of looking around on his own. He went so far as to look up the Baptist anti-slavery pastor, George Waller, with whom he had talked in Clay. Allen wanted to continue the conversations about slavery, the anti-slavery movements, and the churches involved. They had discussed merging his two interests, law and the abolitionist movement, and Allen wanted to see if such thoughts might lead him somewhere that he might consider his future.

George Waller was now back in Louisville, and as he had mentioned to Allen back in Clay, finding him was as easy as finding the Louisville Baptist church. They were both pleased to see each other again, and they discussed again much of what they had discussed in their first meeting. George clearly remembered Allen's experiences with slavery on the Cumberland Trail and at his Kentucky family's farm. Allen briefly sought clarity on two other subjects they had discussed—colonization and manumission. Then George presented Allen with a copy of David Barrow's pamphlet "Involuntary, Unmerited, Perpetual, Absolute, Hereditary Slavery, Examined; on the Principles of Nature, Reason, Justice, Policy, and Scripture", a well-known and passionate defense of the anti-slavery movement. George went on to warn Allen that pursuing anti-slavery legal work in Kentucky, especially for someone whom others would label an outsider and a Northerner, was quite dangerous. He illustrated his point by mentioning that David Barrow's avid anti-slavery views caused a mob violently opposed to those views to attempt to drown him. Barrow had been lucky to escape with his life.

Instead of trying to help a movement in Kentucky, George recommended crossing the river to "free" Ohio where he could get in touch with the new Claremont Baptist church in Lindale. George gave him a letter of introduction to Samuel Tibbets Sr. and Andrew Coombs Sr., founders of the Claremont church and hardworking advocates for the anti-slavery cause. He suggested a stop about halfway at the Forks of the Licking Baptist church in Pendleton County, Kentucky where he would find members sympathetic to the anti-slavery movement who would take him in and help him on his way.

Allen, after making clear to George that Ohio sounded right for him, thanked him for his help. Then Allen returned to the Duncan family. Not many days later, Allen thanked the Duncan family for all they had done for him, especially William who had so fortuitously started him on his way to a law career. Then Allen headed for Ohio where he hoped to eventually practice that career himself and to honor his promise of payment to William.

Chapter Six

"Free" Ohio

Lindale

Allen did stop at the Forks of Licking Baptist Church in Pendleton, KY., and as planned, he met with members who supported anti-slavery activities. They were quite glad to help him on his way to Lindale; they were happy to help anyone recommended by an advocate as well-known as George Waller. Allen stayed the night but then, anxious to be on his way, left early the next morning. His new friends provided a letter of introduction to a flatboat owner east of Cincinnati, also an anti-slavery supporter, whom they knew would willingly transport Allen and his horse across the Ohio River, free of charge, and they gave him enough traveling food (jerky and dried fruits) to reach the river crossing. One of his new friends even traveled most of the way to the Cincinnati crossing, leaving him only after the way forward was clear. Allen found the boatman easily and crossed the river within hours of arriving. Once across, the boatman gave Allen the best directions he could to Lindale; just head east and a little south.

Allen was more than used to that sort of vague help in the way of directions. He thanked the boatman warmly and rode off east and a little south.

Lindale was hardly a recognizable locale at the time, but fortunately Allen's destination was a bit better known; he was headed to Samuel Tibbets' log cabin. Tibbets was one of the co-founders of Lindale and a well-known, local figure. Allen just asked the first person he saw and got exact directions. He arrived about 11:00, tactfully not dinner time, but close enough so that his host would no doubt invite the now hungry traveler to stay for the midday meal. Samuel himself, working on the woodpile out front, saw him coming and held Lundy while Allen dismounted. Samuel Tibbets looked like he spent much of his time working hard—muscular and rugged—even though he was in his mid-sixties.

Allen introduced himself, and, after a few pleasantries, told Samuel why he had sought him out saying, "I've come to see you, and also Andrew Coombs, at the advice of George Waller. He was kind enough to provide me with a letter of introduction knowing we have some concerns in common."

Samuel responded without any questions saying, "George Waller, a fine man. Just hearing his name is all I need in the way of introduction. Let's put up your horse and go on inside; we'll talk some there. This woodpile can wait."

Samuel was a lonely man at this time in his life. His wife died some years ago, and their sons and daughters had moved away, so having someone to spend time with was most welcome. So welcome, in fact, that Allen was encouraged to stay awhile, and he did. Initially, conversation followed familiar patterns. Allen told stories of his travels from New York, as he had so many times before.

Allen saved for last the dream-like, misty view he had experienced while half asleep by the side of the Cumberland gap trail—those chained slaves, the old man wounded and fallen, whipped by the slave driver then helped by fellow slaves. Once again he paired it, as he now routinely did when telling his stories, with the old man slave playing the one string longbow, children dancing to the tune and then followed by the pathos of their song about home.

Samuel immediately felt just how remarkably well these illustrations of slave compassion supported his own views of slavery as an inhumane institution. He implored Allen to write down his thoughts and experiences, hoping at some point to introduce Allen to his like-minded friends. He added, "Look, Allen, someday you might think of turning those experiences into a sermon or at least a lecture—a wonderful aid to our cause."

Samuel managed to provide dinner by just expanding on what he had planned. Allen then helped with chores through the afternoon, and by supper time Allen and Samuel, having become accustomed to working together, prepared some minimal fare. The next morning after breakfast Allen got around to bringing up a more immediately pressing concern. He needed a favor and felt a bit more comfortable now that they'd had some time together and now that he had agreed to begin writing up his experiences, at Samuel's request. He needed a way to convert his law training into a living, so he needed local contacts to help him get whatever legal work might be available for a newcomer.

"Contacts," Samuel mused out loud, "I can certainly introduce you to local lawyers. Most of the action is in Cincinnati, that's local enough. But Martin Pease lives closer, just a bit north of here in Amelia. We could visit him together. I'd enjoy seeing him again."

Allen was pleased. "That sounds good. I'll just work a bit more on writing up my experiences, maybe even finish today. Perhaps we could go on up to Amelia tomorrow or the next day, if that fits your schedule."

Amused, Samuel laughed and simply said, "Schedule, now that's something I haven't given thought to in quite a while. Tomorrow or the next day is fine. Might even stop at Coombs' place on the way back. We arrived here in what is now Lindale about the same time and been neighbors ever since."

Allen finished writing up his lecture and spent the rest of day helping with chores. They left the next day, arriving at Martin Pease's just about mid-day, conveniently repeating Allen's timely arrival at Samuel's. The result was mostly the same, too—an invitation to the mid-day meal and some time for talk. Only some time for talk because, unlike Samuel's lonely existence, Martin's was anything but. His wife, Deborah, pregnant and busy running after three-year-old Mary, while son Leavitt, age 12, running in and out, made conversation just a bit scattered. Still there was time for Allen to repeat a brief version of his Cumberland Gap story. For once, though, Allen's shackled slave stories got a compelling response when Martin decided to tell his own story. Even Leavitt stopped long enough to quietly listen.

Martin recounted his events as follows; "When I was 11, I decided to sail with a privateer. We lived in Martha's Vineyard, and many of my relatives were men of the sea, so going to sea seemed natural to me. I left in 1776 feeling good about contributing to our revolutionary war effort. Of course, at such a young age I had no idea what I'd see and experience; it just seemed dashing and wonderful, exciting; you know. Then came the first encounter with the British. People died, sliced through with swords, even some of the crew I'd come to know. We did our job, I guess, captured several British supply ships, even some weaponry. Gave them enough trouble that they were forced eventually to deploy many of their war ships to protect their supply ships, war ships that could have been used against our troops, or so it was said."

Martin paused, looked at his guests and continued with what seemed like a subdued tone. "Then we had the kind of encounter we all dreaded, even I dreaded by then. Not a simple victim, not a poorly armed supply ship capable of minimal damage to us, no, this time a full British war ship hove into view. We all knew immediately what to do; get out of there fast. Not fast enough, though. That fully armed enemy ran us down, fired two or three cannons, maybe more, and took down a mast. I saw one of our best men mangled by that mast as it crushed him against a railing. That image lingers like no other. Again, the rest of us, those still alive and conscious, knew what to do; we surrendered before they got around to sending us all down to Davey Jones' locker."

Martin glanced at Allen before proceeding. "So, I was captured, thrown into a cabin, locked up, and guarded by three or four well-armed British regulars. I guess I must have felt it was better than being dead, but I'm not sure any such thought actually came to me. I was just plain scared, and I had reason to be. As it turned out, once we landed, we were simply marched off to a prison in New York City, we later found out. No chains, no beatings, like those slaves you saw, Allen, but hardly free, either. We didn't know if we'd ever be free again, if we'd ever see home again."

"Home," Allen muttered. "Interesting that you should mention that particular, universally human yearning. Samuel and I have discussed turning my Kentucky experiences of slavery into a presentation, perhaps at an upcoming anti-slavery event. Home, I could start there. Earlier, I didn't get a chance to mention the other Kentucky story that I usually add to the Cumberland Gap account. At my relatives' farm, I overheard, without revealing my presence, an old man playing a single string longbow instrument I'd never seen before. His audience included young slaves who had been dancing to a lively tune. Then the mood quieted suddenly as he began singing longingly of home. We all miss home; slaves miss home. You got back home; I can still communicate with my folks back home. But slaves? I'm not even sure they can see it in their minds. Maybe it's people they were forced to leave behind, maybe it's just a longing without concrete reference. They may be generations away from anything that we might think of when we think of home. Is home, for them, the last plantation they left? I doubt it. Maybe for young slaves—those born where they still live—home is right there. It's not much of a home. I'll need to work this out. Wonder if I might mention your imprisonment and longing for home. Wouldn't even need to mention your name, if you don't want the story spread. I could just say an American revolutionary war prisoner, as an example, say."

Martin pondered this for a while. Allen and Samuel waited for his response. Surprisingly, it was young Leavitt who broke the mood, jumping up and saying, "I want to be there when you tell my dad's story."

Martin then spoke directly to his son, "I want to be there, too, but I think Mr. Miner's idea to make the point more general is best. These are personal stories I'm telling here, not public. We'll enjoy them together here at home."

Samuel sensed that the subject of Martin's adventures as a young privateer had reached an end, so he took the opportunity to introduce the other important subject that had led them to Martin in the first place, saying as tactfully as possible, "Martin, our young friend wants to get on with his new life here in our bustling state. I had suggested to him that you might be able to introduce him to some people he'll need to know. Back in Kentucky he studied law and worked alongside a lawyer you may know, William Duncan. He'll need contacts here in the Lindale area or more likely in Cincinnati, to get him started on his career."

Martin's response was more than Allen could have hoped. "I certainly can introduce him to our lawyer community, but why not start with me. I've got several cases down in Cincinnati that would be better served if I had some help. More than enough legal wrangling along the docks to keep us both busy. We'll certainly stop in and visit Elijah Hayward. I don't know many in Cincinnati with better connections or wider knowledge of what's going on. I'll let him know we'd like to see him."

Martin and Allen made plans to meet again the next week to make their way to Cincinnati together. Soon it was time to leave; Samuel was beginning to nod off and Martin and family had work to do. On the way back to Samuel's place, Allen could see that the old man was fading fast. It was time to get him home; plans to meet Coombs Sr. could wait for another day.

Cincinnati Docks - Down to the Docks

Allen took a few days polishing his notes for the presentation of his experiences with Kentucky slavery that he and Samuel Tibbets had discussed several times, still hoping someday he would be able to give it in front of some sort of audience. But before any such plans could be made, he thanked Samuel for all he had done and for the many fine conversations they'd had. Then, after packing his belongings, he left with Lundy bound for Martin Pease's place, so they could arrange their proposed trip to Cincinnati. Martin was more than ready to go anyway, and Allen was already packed, so they agreed to leave the next day. Allen stayed overnight, and they left in the morning. Along the way Martin spoke about Elijah Hayward, the man he had mentioned in an earlier conversation as someone uniquely qualified to help Allen start his career as a lawyer. He added, though, a warning about Hayward's possible pro-slavery views. "Best if the subject of slavery never comes up."

They made a quick stop to let Samuel Tibbets know their plans before making their way to the Cincinnati wharf, their first planned stop. It was late summer, and though Allen and Martin might have hoped for a pleasant breeze off the river, the heat, the odor, and the quite noisy crowd of laborers rushing to load or unload goods combined to make it an unpleasant experience. That odor came from the slaughterhouses where hogs were butchered and packed in barrels of brine for shipping. Martin summed up their experience. "Cincinnati commerce may justify calling her 'the Queen of the West', but I'm thinking her other name—'Porkopolis'—comes more readily to my mind today." Allen smiled, held his nose, and added hearty agreement

Martin added another thought, "Allen, think of it this way. The wharf is one quarter mile of intense human activity. Human activity this concentrated means lots of tough interaction leading to lots of lawsuits. But, not from these workers. They are mostly Irish or freed slaves, and while they do have all sorts of squabbles, they settle them in a more personal way. No, the lawsuits will come from the business owners, steamship owners, large landowners—those making the profits here, or trying to. Look up in the hills beyond the squalid quarters surrounding the wharves for them; those folks have the money to take their squabbles to court."

Allen replied, "Good to see so vividly where the real work is done. I'm guessing, soon enough, we'll be heading up to those hills where the money is."

First, though, Martin had another thought. "Before we head up there, let's see if we can talk one the steamship captains into letting us look around on-board. Maybe strike up a conversation; no way of knowing where that might lead."

Dressed as they were—top hat, matching black topcoat and black, baggy fitting pantaloons, pleated white shirts with matching socks rising to just below the knees—so clearly gentlemen they had little trouble finding an accommodating captain. In fact, the captain was quite glad to converse with men not carrying pork barrels for a living. "Welcome aboard the Gen. Clark gentlemen, Captain Vail at your service."

The three men walked together on board, looking into the storage areas, the captain's quarters, the boiler room, the paddle wheel and finally the capstan. Allen, looking for a way to bring up lawsuits, focused on the capstan and asked the captain about its safety. "I heard that back in the spring the Maysville had an accident resulting from a broken line attached to a capstan. Heard the captain was killed and the steamboat destroyed along with all the cargo. Hope you haven't even come close to experiencing such disasters involving this capstan."

"Certainly nothing that dramatic. But ever since I heard about the Maysville, I think nervously about the need to pull this one through those Louisville rapids. I've spent several restless nights trying to decide exactly when I would make the attempt. I'd certainly send my most knowledgeable mate ahead to check before I proceeded. They keep promising a canal but nothing yet. Of course, even if I manage to avoid a rapids wreck, there's always boiler explosions for me to spend time worrying about."

Allen replied, "Lots of lawsuits involved with the Maysville and lots more with boiler explosions I suspect. If I were to speculate on the outcome of the Maysville incident, I'd bet the small crew who did the actual work of securing the line will not fare well. Smaller companies usually don't."

Martin added, "No they don't, but they don't have any money, either. Lawyers would need to find others to sue. With boiler explosions the list of potential clients able to hire lawyers is long—injured passengers, the steamboat owners, the boiler maker, even, sorry Captain Vail, the captain."

Martin then turned the conversation to more directly relevant matters, asking the captain, "Any new issues you've heard about down here along the waterfront?" Reacting to the captain's expression he added, "I know, I know—lawyers, always snooping around."

The captain ended up smiling, saying, "Well, we all must look around for business at some point. But I would guess that you are well aware that you need to scan those hills for cases, up there where the money is, not down here where the work is."

That response amused both Martin and Allen, and Martin just said, "Yes, that's next on our list. Thanks for showing us around and putting up with our curiosity."

Cincinnati Hills - Up to the Hills

On the way up the hill where the money was and where they planned to visit Elijah Hayward after visiting the docks, they stopped to eat a late dinner at a hotel next to the courthouse. Lawyers gathered there after court sessions, and Martin thought there might be someone he would recognize; if so, he would take the opportunity to introduce Allen. Besides, they wanted time to talk over what they had seen and to consider how to approach Hayward about possible legal cases that even Martin knew nothing about. As they had discussed earlier, Hayward was known to hold pro-slavery views, as opposed to Martin and Allen's anti-slavery stances, so they wanted to review their plans about what might be said and not said on that subject, should it come up, hoping, though, that it wouldn't.

The hotel dining room was practically empty. Maybe the court was still in session or, more likely, not in session at all on that day. They sat down, ordered, and began to discuss their plans. Martin started off by stating quite plainly to Allen, "Say nothing about your experiences, those details you so warmly expressed to me. If the subject of slavery does come up, I'll just refer to it in general terms as something I know we have our differences over. He's a curious fellow, though, so he is apt to ask what you think. I'm not sure how comfortable you will feel responding."

Allen seemed ready enough for the question and responded quite quickly, "I think I'll just say I'm new to the ways down here and talk about my home in Steuben, NY, where we don't know much about the subject. Maybe he'll take the opportunity to inform me or just drop it. Either way I get to just listen to him or perhaps to both of you, if that's the way the conversation evolves."

Martin thought a bit before responding, "Sounds good. Will certainly do for now. But I wonder what he'll think if or when you tell your story publicly, as you hope to do. Believe me he will hear about any anti-slavery meeting. He has a reporter's curiosity, particularly on this subject. In fact, not just a reporter's curiosity; he's even talked about starting a newspaper."

"Well," Allen replied, "I hate to fall back on an old cliche', but maybe we'll just have to 'cross that bridge when we come to it'. No knowing at this point how soon that might be."

Martin let that stand, just adding, "As long as you are comfortable with it, I am. Let's finish our dinner and go see the man."

And so, they did. They had planned to meet Elijah at David Wade's nearby residence, definitely an 'up in the hills' place. Elijah and David were partners, and they used David's conveniently located home as their office. Elijah greeted them personally at the door and led them back through David's rather large and roomy residence to the library/study/office in the back. They sat in comfortable chairs placed strategically for a view of the splendid backyard garden. David lived well; lawyering must be profitable here, Allen thought, judging by what he was seeing.

Elijah began by asking Allen how he had managed to end up in Ohio. Travel stories were popular; almost everyone in Cincinnati had one. It always made for a comfortable starting point—with careful editing, even for Allen. Allen talked about leaving home at sixteen, receiving vague directions along the way as he searched for the Cumberland Gap, traveling through the gap itself (eliminating any reference to the slave gang, of course), spending time in Kentucky at his relatives' farm, and finally studying law in Louisville. Why he left Louisville was a bit tricky, but he just glossed over the real reasons and substituted both a general curiosity and suggestions that he might do better as a lawyer here.

That last comment allowed Martin to conveniently take over and steer the conversation. "That's, as I mentioned in my letter, why we came to you. I can help him some, but contacts like yourself would certainly be beneficial. I took Allen down to the wharves on our way here, so he could see just how active they are, action that leads to friction and often lawsuits. We were able to board the Gen. Clark, invited by Captain Vail to look around. When we reached the capstan Allen brought up the Maysville accident, so the three of us talked about those Louisville rapids and the captain added boiler explosions to his own list of major steamboat concerns. We're both wondering if any such cases have come your way."

Elijah responded, "Such cases have come up and they tend to involve many parties. Lots of litigation that tends to last a long time. But I'm finding that most of what I see has to do with land claims these days. The law is evolving, as you no doubt know,

Martin, and each change sets off lawsuits. Allen, the Cincinnati folks, when they arrived here earlier, just settled on unoccupied land, or more accurately land cleared of the Indian tribes. Then that land was bought up by land speculators at very low prices, often from those granted the land as pay for their Revolutionary War service. So, squatters, cheated Revolutionary War soldiers, speculators—all had some sort of claim to the same land. Add in somewhat suspect surveying and you have a mess made for legal wrangling."

Allen responded this time, "I would certainly be grateful if you would help me get started. Any sort of case would be fine; or, if you feel the need of an assistant, I'd be happy just to help with research."

Elijah turned to Martin saying somewhat jokingly, "So, Martin, are you going let me steal this fellow from you? If so, I'll just offer him a night here at the Wade establishment and send you on your way. Allen and I can get started in the morning."

Martin smiled, "Well I suppose we could bid for his services. That would get him started. No, wait, I want to be helpful; you just go ahead and steal him from me."

"Deal," Elijah responded.

Allen, somewhat embarrassed that he had in a sense broken his promise to work with Martin, replied. "Martin, it's a deal, since you've agreed. I'd have stuck with our previous agreement if you had asked."

Martin smiled again. "Off you go and off I go."

So, Allen stayed at Wade's with Elijah, and Martin left, but not before another hour or so of conversation. Amazingly, slavery never came up. "What a relief", Allen thought.

Lindale - A New Home

It was several months before Allen was able to visit with Martin Pease and Samuel Tibbets in Lindale again. The work he was doing for Wade and Hayward, researching several of their cases and studying the related laws, absorbed all his time and substantially increased his legal knowledge. When he did get the chance to visit, Allen finally got to meet Andrew Coombs, Sr., the cofounder of Lindale. This meeting helped settle Allen's decision to locate in Lindale eventually. He met several members of the Coombs family, who were with Andrew at the time. Coombs' daughter, Susanna, was there with her husband Samuel Tibbets, Jr. and their 5- year-old son, John Henry Tibbets.

Allen did make the move to Lindale a year later, after thanking and then leaving Wade and Hayward. During the next few years, Allen's career as an Ohio lawyer grew from a research aide at Wade and Hayward to the full establishment of his own practice. The money was as good as he had hoped, allowing him to move into a small office/home of his own in Lindale. After his experiences with the Kentucky anti-slavery Baptists, it was quite natural for him to join the anti-slavery Lindale Baptist church, founded and actively supported by the elder Tibbets and Coombs and their families.

Joining the Lindale Baptist Church led to what became a long association with the Temple family, including the church pastor, Ichabod Temple and his daughter Sophina. Additionally, as a member of the church, surrounded by like-minded anti-slavery members, he finally found a receptive audience for the presentation of his anti-slavery views. He had wished for a larger venue, something more newsworthy that might reach back to Elijah Hayward and his newly formed National Republic Newspaper, but, in the end, just having the opportunity to share so openly what had become his truth was what he needed to do.

So, on a Sunday morning late in 1823, he was given the pulpit to briefly deliver his views. After introducing himself and thanking his fellow church members and local residents, who had come to hear him, he began by describing the two old men he had linked in his thinking. "As many of you already know, I arrived here in Lindale after traveling as a young fellow from my parents' home in Steuben, NY to visit relatives in Kentucky. Of all that I saw during my travels and my time at my relatives, two images struck me. They were seared into my consciousness and have since shaped my views of slavery."

"The first image came on a drizzly evening as I settled in for the night along the Cumberland Trail. I vaguely made out a line of Blacks that I realized, though I could hardly see them, were chained together. One, a small figure, maybe a boy I thought at the time, was being beaten, beaten without mercy. Horrid. Then others in the line picked him up as best they could while chained themselves and helped him along as they all moved on. So, a despicable White man, as I later discovered, showing no mercy, and Blacks who did show mercy to, as I also learned later, a very elderly, now crippled fellow being. An inhumane White and incredibly compassionate Blacks."

"The second image—another old man. This one I saw while hiding behind a tree at my uncle's farm. Hiding because any sense of a White man's presence completely changed slave behavior, behavior I wanted to see and hear untinged. It was evening, and I was looking downhill to the slave quarters, at the slaves, a family of six, most of whom had finished a hard day in the cotton fields. The old man sat outside playing a longbow-like instrument while the young girls danced. Their pure joy surprised me. How did slaves manage it after working in the fields all day? Then the tune and the dancing stopped, and the mood changed, abruptly, as the old man played and sang a poignant song about his lost home."

"The pathos in his voice while singing of a lost home; I ask myself often, what kind of home could possibly bring up the longing I heard in his voice and those feelings welling up in those around him? What could home mean to a slave? A former homeland? Not likely; even the old man was most probably born here. Those who were ripped from a homeland and shipped here were from earlier generations. Their previous slave quarters—a home? No, at least not one to look back on with such passion. I look back fondly to my family home in New York, but my feelings for my home, well, I simply can't say they match what I heard and saw while watching from behind that tree."

"I ask myself what these two images mean to me, and the answer is clear. Slaves have deep feelings, and they are capable of heroic human actions. But, as important, maybe even more important in the long run for the anti-slavery movement, is what would the actual slave owners feel if they witnessed what I did? Well, I do have some idea, my relatives did tell me what the old man's singing meant to them. Keeping the old man who could not work anymore was an act of kindness. They believed that they treated their slaves well; the old man had a roof over his head, a chair out front, and food to eat. Besides, their act of kindness had the added benefit of keeping the other slaves content. See those happy dancing girls? That's all good for slave morale. The song of home? Just dreams, to be dismissed like all dreams."

"What about the savage beating I saw on the Cumberland trail? Just a guess about this one. I've heard that even slave owners despise slave traders and auctioneers. Even though traders and auctioneers are usually White, to slave owners such scum fall into the lowest levels of White society. White slave drivers, like the merciless one I saw, are the very worst in their opinion. They may need them all, but they don't think of themselves as anything like them. They say their whole way of life depends on the slaves. They simply could not support their livelihood on large or even relatively small farms/plantations, without slaves to do the work."

"So, here's what I've come to convince myself we must do somehow if we really believe in the emancipation of this large body of human beings that slave owners see as necessary to their own survival—slaves, a species they rank below even the slave traders, auctioneers, and slave drivers. If slaves are to be released from their bondage, we need to create an evolutionary change in the minds and hearts of slave owners. But changing those minds and hearts presents us with real difficulties that I don't want to minimize. Think of it, we are asking slave owners to fundamentally change their way of life and that of their families. We are asking them to set aside generations of tradition that has supported them and still does. Our task is about as far from easy as I can imagine."

"The question, then, is how do we, as antislavery advocates, talk to slave owners? Could we start with something like my Cumberland Gap episode and simply ask them what they feel? Chained slaves, ahead and behind that beaten old man, risking similar treatment to help him along the way. Aren't these human beings exhibiting courage and compassion, ignoring their own considerable risk to help another? Slave owners might find some sort of sympathetic way to react without agreeing with our own view of slave humanity. At some level of their souls, they might even be moved. Maybe we might elicit some reaction other than heated resistance at least. Wouldn't that be a start?"

"If you have doubts that owners would be moved, consider their attitude toward slave auctioneers, slave traders, and slave drivers. They despise them. Why? Quite possibly slave owners despise them because such White trash reveals so clearly what they would rather not see in themselves. We need to find a way to help them see more clearly what they may already know, at some level, but need to accept more openly. We know that some slave owner minds have changed. We have examples of slaves freed. In such cases, isn't it likely that owners could no longer ignore their own feelings about their part in slavery? Or maybe there are tiny steps along the way to freeing slaves, steps like no longer participating in auctions or trading, no longer breaking up families, no longer employing cruel over-seers who often damage what they consider their goods, or even paying slaves for their labor to encourage them to stay rather than forcing them to stay."

"You may well think convincing slave owners of any change is a fantasy. Well, maybe, but I don't even want to think about the alternatives. Let me know what you think as we cross paths in the next few weeks or whenever; I like to think I'm open to other opinions." With those words he concluded and was pleased that the audience applauded in church indicating that his words were favorably received. He even managed to convince himself that he received what he took for a smile from Sophina Temple, though of course such approbation from a young lady may have been entirely his own fantasy.

Chapter Seven

Sophina

Life Moves On

One morning in the late Spring of 1824, Sophina decided to visit her friend and mentor Susanna Tibbets. It had been a wet Spring and the trail she needed to take was full of puddles and water-filled ruts. It was rugged with hills to climb, and rocky; not easy to navigate. She considered riding but ended up walking. She thought she'd enjoy the freedom of being alone, in as leisurely a fashion as possible. She was not the sort of prim and proper young lady that etiquette books from the East were fond of describing; at just 15 years of age, she was very much a lady of the West with a mind of her own and spirit aplenty. Some in her family and her church might well have described her action as risky and her attitude as wrong-headed, but her likely response might have been, "A two mile walk along a known road, what could go wrong?"

She was right, for the most part. She did cross the path of a fox that spent a bit too much time eyeing her, but not one bear or panther showed itself. A middle-aged man with a surprisingly long beard did approach, headed the other way, and his glance was a bit long and intrusive enough to put her on guard. When he stopped next to her and took his time addressing her, she stiffened just a bit more, until he spoke, quite politely asking if she needed help. Her guard settled back into confidence, and she replied as blithely as one would expect from her, "Thanks for asking but I'm having a wonderful walk to my friend's house—Susanna Tibbets. Perhaps you know the family?" Of course, everyone from the area knew the Tibbets, as well as Susanna's parents, the Coombs, and no one would want to offend them in any way, as Sophina well knew.

He replied, "Ah yes, I know them well; I just passed their place. Nothing worrisome for the next mile or so you have yet to go."

She nodded and thanked him for the information, then both proceeded their separate ways. The rest of her walk was what she had hoped—a fascinating variety of birds in the trees, gentle breezes, and sun filtering through the forest. By now not even the mud and puddles she had known would be part of the experience troubled her. She practically skipped around them.

She arrived at Susanna's around 11:00 AM and found her alone puttering around in the kitchen. Her husband, Samuel, and their four youngest sons, ranging in age from 6 to 18, were out in the fields pulling out tree stumps to extend their fields for late Spring plowing and planting, once the soil, wet from the rains, dried sufficiently. Even their youngest, John Henry, was out there with his father and brothers. Their oldest son, Charles at 26 was off on his own, and their oldest daughter, Reliance, was newly married. Rebecca at 18 was off visiting her married sister. That left 14-year-old Elizabeth home with her mother, but she was upstairs pouting after a slight tiff. So, Sophina walked in on her friend and found her alone, for the moment at least, and feeling almost as liberated as Sophina did.

They took this unique opportunity to sit down and talk without any interruption. Sophina started by asking about Susanna's family and got a quick review before her friend, somewhat abruptly, switched to a much more interesting subject. She couched it, though, quite generally by simply asking, "So is anyone of interest in your life these days?" When Sophina hesitated uncharacteristically, Susanna gently added, "Now don't tell me, 'No'; I listen to church gossip carefully enough to know what they all think they know."

That did it. "Well," Sophina responded somewhat facetiously, "I guess they know what they think they know. Be nice if they told me. Yes, I have heard a whisper or two about Allen. 'They' seem to think he's courting me. If so, he's very subtle."

"You, however, are not the most subtle person I know; perhaps a little help from you would move him along, should you want him to pick up the pace a bit, that is. You do like him, don't you? At least you liked his antislavery talk; even I saw that."

Sophina had liked that talk and hadn't tried to hide her appreciation at the time or over the next few weeks as she talked to church members about his ideas. She proceeded to reveal more. "OK, my friend and confident, it was not just the talk I liked. Of course, if anyone but you asked, I'd find a way to slither around a full confession, unsubtle though you believe me to be. And I am open to suggestions of the 'push him along a bit' sort. Any ideas?"

Susanna thought for a moment then said, "You've talked to church members about his ideas, why not talk to him directly? Some men may prefer women who don't express ideas of their own, but Allen does not seem like that sort. You couldn't possibly spend your life with someone who did not respect your independent mind, so I'd find out how he reacts. Even go ahead and suggest whatever reservations you might have about his approach toward slave owners. I'm guessing you do have such reservations?"

"Don't you?"

Susanna had to admit she did. "I guess he's right that there are some, even more than would openly admit it, whose consciences are twisted up on their 'need' for slave labor. There are even those who have given up their slaves and found other ways to live. But a wholesale rejection of slavery urged, however subtly, by anyone known as an anti-slavery advocate, well, that seems to me unlikely to influence them."

Sophina agreed. "I'll bring that up the first time I get the chance. Of course, I'd prefer to bring it up when no one else is around; not easy with church members and family watching us so closely."

"You'll find a way," Susanna replied with a smile, "of that I am absolutely sure. Oh, my, the venison stew is boiling over. Shame to ruin the last of the root vegetables in there by over cooking. You will stay for dinner? The husband and boys will be piling in here any moment, so you might as well stay and spend some time with them, too."

"Thought you'd never ask, I'm starved."

As if on cue, the yard filled with the voices and the this and that of the returning—putting up the oxen, arranging equipment for their return in the afternoon, washing at the well—all familiar sounds to Susanna, less so to Sophina. Then Elizabeth came down, having dropped her pique, and joined the family for dinner and even helped Sophina carry food onto the dining room table.

As they entered, all expressed pleasure at seeing Sophina. The young John Henry, in particular, expressed his delight by running over and jumping into her lap. He always sought her out at church gatherings, and she enjoyed his bubbling enthusiasm. All sat down and, in short order, dug into the stew and the always fresh baked bread that they used for dipping and then scooping up the last dribbles.

As hungry as they were, there was not a whole lot of conversation until those last dribbles were gone. But then, they asked about Sophina's visit and mostly about how she managed to get there. No horse in sight made them curious. She surprised even herself by giving a lengthy and upbeat description of her walk, including a reference to the long bearded, old man and to her various reactions to him. They knew him and vouched for him. Then, as suddenly as they appeared, off they went back to work. John Henry dragged his feet a bit, but he went along with the others, waving goodbye at last.

Elizabeth, though, stayed and helped with the dishes, but her presence meant that Susanna and Sophina found themselves unable to pick up their conversation where they had left off. Susanna did say, "I'll be interested to hear how it goes" without specifying what 'it' was. An hour or so passed without anything of interest coming up, except perhaps the cheering of Elizabeth. Both women took turns at making her feel better until they got down-right smiles.

Sophina finally got up and made it clear that she was ready to leave saying, "Guess I'll be going, need to slosh on home before dark." Off she went, and her trip back home was completely uneventful, though filled with thoughts about what she had discussed with her friend and with a kind of new contentment, knowing now what she was determined to do next about Allen.

Courting - Western Style

Sophina had to wait longer than she wanted before she got, or maybe manufactured, an opportunity to speak privately with Allen. She chose a Sunday when her younger siblings were visiting a friend's family and when, for once, Allen did not leave the post service socializing early. In fact, he stayed until only a few stragglers remained and then by luck, or good planning by both perhaps, they found themselves almost alone. One old lady remained, chaperoning it would seem, along with Sophina's father, who was outside seeing parishioners off. Her Mother, Mary, as usual, left as soon after the service as she could without offending the congregation to prepare dinner.

Sophina spoke first. "Allen, why don't you come with us over to our place? Stay for dinner; we'd love to have the chance to talk and spend some time with you."

Allen, quickly turning Sophina's 'we' to 'I' in his mind, accepted without hesitation. "Thanks," he said, "that's very kind of you." That 'you' definitely did not include her father as he spoke it.

Sophina and Allen walked out of the church, shedding their 'chaperon' on the way, and picking up her father, Ichabod. Sophina told him her good news. "Allen has been kind enough to accept my invitation to stop over for some conversation and dinner."

Her father responded, "That sounds splendid, let's go and see what's cooking." They walked together the short distance home and arrived at the front porch moments later. Ichabod sat down immediately in his favorite porch chair; the preaching and then being a pleasant pastor apparently wore him out. How convenient. Sophina and Allen simply slipped inside; and, after greeting Sophina's mom and after asking her if they could include Allen as a dinner guest, as well as offering to help, Mary simply said 'yes to Allen staying' and 'no' to help in the kitchen, freeing Allen and Sophina to leave the kitchen and sit themselves down in the living room to talk alone.

Allen started with some sort of pleasantry about the weather, but Sophina did not allow that sort of conversation to last much more than a minute or two. She came right out with, "I wanted to talk to you about your anti-slavery presentation. I've talked to others in the church and in town, but I haven't had a chance to talk to you. You may have heard that I liked it, but I do have questions I wanted to ask you without others around. Hope you don't mind."

Allen was pleased. That smile he thought she gave at the end of his talk, maybe it was real. His response came even more quickly than her question. "Don't mind at all, in fact I'd welcome hearing what you think."

Sophina, encouraged, though she didn't really need encouragement, started with what she knew were areas of agreement. "I think we all would like to feel that slave owners will come to see what we see, and I liked the less confrontational approaches you suggested. Some have come around and found ways to exist without slaves. Maybe some others have new, uncomfortable questions about how they were reared and what they were taught to believe. You were right to point out how they rank slave traders, auctioneers, and slave drivers at the bottom of White society; that does indicate a certain sense of what slavery is. We might even go so far as to think some even feel guilty at some level. I would hope some might even act on what they feel rather than on what they think supports their way of life."

Allen interrupted, "But not many. I know and I do understand what a long time such a life change will take to become widespread."

"Yes," Sophina responded, "that's the problem. How long will slaves have to continue just enduring? Generations?"

Her response caused Allen to think beyond what he had said in his talk and even beyond what he had said to others since. "The whole process, as I see it, will be a mess. Some, maybe many, slaves won't wait. They'll attempt, by whatever means, to escape, as some already have. Some slave owners may fear retaliation, even fear for their lives or the lives of family members. They might well react by taking harsher measures like public beatings, even hangings or selling the slaves further south and splitting up the families. Such measures might well begin a vicious cycle, increasing the pressure on the slaves to escape or even fight back and by doing so increase the fear and retaliation by the owners. I try to be hopeful, but I'm finding hope difficult."

Sophina felt a certain level of confusion. She hadn't expected to find that she and Allen were so close in their feelings about the future of slavery. Maybe there was nothing more to say right now, or maybe there was more to say, just not about those feelings. She searched around for a transition and finally came out with a very clumsy one, but that fact did not stop her. "Yes, sounds like our feelings about slavery are very close. I'd guess we have other feelings in common."

Even Allen couldn't avoid that spur. "I'd guess I could find some way to talk about how I feel, novice that I am in the feelings I very much want to express. I think you know that I really enjoy your company. See, I'm not good at this. I'll try again, I like you and enjoy talking with you."

Sophina couldn't help laughing but ended up letting him off the hook. "I like you too. We should spend more time together, don't you think?"

Allen reached out and touched her hand. "Yes, for sure."

Just then they heard Ichabod rise from his chair; Allen withdrew his hand as Ichabod entered and in a loud enough voice for Mary to hear said, "About time we find out what's cooking; I'll check."

Mary pertly responded almost as loudly, "You will find out when you prepare to eat and sit down. Why don't you make yourself useful and set the table?"

Shortly, Mary walked into the dining room with a spit roasted chicken and then went back for greens and roasted new potatoes. She'd even baked some muffins. Sophina caught that fresh muffin aroma she knew well and jumped up to retrieve them.

After grace offered by Ichabod, dinner conversation started off with the usual praise for the cook as Ichabod carved and served chicken and the other dishes got passed around. They talked about their morning in church, and Ichabod complained that after-church-socializing had dragged on too long, making apologies for resting on the porch instead of joining the conversation inside. Allen and Sophina stumbled over each other's responses, both saying as politely as they could manage that they hadn't minded, then smiling as they realized that Ichabod knew quite well that he hadn't been missed.

Then Mary countered their amusing routine saying quite openly that she had caught parts of the conversation from the kitchen. "I admit that I did not pay close attention to the anti-slavery discussion, but my hearing seemed to improve toward the end, just before

Ichabod interrupted the much more interesting exchange between you two, at least more interesting to me. Shall I just blurt it out in your own style, dear Sophina? That look says 'no', but I'll just ignore it. I heard words like 'get together more often' and even, oh my, 'I like you'."

Since it was Sophina's mother who brought up the budding relationship and since even her father apparently realized that something was happening between his daughter and Allen, Sophina took the lead in response. "We have a good time together and we want to enjoy more such times. Maybe even outside the reach of curious ears. A long walk alone, perhaps. I do enjoy walking, now don't I. Walking with pleasant company sounds very good to me. And Allen is pleasant company."

Ichabod couldn't resist adding, "Perhaps your good friend Susanna would like to join you two. She's pleasant company, too, and of course a third would restrain wagging tongues, particularly those at the church who whisper within my hearing already."

"Well, perhaps we'll give that some thought," Sophina responded, knowing quite well that she, at least, would not give it much thought at all.

Allen was wise enough to add nothing, simply repeating, "'some thought', yes."

Dessert followed—fresh strawberries, newly in season, and cream. Soon afterward Allen thanked all for a pleasant time and Mary for dinner before leaving. He did manage something that others could interpret as a handshake with Sophina, but it lingered and became for her a gentle squeeze.

They saw each other often over the next several months, and the courting continued over the next year or so, though how it went day to day or even month to month was left entirely to the imagination of church tongue waggers. Delicacy to Allen seems to have required that a 'tell-all' was not even permissible in a private diary. At first, Sophina did invite Susanna along on walks, but they dropped that nod to convention soon enough and walked together, alone. Tongues did wag some, but they were in love by then and didn't really care. Eventually Allen knelt and proposed. To no one's surprise and to the delight of family and friends, Sophina accepted. On Thursday, August 4, 1825, Martin Pease, JP prepared and signed the legal marriage papers.

The next Sunday Ichabod performed a church ceremony attended by church members and quite a few other friends and acquaintances, some from Allen's legal activities. The ceremony was followed by a buffet style reception at Allen's home, now Sophina's new home, attended by a limited number of close friends and church members. Mostly finger foods were served—bread, fruits, hard boiled eggs with a honey dip, and apple pies, the latter brought by church members. One 'lucky pie', baked by Mary herself, contained a glass ring. This pie was reserved for unmarried young men and women, and the one 'lucky' enough to discover the ring in his or her piece was traditionally supposed to be the next to marry. Susanna's young daughter, Elizabeth, no longer the pouting 14-year-old, got the ring. She responded with a smile and a very charming blush.

The evening eventually did come along followed by the much-anticipated wedding night that Allen and Sophina tried to pretend they did not anxiously anticipate. One that they could have celebrated that night without the usual ruckus, but the times did not allow it. They were up what seemed like half the night listening to their 'friends' sing and jeer under the window of their modest home.

Chapter Eight

Changing Times

Pro-Slave Backlash

Life within the new Miner family grew. Their first son, Jacob, was born in the winter of 1827 followed by Ichabod in 1829, David in 1833, and Elizabeth in 1837. They remained active members of the Lindale Baptist Church. They added on to the small home/office as the family grew. In 1832 profits from Allen's legal work and cheap prices made possible by the 1820 Land Act allowed them to purchase 14+ acres in nearby 10-Mile-Creek. Perhaps they meant to move there, but instead, three years later, they sold it for almost twice what they paid; not a bad investment as it turned out. Times were changing, the population around Lindale was increasing, so land quite naturally became more valuable.

But those changing times and the Miner's successful family life did not mean all was well. Ohio in general and particularly Cincinnati and the surrounding areas like Lindale were changing in other ways that could be described as sinister. The pro-slavery vs. anti-slavery conflict intensified significantly, and the Miner family shared in that conflict.

Allen, remembering well his discussions in Kentucky with George Waller about using his new legal skills to aid the anti-slavery movement, spent a good deal of his time studying related laws in Ohio. From time to time, he talked over his studies with Sophina, and as tension between pro-slavery interests and abolitionists intensified, Miner family discussions did, too. One evening in late 1831 Allen received a letter from his New York family reporting on a letter they had received from their Kentucky relatives. The August Nat Turner rebellion had shaken their Kentucky relatives seriously, causing them to fear their slaves for the first time and putting an abrupt end to their "happy slave" notions.

Allen read the letter to Sophina and then leaned forward in his chair and launched into an extended explanation of Ohio law as it stood at the time, expressing his fear that the conflict might well get worse as both sides escalated their responses to each other.

"You know, we've discussed just how restrictive even Ohio's 'free state' laws are. That 1803 free state law was already getting worse by 1804. Just the 1804 name bodes ill—Black Slave Code. Here it is I'll just paraphrase. That code meant Blacks needed to produce a court document attesting to their freedom and to register with the Ohio county clerk's office in their county of residence giving names, including the names of children, and addresses in order to get a certificate of residency. Without that certificate no one could employ them upon penalty of a fine of up to $50.00."

Sophina gasped, "That's nearly half of what we paid for our 14+ acres. Makes you think twice about breaking that law."

"Right, but it's way worse than that. Informers got half of that money as an incentive to report employment abuses. But think of this; they got $500 dollars, if they informed on someone who was successfully prosecuted for transporting an unregistered Black out of state. And the Blacks themselves? Let's just say they did register, obeyed the law fully, had their proper county certificate. That certificate, registered in the county office, put themselves and their families in severe danger. Slave hunters are out there to make money, but first they need to find former slaves. All they need to do is go to the county office and get addresses. Then they can make up ways to seize even freed slaves and their children let alone any runaways who might have sought shelter in their homes. Sad to say that holding slave hunters to the actual law against a Black of any kind as a defendant, well, all I can say is good luck."

Sophina asked, "Have you heard of any Blacks having a successful case? Think I know the answer; you'd have been right there, and I'd have heard about it at length if one had come up that you thought had even a slight chance."

"Right, not a one yet with the slightest chance of winning. And what do you think, could it get any worse?" As Sophina's facial expression along with a slight nod indicated probably yes, Allen continued, "Right again. The 1807 addition to the 1804 law really did it. The 1807 law required Blacks entering Ohio to post a $500 bond guaranteed by two White people who would ensure the African American's 'good behavior'. 'Good behavior', well, I believe the law includes examples of bad behavior like, say, owning a gun or, heaven forfend, marrying a White.

"By 1807, you know, Ohio and particularly Cincinnati, well, business ties with Kentucky were underway, and currently there are so many White Kentuckians here in Ohio doing business that some of those old 1807 laws will actually be enforced, in fact are being."

Sophina paused for a while, seeming to consider asking a question. Allen leaned back in his chair knowing well the signs of Sophina thinking hard before phrasing her thoughts. Then she came right out with her concerns. "I've heard, church members do talk after all, anyway, there seem to be some who believe members of the church are breaking the law. There's talk that younger members, like maybe Andrew Coombs and others, may actually be transporting slaves across state lines. Dangerous, if true, don't you think."

"So dangerous that, sympathetic as I am, I wouldn't do it. Younger members, right, no wives and children to consider. Guess, if it's true, they figure the harm will fall on themselves alone. Oh, and I think it is true. Someday I may talk to Andrew about it, but for now I like being able to say I know nothing."

Sophina agreed, "Right and I can safely say, if it ever comes up in a legal case, that I know nothing—just rumors. Well, getting a bit late. Let's check on the children and get some sleep ourselves. Busy day tomorrow."

Allen simply nodded and picked himself up out of his chair, ready as always for bed and even sleep.

It was late 1832 before he got around to having the discussion with Andrew Coombs, Jr. about his involvement in transporting Blacks across state lines, in what had become known generally as the Underground Railroad. By then most church members, particularly those who were avidly anti-slavery advocates like Allen, could hardly avoid knowing about Andrew's activities. Allen and Andrew discussed directly Andrew's participation at Andrew's house after supper one evening. They were about the same age; Andrew was 27 and Allen 28. By then Allen had two young sons, Jacob and Ichabod, and Sophina was pregnant. Andrew was courting Kitty, his soon-to-be wife.

Andrew started by stating the obvious, "I guess you and many others in the church know what I've been doing for the last couple of years. We are just too close a community for activities like mine to go unnoticed. I felt strongly that I needed to act and actually help escaped slaves on their way to freedom, real freedom, even if they have to make it all the way to Canada to achieve it. That seems to me to be the kind of action needed."

Allen was just about to respond when John Tibbets knocked on the door seeking Andrew. Though John was young, a 14-year-old, both Andrew and Allen were fully aware that the youngster knew almost everything about Andrew's activities. Allen simply proceeded.

"Hi John. Andrew and I were just beginning to discuss his Underground Railroad Activities. He believed he needed to act and act he has, as you know. I have several thoughts about this. We are good friends and sometimes good friends sit down together and talk, even when they disagree. I have several concerns. I'll just list them and then we can all discuss them. One; these activities are illegal and eventually the law may get around to acting. We know there are informers who would willingly turn Andrew in for the good bounty money. There's no telling where a legal case might lead, even uninvolved members of the church might be dragged in. Two; nothing could possibly make slave owners, or even pro-slavery advocates, more angry than White people aiding escaped slaves. Tensions are already escalating; we can expect even worse as those aiding the escapees increase in number and daring. Three; in such a charged climate, any lingering hope that we might be able to convince slave owners to see their ways for what they are will diminish and perhaps disappear altogether."

Andrew was about to respond but John couldn't wait. "Illegal? The laws are illegal. We're a free state, right? Why aren't freed slaves free here?"

Andrew took up John's thought but polished it some. "Our Constitution labeled Ohio a free state, but subsequent laws, approved by men we elected, mind you, all but erased any meaning that "freedom" might have had. Allen's right, there's real risk involved. I'm concerned, though, Allen, that you think the risk might extend beyond me to sympathizers like yourself or others."

Allen toned down that thought a bit by saying, "Perhaps, as a family man with a wife and soon to be three children to support, I've allowed myself to imagine concerns where they are unlikely. I just don't trust the pro-slavery factions who created those laws not to stretch them as far as they can. Add in my second point about increasing pro-slavery anger and I guess I can't help being concerned."

Again, John jumped in before Andrew could respond. "I'm angry, too. I'll fight them."

Andrew once again gave a more reasoned reply. "Fight we must, but we need to keep in mind what we are fighting for. My fight is to aid slaves who have the raw courage to seek a better life of freedom. A pitched battle with slave owners seems to me like a distraction."

Allen added, "I see it as even more than a distraction. An out and out fight leaves all reasons behind. Each side becomes more and more angry and set in their ways. Ask yourself just how harsh will slave owners become toward slaves they even begin to suspect will seek their freedom? Do we end up making life harsher for the majority of slaves left behind? Do we accelerate the tendency of slave owners to defend what they call their culture? If they also see their slaves as a serious investment, so serious that losing them might even cause financial collapse, do they end up protecting that investment by selling them to more secure regions further south? And you know what? Selling slaves south or helping them flee north, both often split up families."

This time Andrew, agitated, jumped in immediately without letting John get in a word. "The slaves need to make these decisions, not us. If they decide to seek freedom, knowing the potential consequences far better than we do, then we help them. For me, it's that simple."

Allen couldn't help but feel the passion in his friend's response and yielded as gracefully as he could without fully agreeing. "Your point is well put; it is their decision, not ours. But I do hope we keep our help as quiet as possible, not only for our own safety but theirs, too, and for the safety of those left behind. We don't want to become like Rankin and his family, already too well known as prime actors. They're so well known that their home has a unique name, 'The Beacon on the Hill'. And, Rankin has experienced real violence, as have others."

Andrew's response was short. "No beacons here." Both Andrew and Allen seemed to understand that this conversation had run its course. Both signaled an end by standing up at the same time. John was about to speak, but even he understood that standing up was a signal that it was time to end the discussion, say goodbye, and depart. And they did.

Organize? - How

Despite his reservations, Allen admitted to himself that The Underground Railroad certainly added excitement and intrigue to the abolitionist cause. But he was pleased to note that in terms of the sheer number of people involved, it was dwarfed by the organized anti-slavery societies which were spreading throughout the country. Clermont County's organized activity certainly flourished in the 1830's, and he knew that its Lindale chapter had a history with anti-slavery societies. He'd learned from his discussions with George Waller in Kentucky that as early as 1812 Andrew Coombs, Sr. and Samuel Tibbets, Sr. had seen to it that the Lindale church established a relationship with Kentucky based anti-slavery societies.

Allen's worries about the risks he had expressed in his conversation with Andrew and young John became even more pronounced as the 1830's progressed. He read about the riots in Cincinnati noting that they led to the deaths of Blacks, both escaped slaves and Blacks "freed" by their masters. He knew that if they survived, they were very likely to suffer from the destruction of their property and/or from chilling threats, both physical and legal. In his conversations with Andrew and John, he'd brought up the risk to Whites, too. Certainly, those who operated the Underground Railroad, actually flouting the law to do so, were at most risk; but, as he had cautioned, those who just supported, joined, or even simply made known their approval of anti-slavery activities were at risk also and experienced their share of harassment. He had heard of Theodore Weld, a well-respected anti-slavery lecturer but in no way an advocate of violence and not known as a member of the Underground Railroad, who none-the-less had been called, in local newspapers, the "most mobbed man in America". Allen read the stories. Weld had reported one incident where he was stoned by rocks thrown at him through windows, another where men chased his audience from one venue and then, when the lecture continued elsewhere, they interrupted again with bells, tin pans, tin trumpets, and a barking dog.

As tensions between pro- and anti-slavery advocates heated up, the Temples, Coombs, and Miner families, and at times John Tibbets, began to meet on a somewhat regular basis. They talked and thought together about what they might do in the future, and they read aloud articles from newspapers or passages from books. Among their favorites was William Lloyd Garrison's Boston paper "The Liberator" which had grown since its inception in 1831 to become the premier anti-slavery paper in the country. Their interest was piqued when they received and spent most of a long evening reading from a recent January 10, 1835 edition. That edition carried the full "Statement of Reasons" expressing, when the anti-slavery students left Lane Theological Seminary, their reasons for doing so, endangering their own theological careers and, if Weld's own experience was any indication, their own personal safety. Weld did not reveal his authorship of the "Statement of Reasons", fearing more of the attacks he had already experienced, and the Liberator article just listed his name with the Lane students who had chosen to leave the seminary.

Andrew Coombs, Jr. began that reading with its introduction, "We prayed much, heard facts, weighed arguments, kept our temper and after the most patient pondering, in which we were sustained by the excitement of sympathy, and of anger, we decided that slavery is a sin, and as such, ought to be immediately renounced. In this case, too, we acted. We organized an anti-slavery society, and published facts, arguments, remonstrances and appeals."

Allen responded, "I've thought often about how to approach slave owners to convince them that slavery is wrong. What you just read, Andrew, seems to me to express two approaches. One: calling it a sin, which leads often to endless biblical talk and two: acting by organizing in order to publish facts and then to make arguments based on those facts. My preference has always been to present the facts, period. Slaves are human beings and must be allotted human rights. I'm not sure arguing about what the Bible says and bringing up sin is as productive. Look what these former students say they actually do in the next paragraph."

Allen continued reading the passage. "We threw ourselves into the neglected masses of the colored population in the city of Cincinnati and that we might leave it up to the light of the sun, established Sabbath day and evening schools, lyceums, a circulating library, &c.; choosing rather to employ our leisure hours in offices of brotherhood to 'the lame, the halt, and the blind' than to devote them to fashionable calls and ceremonial salutations." Nothing there about the Bible, except the somewhat odd quote from Luke; no, it's all about learning to know freed Blacks and then helping them." Allen had remembered that paragraph from a previous reading because it had so perfectly echoed his thoughts.

Young John Tibbets, puzzled by a portion of Allen's comment, asked, "Why is choosing the biblical phrase 'the lame, the halt, and the blind' odd?"

Allen responded, "I've been to the colored section of Cincinnati several times over the years, where the former Lane students were working, and what I saw were the healthy, hefty, and sharp sighted. But the students meant it, no doubt, as a way of expressing the 'neglected masses', and, yes, the Blacks down there are certainly neglected. That other phrase they use and reject, 'fashionable calls and salutations', I'd translate as acceptable Bible talk. Of course, I have nothing against the Bible, but I want action and so it seems do these former Lane theology students."

Susanna Tibbets pressed Allen on just what sort of action he had in mind for their small group. "Perhaps you men can go on down to Cincinnati and find a way to join the ex-Lane students' projects there. Apparently, no women are helping now, and I know I don't want to be the first."

Allen, certainly not wanting to aggravate his wife's best friend, responded, "Guess we might be wise to leave those projects to Weld and the young men currently performing them so well. But, I believe I heard that one of them is colored. Wonder if we could get him to come here and speak to us. Just getting to know one non-white, educated at Lane Theological Seminary no less, should help even skeptics see their worthiness. Seeing and experiencing that first-hand is at the center of my experience, as I've bored you all with so many times."

Ichabod Temple then took charge by saying, "Looks like we have an agenda, and I don't mean the usual one—when we meet next. Allen, why don't you check on that student and see if he will join us some evening. When we find out if he can join us, we can invite other sympathetic members of the community, too. We'll ask him about the anti-slavery society they started and consider what we can do in that line."

The next day Allen got to thinking about his assignment. He needed to consider how to contact them, particularly James Bradley who was mentioned as the colored student in "The Liberator" article. Sending a letter would be easiest, but he had no address. Besides, he wanted to invite James personally. He would need to go to Cincinnati, inquire about his address, and then, since he was there anyway, he'd take the opportunity to visit the other former Lane students. Being an honest fellow, he would need to tell his wife, at least, that he would be going to the colored section after all, despite what he'd said to Susanna Tibbets at the meeting the previous evening.

The discussion with Sophina went much better than he expected. She responded by agreeing and adding, "Just be careful, and I know what you haven't said, 'will you let Susanna know', yes, I will."

Allen, knowing full well when to take "yes" as "yes", left as soon as possible after taking care to arrange his work and family affairs. He figured he would go down to the docks first, an area he knew relatively well. Many freed Blacks, with all their papers in order, worked the docks and the steamboats; they'd be his best bet for information about where to find those he wanted to find and in particular James Bradley. Allen packed saddle bags with some extra clothing and food and loaded them onto the somewhat aged Lundy to make the nearly 30-mile trip.

He arrived in Cincinnati late in the evening, boarded his horse at a stable near the hotel, figuring he'd go down to the docks to make his inquiries early in the morning. That next morning proved to be ideal, cool but sunny and pleasant; Allen felt good and people down at the docks seemed to be in a pleasant frame of mind. As casually as possible, he asked several colored workers about the Lane students, but for quite some time he was unable to find anyone who knew what he needed to know. Finally, Allen found a young Black named Alfonso willing to talk at some length. He'd been to what he called the Ludlow House, even studied math under some of the former Lane students there. He told Allen that the Ludlow House had become known as The Hall of Free Discussion, and he enthusiastically praised it as such. He even suggested that he planned on going there after work as he usually did, offering to show Allen the way. Allen, knowing good luck when he heard it, accepted the offer and arranged to meet his new friend that evening, right where they were currently standing.

Allen spent most of the day walking around the docks. He did visit Lundy, just to see if all was well, and he found a local place to dine. Finally, it was time to meet. Allen and Alfonso arrived within minutes of each other at the place arranged, greeted each other with smiles, and left with the sun declining but still lighting their way.

As they walked, Allen asked Alfonso if any of his teachers had been particularly helpful to him in any way, hoping Alfonso would mention James Bradley. Instead, Alfonso responded by suggesting a new possible contact unknown to Allen, "Mister Thome, he help me most. Heard tell he come from slave owners, but he treat me fine."

So, Allen took what he could get from what Alfonso said and finally asked about James Bradley directly, "From a slave owning family and converted to anti-slavery, good. Speaking of slavery, I heard one of those who might be working with your Mister Thome is a freed slave. Do you know him?"

"Sure do, he Mister Bradley. Help me write, he be a good man."

"I'd like to meet them both. I am hoping they will be willing to speak to those members of my church interested in our own anti-slavery movement."

"Mister Thome he make speeches, Mister Bradley, he, too."

As they talked, they made their way into the colored section of the city. It wasn't just the lack of White faces that was different, the buildings told something about where they were; well-kept homes were right next to those in need of lots of work. It seemed the community had successes and failures made much more obvious, side by side, than in White communities where the successful isolated themselves into whole neighborhoods as far away as possible from their less successful fellows. It would seem that being colored was clearly isolating enough; no need to isolate further by separating successful from unsuccessful. Allen noted this but put it away in the back of his mind for later thought.

By then they were well into the area named Cumminsville, nearing the ex-Lane student's aptly designated Hall of Free Discussion. Allen focused his thoughts on the matter at hand. Alfonso led him into the hall and, after a few minutes, found James Thome. Alfonso's introduction was brief but to the point. "Mister Thome here be Mister Miner, he want to talk to you."

Allen and James Thome shook hands, then Allen explained his mission to James with Alfonso patiently listening. "I've come as a representative of members of my community who support the anti-slavery movement. We thought we might be able to learn from involved people like you how we can become more engaged. We read about what you have been doing in a recent copy of the 'The Liberator' and we were impressed."

James replied, "I bet you may have guessed that the anonymous author of the 'Statement of Reasons' for leaving Lane is one of our brightest and most vocal, Theodore Weld. He's out there spreading the word right now, as he so often does."

Allen responded, "Speaking of spreading the word, that's what I hope you might be willing to do at our church. We have several members, including myself, who meet and talk about anti-slavery activity. We read together, discuss issues, weigh approaches to slave owners, but at this point we want to do more. A good number of other church members and members of the community would show up, if we had someone from your group give a talk and perhaps give us some new ideas and perspectives."

James responded enthusiastically, "I'd be more than willing to do that myself."

Allen took a few moments for thought after thanking James for the offer. "Alfonso told me that your family owns slaves. That gives you an important perspective, if our aim is to convert slave owners, as I believe it is. Members of my family I visited in Kentucky own slaves, and I got to hear their notions of slavery while witnessing the slaves they owned. The contrast between what my family said and what I saw the slaves doing was striking. Even more striking was what I saw on the way to Kentucky from my home in Western New York. I saw an old man, chained in a line of chained slaves, fall from exhaustion, then beaten by a slave driver. He was saved by the slaves he was chained to; they practically carried him on down the trail. Those slaves showed me a simple act of humanity etched in my mind against the White slave driver's inhumanity. Recently my pro-slavery friends and I in Lindale have been expressing our concern over escalating pro- and anti-slavery antagonisms. We need to figure out how to face this increasing conflict."

That passionate response inspired James to propose exactly what Allen had hoped it would. "I have an idea that might lead to an excellent presentation for your group. I know from family experience what slave owners think and what a convert thinks, and we have a former Lane student, James Bradley, who knows as personally as possible what slaves themselves think. He was a slave himself before he managed to buy his own freedom and reach Lane. Theodore Weld took him in and saw to it that he joined our class. Why don't we both come and speak to your group? We've teamed up together before for talks, and I know how willing he would be. We're both free, let's see, not this coming weekend, maybe the following weekend, Saturday evening say, would that work?"

"Yes," Allen responded, "that would be perfect. Alfonso mentioned James Bradley. 'The Liberator' article mentioned him, too. What a pleasure it would be to have both of you over to our church. Is he here this evening?"

"No, he's out with another ex-Lane student doing just what we're talking about, speaking. He'll be back in a couple of days and ready to go by then."

Allen turned to the oh-so-patient Alfonso and said, "Seems like we have talked away right through your time for your evening math class here with Mr. Thome. I owe you for bringing me here, and I'm so happy it's all working out. I know, I'll make up a bit by letting you in on a little numbers game I've played with my oldest son. You need to figure out the numbers pattern after I give you some of the numbers. Then you complete the pattern. Ready? Here we go. 1-10, 2-9; so, now it's your turn."

Alfonso picked it up immediately. "3-8, 4-7, 5-6. That good?"

"Sure is. Now let's try it using 1 as the low number again but 11 as the high one this time. Go on, you're good at this."

"1-11, 2-10, 3-9, 4-8, 5-7, 6-. Oh, don't work right."

Allen couldn't help but smile. "Now that's odd, right?"

James jumped in. "Amusing; odd numbers, odd folks—one might say neither work right. Good Allen and very good Alfonso. I think that about sums up our evening. Allen, you can join me for a little supper, sleep overnight, and get a good start in the morning, if you'd like. Alfonso can guide you back when he returns to the docks for work in the morning."

Allen replied with thanks but couldn't help adding one more problem for Alfonso. "Alfonso, I have favorite times of the day like twelve thirty-four, the only time possible with four numbers in order, '1234'. Now guess why I like twelve forty-eight. Hint, it's '1248'."

Alfonso seemed stumped for a few moments, so Allen simply said, multiplication.

"Ise got it. Two times one, two; two times two, four; two times four, eight. Dat right?"

Allen and James in tandem, "right". And that did end the evening.

The next morning all went as planned. Alfonso led Allen back to the docks where Allen retrieved Lundy and set off for home, having successfully accomplished his mission. He could even say to his wife and Susanna that he didn't go into the colored section alone but with an excellent guide. No need to mention the guide's age, he guessed.

Chapter Nine

Cincinnati Slavery

Timorous Cautionists or Not

Once Allen settled in at home, it did not take long for news to spread throughout the church, and then the wider community, that anti-slavery speakers, formerly from Lane Seminary but now working in the Black section of Cincinnati, would be coming to Lindale to speak. Even the newspapers picked up and spread the news. Most of Allen's Lindale fellow church members approved, but a few and many non-members in the surrounding community protested the whole project to varying degrees. When the newspapers printed that one of the Lane members scheduled to speak was a freed slave, the protests became even more widespread.

Despite the opposition, which included personal threats to them, James Thome and James Bradley arrived in Lindale safely, as when visiting even more hostile areas. James Bradley always traveled with a White cohort; it was simply too conspicuous and thus dangerous in the 1830's for Black men to travel alone any distance from their Cincinnati enclave, no matter what papers they might carry. Both were heartily greeted by the avid anti-slavery members of the church—the Tibbets, Temples, Coombs, and Miners especially. Allen made a point to welcome and thank James Bradley for coming, to let him know how glad he was to finally meet him. He took care to introduce both to each of the church members present.

Ichabod Temple invited both guests to his home for supper and time to relax. Plans had been made for them to stay with Ichabod's family Friday night and through Saturday before the evening event. Others might stop over during the day, if they wished, but Ichabod made it clear that he wanted to give his guests time to settle in. All would be able to spend time with them at the meeting. Ichabod had decided, given the level of interest both good and bad, that they should hold the meeting in the church where he hoped any possible conflict would be modified by the holy environment, even though space was limited.

Friday evening and the next day went as Ichabod had hoped. His guests were well rested and ready for their evening talks and subsequent discussions. Allen did stop by in the afternoon, primarily to go over his introduction of his new friends. They all decided on a very brief run-through of the Lane student revolt followed by an even briefer description of James Thome's slave-owning family background as it contrasted with James Bradley's slave background, emphasizing how close their friendship had become.

It was early evening, and the church was crowded with both members and non-members. The press was there, too. When Allen stood up and began speaking the crowd settled in and hushed. "We are privileged this evening to hear from two former Lane Seminary students on the subject of slavery. As most of you already know, a number of Lane students left the seminary in protest when such discussions as we will hear this evening were essentially banned on campus. These students had done all that the seminary required of them in the way of civility; they had been respectful and diligent.

But, despite the orderly nature of their debates on the future of the anti-slavery movement, they were denied the right to speak freely on the subject by the board of trustees, even though backed by a well-known mentor, Theodore Weld, and the school's president, Dr. Beecher."

"Let me introduce James Thome and James Bradley to you all, the former from a slave owning family background and the latter a freed slave. That's quite a contrast and one that seldom, far too seldom, leads to civil discussions let alone friendship. But as young students these two became close friends at Lane and then that friendship deepened while they worked together, as they are working together here tonight in our church. Please welcome them. Mr. Thome, I believe you wished to speak first."

"Thank you, Allen, and thanks to all here willing to listen to what I have to say. Let me first summarize the findings of those students who left the seminary after their freedom to speak in opposition to slavery was denied. Though I knew about some of what follows from my slave owning experiences, I want to emphasize that what follows comes from the Lane debates summary, from the testimony of participating anti-slavery students. Several of those students knew slavery as slave owners or members of slave owning families, as I did. One was a slave himself. Others studied slavery extensively in various areas of the slave-infested South. The following facts and premises were agreed upon and written as part of the summary.

"I will include as much as I can recall. Slaves long for freedom; it is very frequently the subject of conversation among them. They know their masters have no right to hold them in slavery despite laws to the contrary, and they keenly feel the wrong, the insult, and the degradation which are heaped upon them by the Whites. They feel little interest in their master's affairs because he is their oppressor. When performing acts related to their master's affairs they practice indolence, because nothing they earn is their own. They pretend to be more ignorant and stupid than they really are, so as to avoid responsibility, and to avoid the lash for any real or alleged disobedience to orders. Yet when inspired with a promise of freedom, they will toil with incredible alacrity and faithfulness. They tell their masters and drivers they are contented with their lot, merely through fear of greater cruelty if they told the truth. No matter how kind their master is, they are dissatisfied, and would rather be his hired servants than his slaves. The slave drivers are generally low, brutal, debauched men, distinguished only for their cruelty and licentiousness. Unfortunately, these brutes generally have despotic control of the slaves. Slave owners attempt to conjure up slavery's bright side. Its darker side is only known fully by slaves, slave traders, and drivers; they know the horrid facts, the whipping and murdering of slaves, though owners can't help but know at some level what's happening. God sparing my life, all these facts shall be broadcast to the public so everyone will know.

"No group of people in the country has stronger family ties than slaves. Nevertheless, those ties between parent and child, husband and wife, brother and sister, are torn asunder by this bloody traffic. A husband has been known to cut his throat deliberately, because this damnable traffic was about to separate him from a wife whom he tenderly loved. Think about this fact; the horrid character of Louisiana slavery was developed in some degree because of one crop grown there—sugar. The planters in that state, when sugar commands a high price, do not hesitate to kill a few of their negroes by overworking them, if by that means they can bring more sugar into a favorable market. In consequence of this, one of the usual prayers of the poor negro is that sugar may be cheap.

"Multitudes of slaves are being carried into Louisiana from other slave states. Blacks are kidnapped from free states and sold into slavery. If slaves are offered freedom on the condition of moving to Liberia, they are decidedly hostile to the idea and only consent to go there to escape from the horrors they experience here. Masters are generally opposed to their negroes being educated as well as to the notion that they are abundantly able to take care of and provide for themselves or that they would be kind and docile if immediately emancipated. These points, with many others equally important, were established in our summary, so far as a multitude of facts could establish them.

"James Bradley, the emancipated slave alluded to above and here with us tonight, addressed the Lane students at length. I wish his speech could have been heard by every opponent of immediate emancipation, to wit; the notion that it would be unsafe to the community, that the condition of the emancipated negroes would be worse than it now is, that they are incompetent to provide for themselves, that they would become paupers and vagrants, and that they would rather steal than work for wages.

"This shrewd and intelligent Black cut up these White objections by the roots, and withered and scorched them under the sun of sarcastic argumentation, for nearly an hour, to which the assembly responded in repeated and spontaneous roars of laughter, which were heartily joined in by both Colonizationists and Abolitionists. Do not understand me as saying that his speech was devoid of argument. No, it contained sound logic, enforced by apt illustrations. I wish the slanderers of negro intellect could have witnessed this unpremeditated effort.

"Now, I understand that some among you have begun to consider creating an anti-slavery society as the students from Lane seminary now working in the colored section of Cincinnati have done. I want to make two points about such efforts, points I try to make whenever I speak on slavery.

"First; I can give you but a faint idea of the notions that are entertained about abolition principles by those who support slavery. Here are some of the words they use to describe us. Reckless, false estimate of right, fanaticism, Quixotism, sublimated austere bigots incessantly harping upon abstract principles, incendiaries, officious intermeddlers, arrant knaves who would break up all well-ordered society, set every slave at his master's throat, and enjoy the massacre with infinite delight; outlawed renegades who, having themselves no interest at stake, would bankrupt the honest planter, and most horrifying of all, introduce a general system of amalgamation.

"These notions, so monstrously perverted, have not been spread haphazardly, but most faithfully instilled by pro-slavery advocates as well as the timorous cautionists of our day. But from whatever source they may have come, they clamor for correction, immediate correction. It is of immense importance that the public mind should be disabused by a faithful presentation of facts. If you proceed in establishing an anti-slavery society and fearlessly broadcast the facts, you, too, will hear such lies about your intent.

"Second; Ang yet, despite being plagued by all these disadvantages, you will be capable of doing much. The very little leaven which others like you have been enabled to introduce is now working with tremendous power. One instance has lately occurred within my acquaintance, of an heir to slave property; a young man of growing influence, who was first awakened by reading a single copy of the Anti-Slavery Reporter, sent to him by some unknown hand. He is now a wholehearted abolitionist. I have facts to show that cases of this kind are by no means rare. A family of slaves in Arkansas Territory, another in Tennessee, and a third, consisting of eighty-eight, in Virginia, were successively emancipated through the influence of one abolition periodical.

"So, I implore you do not hesitate as to your duty. Do not pause to consider the propriety of interference. It is as unquestionably the province of those who choose to labor in this cause, as it is the duty of the church to convert the world."

James Thome then turned toward James Bradley, preparing to introduce him. The audience took his turn toward the next speaker as an indication to give him scattered applause. Applause within the confines of a church was an unusual occurrence, but in this case the scattering caught on and became general. After thanking the audience for their demonstration of approval, he proceeded, "Now, let's hear from James Bradley himself. Nothing more I could say could be as convincing as the personal testimony of such a man. Mr. Bradley..."

Mr. Bradley began, "First, let me thank you all for this chance to speak out freely. I will tell you what slavery was like for me, one of so many thousands. I will begin as far back as I can remember. I think I was between two and three years old when the soul-destroyers tore me from my mother's arms, somewhere in Africa, far back from the sea. They carried me a long distance to a ship; all the way I looked back and cried. The ship was full of men and women loaded down with chains; but I was so small, they let me run about on deck.

"A slaveholder bought me and took me to Pendleton County, Kentucky. I suppose that I stayed with him about six months. He sold me to a Mr. Bradley, by whose name I have ever since been called. This man was considered a wonderfully kind master; and it is true that I was treated better than most of the slaves I came to know. I never suffered for food, and never was flogged with the whip; but, oh my soul! I was tormented with kicks and knocks more than I can tell. My master often knocked me down when I was young. Once, when I was a boy, about nine years old, he struck me so hard that I fell down and lost my senses. I remained thus some time, and when I came to myself, he told he thought he had killed me. At another time he struck me with a curry comb and sunk the knob into my head. I have said that I had food enough; I could say as much concerning my clothing.

"My master kept me ignorant of everything he could. I was never told anything about God, or my own soul. Yet, from the time I was fourteen years old, I thought a great deal about freedom. It was my heart's desire; I could not keep it out of my mind. Many a sleepless night I spent in tears because I was a slave. I looked back on all I had suffered, and when I looked ahead, all was dark and hopeless bondage. My heart ached to feel within me a life of liberty.

"After the death of my master, I began to contrive how I might buy myself. After toiling all day for my mistress, I used to sleep three or four hours, and then get up and work for myself the remainder of the night. I made collars for horses, out of plaited husks. I could weave one in about eight hours; and generally, I took time enough from my sleep to make two collars in the course of a week. I sold them for fifty cents each. Then one summer, I tried to take two or three hours from my sleep every night; but found that I grew weak, and I was obliged to sleep more. With the money I'd made I bought my first pig. The next year I earned for myself about thirteen dollars; and the next about thirty. I bought more pigs. There was a good deal of wild land in the neighborhood, that belonged to Congress. I used to go out with my hoe, and dig up little patches, which I planted with corn, and got up in the night to tend it. My hogs were fattened with this corn, and I sold a number each year. Besides this, I used to raise small patches of tobacco, and sell it to buy more corn for my pigs. In this way I worked for five years; at the end of which time, after taking out my losses, I found that I had earned one hundred and sixty dollars.

"With this money I hired my own time from my mistress for two years. During this period, I worked almost all the time, night and day. The hope of liberty stung my nerves, and braced up my soul so much, that I could do with very little sleep or rest. I could do a great deal more work than I was ever able to do before. At the end of the two years, I had earned three hundred dollars, besides feeding and clothing myself. I then bought my time for eighteen months longer; and, with thorough documentation in hand, I went two hundred and fifty miles west, nearly into Texas, where I could make more money. There I earned enough to buy myself from my mistress, which I did in 1833, about one year ago. It cost me, including what I gave to her for my time, about seven hundred dollars.

"As soon as I was free, I started for a free state. When I arrived in Cincinnati, I heard of Lane Seminary, about two miles out of the city. I had for years been praying to God that my dark mind might see the light of knowledge. I asked for admission into the Seminary. They pitied me, and granted my request, though I knew nothing of the studies which were required for admission. I was so ignorant, that I supposed it would take me two years to get up with the lowest class in the institution. But in all respects, I was treated just as kindly, and as much like a brother by the students, as if my skin was as White, and my education as good as their own. Thanks to the Lord, prejudice against color does not exist in Lane Seminary. If my life was spared, I planned to spend several years there and prepare to preach the gospel.

"In the year 1828, I had met some Christians who talked with me about my soul, and the sinfulness of my nature. They told me I must repent and live to do good. This led me to the cross of Christ; and then, oh, how I longed to be able to read the Bible! I got an old spelling-book, which I carried in my hat and studied when I could for many months, until I could spell well, and read easy words. When I got up in the night to work, I used to read for a few minutes, if I could manage to get a light. Indeed, every chance I could find, I worked away at my spelling-book. After I learned to read a little, I wanted very much to learn to write; and I persuaded one of my young masters to teach me. But the second night, my mistress came in, bustled about, scolded her son, and called him out. I overheard her say to him, 'What are you doing? If you teach him to write, he will write himself a pass and run away.' That was the end of my instruction in writing, but I persevered, and made marks of all sorts and shapes that I could think of. By turning every way, I was, after a long time, able to write tolerably plainly.

"I have said a great deal about my desire for freedom. How strange it is that anyone would believe any human being could be a slave, and yet be contented! I do not believe that there ever was a slave who did not long for liberty. I know very well that slave owners take great pains to make the people in the free states believe that their slaves are happy; but I know, likewise, that I was never acquainted with a slave, however well he was treated, who did not long to be free. There is one thing about this that people in the free States do not understand. If they ask slaves whether they wish for liberty, slaves answer, 'No'; and very likely they will go as far as to say they would not leave their masters for the world. But at the same time, they desire liberty more than anything else, and have, perhaps all along been laying plans to get free. The truth is, if a slave shows any discontent, he is sure to be treated worse and forced to work harder, and every slave knows this. This is why they are careful not to show any uneasiness when White men ask about freedom. When they are alone by themselves, all their talk is about liberty, liberty! It is the great thought and feeling that fills their minds full all the time. Thank you all once again for giving me the chance to act on my liberty so openly before you."

The applause, this time, was spontaneous and quite hearty. James Thome then stood up next to Mr. Bradley and opened the session for questions saying, "We had promised to respond as openly as possible to any questions you may have for us."

Two or three hands went up, but they deferred to Ichabod, who spoke first. "We certainly thank you both for such a compelling defense of the universal humanity felt now even more strongly by those of us who support the anti-slavery effort you both so cogently represent. At some point, perhaps not now, I'll be interested in discussing more fully the anti-slavery society efforts you have advocated."

James Thome responded. "Yes, we could discuss formation of an anti-slavery society here in Lindale later this evening at your place, if possible, with a smaller interested group. That's probably the best way to handle the many specific questions you might have on the subject."

Andrew Coombs, Jr. was recognized next. "Mr. Thome, you used a phrase that caught my attention, when you were talking about what those who advocate abolition would be attacked as supporting including Black and White amalgamation. You attributed some of the blame for all sorts of horrible thoughts related to amalgamation to 'timorous cautionists'. Just wondered who these 'timorous cautionists' are and what they stand for."

James Thome hesitated a moment and then answered, "Well, that's sort of a broad term for all those who, for whatever reason, feel that Blacks and Whites will not be able live side by side. And, yes, most assuredly it includes those whom the Lane students eventually rejected in their debates—those who supported and argued for The American Colonization Society. We do not need to send former slaves to Liberia; in fact, doing so would be our loss, as my friend James Bradley's cogent speech has made so clear here tonight."

Allen then jumped in, "It is a denial of their compassion, and ours, to believe we can't live together. We can do it. We can recognize our common humanity. Some have already done so; others will take convincing. That's the work of anti-slavery societies in general."

That simple statement seemed to end any further questions that might have been percolating in the minds of others. Interestingly, no one felt the need to question the very personal account James Bradley had given them. They waited to simply congratulate him upon leaving. James Bradley and James Thome stood with Ichabod at the church door as attendees filed past. One might expect the newspaper personnel to ask James Bradley in particular more probing questions, but they seemed to have heard all they needed to hear, even if they didn't all share the sentiments or the spirit they'd just heard expressed.

Anti-Slavery Societies
Immediate Emancipation

That evening, Mary Temple provided their guests, James Thome and James Bradley, and her family with supper, even though it was well beyond the normal time for the evening meal. After supper, Ichabod, along with a select few he had invited, gathered to listen further to what the two guests might have to say about the anti-slavery society they and their fellow students had created, and how their experiences might aid efforts in Lindale.

The conversation began with some general principles of slavery. Most present knew how fervently the ex-students felt their disgust for what they had no hesitation calling "the sin of slave ownership". Many had read the "Liberator" article, and several remarked on it. Finally, James Thome said that he had brought along with him the preamble and the constitution of the ex-Lane student's Anti-Slavery Society in Cincinnati and suggested that reading a few passages from the preamble might be in order. "Let's see, first:

'Our objective is the immediate emancipation of the whole colored race within the United States: The emancipation of the slave from the oppression of the master, the emancipation of the free colored man from the oppression of public sentiment, and the elevation of both to an intellectual, moral, and political equality with the Whites.'"

"Second: 'We advocate for the immediate emancipation of the slave for the following reasons. First: He is constituted by God a moral agent, the keeper of his own happiness, the executive of his own powers, the accountable arbiter of his own choice; personal ownership his birth right, unforfeited and inalienable; liberty, and the pursuit of happiness, his chartered rights, inherited from his Maker and guaranteed by all the laws of his being.'"

Then he handed the document over to James Bradley, saying that it quite simply summarized what the former slave had suffered personally. James Bradley read the following with the passion it deserved. "Slavery robs himself of himself, body and soul; and though he is immortal, created in God's image, the purchase of a Saviour's blood, visited by the Holy Ghost, and invited to a citizenship with angels and to fellowship with God, it drags him to the shambles and sells him like a beast, goads him to incessant and unrequited toil, withholds from him legal protection in all his personal rights and social relations, and abandons to caprice, cupidity, passion, and lust, all that is dear in human well-being. It crushes the upward tendencies of intellect, makes the acquisition of knowledge a crime, and consigns the mind to famine. It stifles the moral affections, represses the innate longings of the spirit, paralyzes conscience, turns hope to despair, and kills the soul."

James Thome then added that slavery destroyed the slave owner, too, and the country itself, reading a couple of passages that included comments about how the opinions of none other than the slave owner Thomas Jefferson evolved over his lifetime, before offering to leave a copy so they could read the whole much more damning preamble later when they gathered for their next meeting. He selected the following line from the preamble. "It tends to blunt the sensibilities of all who exercise authority over the slave, and to transform them into tyrants. That whole process is drawn to the life by the younger President Jefferson, who, despite changing his opinion of slavery, lived and died a slave holder."

Then he read the section that included a quote from an older, better-informed Jefferson on what slavery does to the nation. "'I tremble for my country when I reflect that God is just, and that his justice will not sleep forever.'"

The initial response from the Lindale members was silence accompanied by a good number of nods signifying approval. James Thome then encouraged them to ask any questions that occurred to them, even if they thought their questions might be troubling. "Please ask questions, whatever concerns you. We've handled responses from those who were outright hostile; we can certainly handle questions from you who have been so welcoming."

Allen began by asking about the issue he and his wife had discussed so often. "Sophina and I have struggled with a question that underlies the whole notion of anti-slavery societies—that conversion of slave owners, that releasing them from what you rightly call the sin of slavery, is possible on anything but a very limited scale. We are aware of a few examples of conversion, yours included James, and you have cited examples, but we continue to struggle with doubt about whether enough conversions can occur to make the fundamental changes that are necessary, when slave owners believe that their whole way of life depends on being unable to see what to us is so obvious."

James Thome responded, "That's a doubt we all feel from time to time. There really is no answer we can offer that would be in any way absolute. All we can say to ourselves, when doubt occurs, is that we must just work through it by continuing to express in every way we can what we, ourselves, believe. We can't stop trying because of doubt; we can't surrender to falsehoods. We just keep telling the truth and continue to hope."

He continued, "Perhaps the main answer to the economic arguments so adamantly offered by slave owners is to start slowly. Start paying the slaves something, as if they were employees. Getting slave owners to let slaves make decisions about staying while receiving pay or leaving as free souls—well, that may be a much more distant hope."

James Bradley took up the question. "A 'distant hope' and yet we almost always use the words 'immediate emancipation', even in our preamble. Personally, I didn't wait, and I believe many other slaves won't wait either. Some simply run for it, and some make it here. They need help, too."

Several in-the-know members of the church turned expectantly to Andrew Coombs, and he responded. "Indeed, run-away slaves do need help, and they do get it but not through anti-slavery societies. These organizations emphasize activities within the law, as I understand them. That's, unfortunately, within laws that have little to do with God's laws."

James Bradley agreed but added, "There's no doubt that ending slavery will take more than one approach. Anti-slavery societies emphasize persuasion, others emphasize action. We believe in both. We work with former slaves, as we have made clear in our talks, and we certainly don't deny our aid to those who have run for their lives."

A new voice, that of William Doan, then spoke up. As a State Senator, he commanded attention. "To be persuasive, anti-slavery societies must be as open to public view as possible. We had the press here this evening, so what we said at the church will be reported, for better or worse. We need to engage the press, support them when they support our goals and debate them when they do not. So, yes, anti-slavery societies need to be lawful to speak as lawful citizens."

Another new voice, Morgan Dickenson, Jr., countered with, "Yet I remain with Allen; doubtful, very doubtful. I think, as Mr. Bradley does, that we will see more, perhaps many more, brave slaves running for freedom. Slavery is a law in slave states, and I cheer those brave slaves who break it. Sure, I'll join an anti-slavery society, and when acting as a member, I'll not break the law. But, as a citizen of a 'free' state, I might well be tempted to follow my conscience, and following my conscience could well mean breaking the law."

That statement evoked a general nodding of heads, signaling a basic understanding of what those present would want their society to endorse and what they would choose on their own to do or not to do. Ichabod took charge again. He thanked his guests and encouraged those interested in a future Lindale anti-slavery society to let others, whom they thought might be interested, know what had been discussed. He then asked if all thought they were at a point where, in a couple of weeks, they should meet again along with those who might consider joining, to work out what their own anti-slavery society constitution should include.

Again, agreement was general. They now had the Lane constitution as a model, and they thanked their Cincinnati guests for it once again. Slowly those who had been invited began leave-taking, and on the way out they thanked Ichabod and Mary and shook hands with both speakers, heartily congratulating them.

A Balm in Gilead
Lindale Baptists Heal Themselves

It would have seemed likely that after the talk at the church and the smaller meeting of interested members at Pastor Temple's home focusing on the nature of anti-slavery societies and with the Lane preamble and constitution in hand, that they would form one for themselves soon. The next meeting scheduled took place two weeks after the first, and another a month after that, but no formal society emerged in Lindale for two more years.

During those years they were struck again and again by how extreme the dangers around Cincinnati were for anyone opposed to slavery in any way. They saw an explosion of anger among pro-slavery citizens, many of them new residents from Kentucky pursuing business opportunities in the thriving city. That anger culminated in 1836, leading to a mob attack against the colored section of Cincinnati, or "the swamp" as the pro-slavery attackers called it. Houses were burned, and Blacks were attacked and driven from their homes. The Lindale sympathizers feared for the Blacks as well as for themselves. In early July pro-slavery forces attacked the anti-slavery paper The Philanthropist, destroying the office and the printing press. At the end of the month, they attacked the paper again and threw the press into the Ohio River.

Eventually the increasing violence in Cincinnati led Lindale's anti-slavery supporters to react, but not as the pro-slavery forces had hoped. Days before the second attack on The Philanthropist, the small but dedicated group held a meeting to discuss the formation of an anti-slavery society of their own, the one they'd put off for so long. They kept the meeting small so they could vent their feelings about recent events and then actually map out what the society they were now determined to start should emphasize in its constitution. The members at the meeting were Ichabod Temple, Samuel Tibbets, Martin Pease, Andrew Coombs, Jr., John Tibbets, Allen and Sophina Miner, Joanna Doan and her father William Doan Sr. They met in the evening at Ichabod's centrally located home, after making whatever arrangements were necessary for the safety of their own families and homes.

Ichabod, as the recognized elder and church pastor, began the meeting with a prayer that ended with, "... let us pray for the Blacks who suffered from the destruction of their homes during the vicious attacks against what their attackers derogatorily call "the swamp" and what we know to be a remarkably fine community. Several community members died in the attack. We send our sincere sympathy to their loved ones and pray that they may reap their just heavenly reward."

William Doan Sr. added to the prayer by mentioning the attack on The Philanthropist and then, after hearty amens from all, proceeded by suggesting a reading from the placards that had appeared around town. "Here's the perfect quote that provides evidence of just how vicious the pro-slavery opposition in Cincinnati has become. 'The Citizens of Cincinnati ... satisfied that the business of the place is receiving a vital stab from the wicked and misguided operations of the abolitionists, are resolved to arrest their course. The destruction of their Press on the night of the 12th instant, may be taken as a warning.'"

Joanna then jumped in saying, "and that's not all. They went after the publisher, James Birney, personally, a few days later with this placard. I pulled it off a store front right near here when no one was around; look at it. 'FUGITIVE FROM JUSTICE, $100 REWARD. The above sum will be paid for the delivery of one James G. Birney, a fugitive from justice, now abiding in the city of Cincinnati. Said Birney in all his associations and feelings is black, although his external appearance is white. The above reward will be paid, and no questions asked by OLD KENTUCKY.'"

John Tibbets responded by referring to what he saw as a significant connection between the two placards. "Note that the first placard refers to 'the business of the place receiving a vital stab wound' and the second claims the award will be paid by 'Old Kentucky'. We all know that a main source of pro-slavery anger against us comes from Kentuckians who moved here relatively recently to take advantage of 'The Queen of the West', the well-deserved name of our vital port city and manufacturing center. There are far too many of those newly arrived pro-slavery Kentuckians around here now, and they simply rile up our relatively peaceful, home grown slavery advocates, turning them towards hate against anyone who in any way advocates or supports anti-slavery activities."

Allen added, "Hard to imagine converting haters to what we believe about slavery as I'd always hoped we might convert slave owners. Haters, like too many have become, simply don't listen.

On the other hand, conversion is not yet completely hopeless. We have been talking about James Birney, never a hater, but he does freely admit that he went from a slave owner to a supporter of colonization and then to an abolitionist. Peaceful abolitionists using persuasion helped him along that healing path. It can be possible; we shouldn't give up entirely."

Sophina agreed but with her usual reservation added, "No, we shouldn't give up, just realistically understand that times are changing and not in a way that helps slavery advocates change their minds and save their souls, as Birney did. In fact, I can't even imagine talking to these 'business minded Kentuckians' now."

Samuel Tibbets then took charge, turning the discussion toward the main purpose of their meeting. "OK, we don't give up. We form our own anti-slavery society. And its purpose will be to convince anyone we can convince, even if the number of successes is discouragingly small."

Andrew Coombs, Jr. then stated in a firm and authoritative voice, "We start by unequivocally stating that we will not, as a society, use violence; as society members we will not advocate in any way what these hate-filled, pro-slavery folks have advocated by their recent actions and threats."

Martin Pease finally entered the conversation with a lawyerly speculation. "What if, let's just say, a Black man peacefully residing in his own home, a freed Black man even, suddenly hears a commotion outside and shouts of 'we've got them all trapped inside'. He'd know what that meant, right? He and his family were all in danger of being captured and sent back to slavery no matter how illegal it might be for those slave hunters outside his door to do so. Oh, 'we will not use violence', is not what would occur to me if I faced what he was facing. I'd get any guns I had and any other weapons I could get to and shoot the minute they burst in. My question: How far do you intend to extend the rule of non-violence?"

John Tibbets added, "And, I can imagine a case where, in the act of aiding in some way a fellow human being who happens to be Black, I might have to ward off slave hunters violently, too."

Andrew, judging from the way he held his head and squinted his left eye, was trying to figure out an answer. "That's a tough one. I still think the society must be non-violent and we need to say so. Our purpose must be to save souls, not destroy sinners, whatever we may think of them. But, on the other hand, I certainly understand, perhaps as well as anyone, that as individuals we may, no, probably will, encounter moments when self-defense requires violence and certainly our African American brothers and sisters will. Any ideas about how to write about this in our constitution?"

Martin Pease responded. "Well, wording, yes, let me try. Guess I'd start by defining slavery as a sin. Pro-Slavery advocates are in support of horrendous sins against fellow humans. Start there and the implied Christian solution is to save their souls by helping them move forward toward an understanding of the current disastrous state of their souls. Violence on our part is just plain counter to that purpose. And violence for our colored brethren, well, let's just say, this society will never encourage the coloured people to assert their rights by force. 'Encourage' that's the way to put it. We don't encourage violence even though given certain circumstances we certainly understand it."

There was an expression of approval from the attendees. All seemed to agree that wording of the sort Martin suggested got them past the issue. Allen went a step further. "I think Martin, Andrew, and John may have shown the way to address other issues. For instance, what about Federal regulations? We convince there too. We acknowledge that states have their own rights, but we must encourage federal action to keep new states free, even though we acknowledge their right to make their own laws. Seems to me that we must keep 'encouraging'."

Again, the agreement was general. Given the contributions of Martin, Andrew, Allen, and John, all agreed with Ichabod's suggestion that those four go ahead and work out the wording in preparation for the next meeting, scheduled in a couple of weeks. It was time to go home, and they were happy to do so, especially after making such promising progress.

The four got to work together the next day and created what they considered satisfactory wording for the constitution within a week. It was well that they moved quickly given that the second attack on The Philanthropist occurred that week. That attack spurred anti-slavery Lindale church members and friends to act. They were so incensed by this further provocation that they went so far as to preserve their meeting notes with the names of their members prominently listed. No meeting notes from any of the other Ohio based Anti-Slavery Societies exist, though they all made their existence and their cause well-known through local anti-slavery papers. All were part of the movement now; joining other Anti-Slavery Societies across the country that trace their origins from these years. There were eleven in Clermont County alone. The Lindale branch members were proud to be part of the Gilead Society of Clermont County, so proud that they risked letting the world know their individual names.

The four also worked out wording for several issues less fully covered at previous meetings, knowing what the overall group consensus would be when it came time to vote on the constitution. They soundly rejected colonization or any such suggestion that Blacks and Whites needed to be separated, by stating clearly, "The object of this society is the entire abolition of slavery in the United States. While it admits that each slaveholding state has, by the Constitution of the United States, the exclusive right to legislate in regard to the abolition of slavery within its own bounds, this society will endeavor, by arguments addressed to the understanding and conscience, to convince our fellow citizens that slave holding is a heinous sin in the sight of God, and that the safety and best interests of all concerned require its immediate abandonment without expatriation."

Knowing full well that expanding slavery to territories and on to new states would tip the federal government toward slavery, they used another non-violent word, 'influence', to describe their approach. "This society will aim to influence Congress in a constitutional way to abolish slavery in the district of Columbia and in the territories of the United States, and to prevent it from extending to any state that may hereafter be formed and admitted into the union."

The Gilead constitution insists on non-violent and lawful means. Yet the first speaker to the Lindale branch was John Rankin, whose home was known quite openly as the number one Underground Railroad point of light. It's the first place run-away slaves, who crossed the Ohio River from the slave state of Kentucky, would search out. He was not the only one there who showed, by his actions, that he advocated means that were specifically unlawful in Ohio and that might well lead to violent clashes. Andrew Coombs, Jr., now acting as pastor of the church as Ichabod Temple's health declined, was part of the same "unlawful" and potentially violent path to freedom.

Of course, nothing John Rankin said that day openly acknowledged the existence of those who pursued these 'legally' unlawful actions. His speech emphasized what the Society's constitution emphasized, the offense of slavery to God and the church. But he did advocate excluding slave owners from the church. He would turn the tables on them by questioning the lawfulness of slavery itself rather than the lawfulness of protecting and aiding run-away slaves. He went so far as to advocate resisting the law, arguing that aiding run-away slaves was a Christian duty, without going on to say that anyone was involved in such aid locally.

No doubt Lindale Anti-Slavery Society members, as well as much of the wider community, held varying degrees of both approaches, some all the way behind the anti-slavery society attempt to bring the sinners in line with Christian teaching by altering slave owners' convictions, some holding that the laws supporting slavery had to be opposed by actions, even violent actions, against those who enslaved others, and a few who firmly believed that sinners against

God and the church simply should be attacked whenever necessary and by whatever means.

In the Spring of 1837, Allen and John decided that they might be interested in purchasing land in Indiana. The 1820 Land Act no longer allowed credit purchases, but to counter the chilling effect of that change it also reduced the per acre price from $2.00 per acre to $1.25 and the minimum size from 160 to 80 acres, well within Allen's financial range and within the range John thought he could handle. Fortunately for Allen, Sophina had lived her earliest years on a farm in Maine and had nothing but fond memories of those times. When they discussed reducing the sort of multiple activities they had pursued in Lindale and instead living a simple farm life in Indiana, she surprised him with her enthusiasm.

Allen decided to check down at the Cincinnati docks to see if his old steamboat captain acquaintance, Captain Vail, might still be around guiding the Gen. Clark up and down the Ohio River as he had some 16 years ago when they first met. He'd always wanted to take a steamboat down the Ohio past the Louisville rapids; this was his chance. Besides, he figured John would love it. When he asked around the docks, he was given the Main Street address of Captain Vail but no information about his steamboat the Gen. Clark, so Allen went to visit the captain himself.

Captain Vail remembered Allen immediately, welcomed him, and suggested a stay for lunch, which Allen accepted. They talked as they ate, mostly about steamboat boiler accidents. Many had occurred since they last discussed the dangers of steamboats. Captain Vail had retired. He didn't exactly say boiler accidents played a part in his decision; Allen just assumed from the discussion that they had. As Allen readied to leave, the captain gave Allen a letter of introduction to a young captain he highly recommended, Captain Perrin of the Moselle. The Moselle was well known as the fastest steamer on the river, and it could accommodate as many as 300 passengers. Its reputation meant the letter from a well-known former captain to a well-known newer captain might be helpful in obtaining passage in a timely manner, whenever Allen decided to head to Indiana.

The Spring of 1837 had turned to Summer before Allen was able to clear up his law practice sufficiently to travel. Sophina and their sons were left with the farm work in Lindale, much reduced from former years when it had been more central to their life. As hoped, Allen and John were able to leave for Indiana on the Moselle. The letter from Captain Vail assured excellent accommodations, and fortunately the passenger list was well below capacity, leaving Allen and John room aplenty on deck to relax, enjoy the scenery, and to talk at length. Allen, with a wife and children to consider, and John Henry Tibbets, years younger with no family of his own, held quite different views. A few snippets of their conversation could be heard over the noise of the steam engine and paddle wheel whisking them rapidly down the river.

John began, "You know that Coombs has been helping run-away slaves for quite a while now. You may not know just how interested I've become in his work, what shall I call it, his 'sacred' work. That's how I see it anyway."

Allen knew well enough just how interested his young friend was, so he couched his response accordingly. "I agree that owning slaves is a sin, yes, and so countering slavery is sacred work, as you say. But I do wrestle with how aggressively to address 'sin' in others. That, for me, is the issue, and I've not resolved it yet and maybe never will."

John considered some before replying. "What to do about sin in others, hmm, even Jesus seems to have held different views on that one at different times. He threw sinners out of the temple with considerable energy. Do I dare say anger? Well, let's keep my thinking so to ourselves, anyway. He also welcomed sinners to repent."

Allen couldn't help adding, "Yes, true, and I believe the younger Jesus took the more direct approach and the older the more accommodating one."

John let that go responding, "Well, look, in most cases one person's sin hurts not only that person, but others too. In the case of slavery, the damage done to slaves is, as Rev. Rankin describes, both physical and moral. The sinners not only degrade themselves, they bury others in sin—bury, maybe even literally. I'm for saving the slave first. Slave owners, second, and some days, I'm ashamed, I guess, but I do find myself thinking, let them save themselves."

Allen had to agree but with reservations, "Save the slaves first, certainly makes sense. But saving them by breaking the law and infuriating slave owners may well put the large majority of slaves who have not yet become runaways in even greater danger. Hard to know how slave owners might react, but I'm thinking encouraging harsher overseers may be one way. 'May' is probably too tame a word, slave owner anger 'will' put slaves remaining behind in greater danger, 'will', that's better."

John had no direct response and admitted it. "Yes, the slaves left behind will pay a heavy price. But I know that you have reservations that merely relying on convincing slave owners to repent has serious repercussions for the slaves, too. For instance, convincing takes a long time, meaning slaves remain years longer in slavery. I'd even say, no not years, more likely generations."

Allen and John had reached a familiar standstill in their discussion. They just stood quietly for quite some time and then walked to the other side of the deck. They were approaching the new Louisville canal that had been finished at long last. They could view the falls best on one side and Louisville on the other as the Moselle glided along so easily through what would have been hard going years ago when Allen last saw the area. The topic of slavery would come up again as they traveled toward Indiana, but as they cleared the canal, Indiana and their tentative plans took precedence.

Beginning of the Gilead Anti-Slavery Society Constitution

Constitution

Of the Gilead Anti-slavery Society

Art. 1st This society shall be called the Gilead Anti-slavery Society of Clermont County auxiliary to the Ohio Anti slavery society.

Art. 2nd The object of this society is the entire abolition of slavery in the United States. While it admits that each slaveholding state has by the Constitution of the United States, the exclusive right to legislate in regard to the abolition of slavery within its own bounds, this society will endeavor, by arguments, addressed to the understanding and conscience to convince our fellow citizens that slave holding is a heinous in the

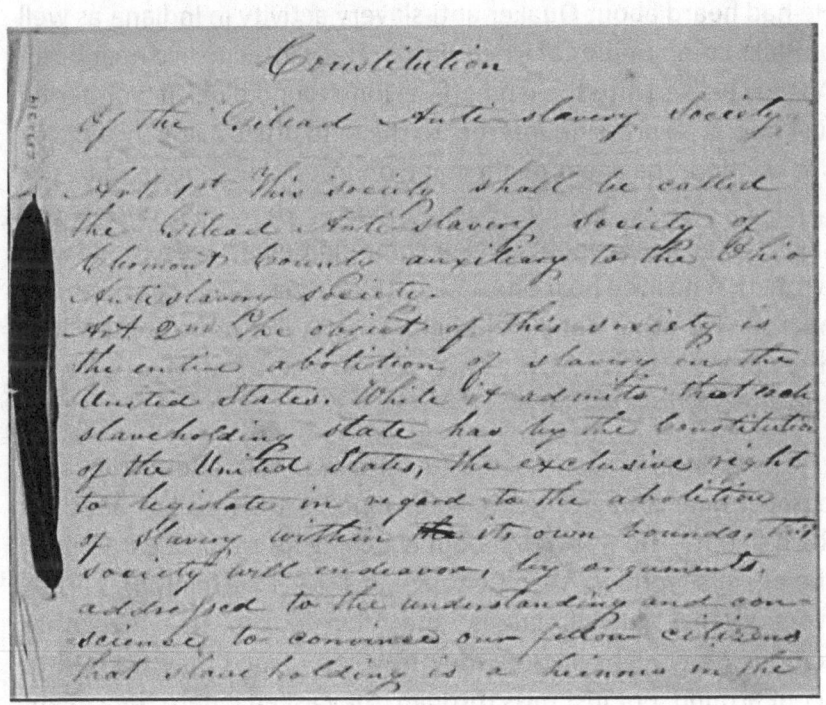

Indiana Tour - Ripley, Believe It

The Moselle docked at Louisville, Kentucky. Allen and John took a skiff across the Ohio River to Jeffersonville, Indiana, where they planned to look through land office records to get some preliminary ideas of what was available. The skiff crossing proved worth every bit of the somewhat unexpected high price. The two burly fellows in charge seemed mischievously pleased to give their passengers the full crossing experience. They could have gone a little further down river to avoid the roughest rapids but didn't. Actually, John and Allen were pleased, too, once the turbulence stopped and they realized they would survive. John said, "So this is how navigating the river used to be before the canal route. We have one more story to tell."

That afternoon they reached the land office in Jeffersonville, and John thought again about the specific objectives he had in mind. He had heard about Quaker anti-slavery activity in Indiana as well as Black communities of freed slaves. He wanted to live near both. As they walked into the land office, John found himself wondering just how to express his interest to the land office agent. He didn't know where the agent might stand on freed slave communities or Quakers, but he figured he could guess. He asked, tentatively, saying, "I've heard about Quaker communities. I have a friend who wrote that he lived near one and that there was a negro community nearby. No other details, though. I might like to be somewhere near my friend. Any place you know of that might fit the description he sent?"

Clever little lie and successful. He was told about a Quaker outpost near a negro 'dumping ground', a town called Beech in Rush County. He was right about couching his request carefully; if the agent's wording wasn't enough, his sneer certainly was. They were given vague directions, and Allen looked at a few other options they might pass as they traveled. Since they wanted to scout around, not just pass through, they asked where they might hire a couple of horses and got a less surly answer. Good for local business Allen figured.

They hired two horses along with saddle bags and purchased enough supplies for at least the first few days. Heading north they would pass through an area Allen had noted at the land office as open for purchase. It was in Ripley County on the way to Rush County where John wanted to check out Beech. They reached Ripley County on their second day with nothing of note slowing their progress. The weather could not have been better—perfect summer days, sun shining, pleasant breeze, perfect for just taking their time looking around. So fine, in fact, that they traversed the whole of Ripley County finally reaching the area Allen had noted called Otter Creek. Somehow it echoed home, home as in his childhood home of Steuben County, NY. Maybe it was the rolling hills or the streams; whatever it was he liked what he saw, and he was taken by it.

They camped for the night, and when they awoke Allen seemed intent on further exploration of Otter Creek, but John fidgeted enough to get Allen's attention, finally saying that they ought to get on their way. The next day they did stop outside a house that seemed to serve as a Baptist church, judging from a sign outside advertising a service Sunday. A man was about to enter but greeted them instead. He introduced himself as Ichabod Sheldon and added that he was a traveling preacher stopping here for the upcoming Sunday service. They had a brief discussion of their shared anti-slavery positions. After finding many areas of agreement, Ichabod kindly offered the church address so, if they ever wanted to contact him, they could. Allen thanked him and then they continued on their way.

When they had passed through Versailles on their way to Otter Creek, they noticed a newly constructed "highway", (highway—well, enhanced trail might be a more accurate description). At least it headed roughly in the direction they needed to go to reach Beech. They decided to go back to Versailles, resupply, and then start toward Beech using the highway. They figured they would ask for further directions in Versailles and along the way north. They reached Versailles without incident, resupplied, and even found out from locals that the highway was originally designed to go from the Ohio River all the way north to Lake Michigan. Along the way they got instructions from other travelers when to leave the highway (it headed too far west) and head for Rushville instead. They could resupply again there and head a bit northwest to Beech by eventually locating and following what the travelers called the Big Blue River. Though John found the directions a bit vague, Allen encouraged him by mentioning once again the vague directions he had navigated when heading for Kentucky all those years ago.

They reached what they took to be the outskirts of Beech a few days later with just a couple of wrong turns and misdirections trying to locate that Big Blue River. They arrived mid-day. John had no qualms about stopping at the first farmhouse that he saw. He was greeted at the door by Willis Rogers, shotgun in hand. That greeting was clearly not friendly; Willis, a Black man, had learned to be as cautious as he had to be, even though the 1816 Indiana state constitution included a free state clause. Allen stepped back but John just smiled, introduced himself and Allen, and continued talking. "We've come a long way hoping to find out more about your community—Beech, right? We're from Ohio, members of a newly formed Ohio anti-slavery society. We've visited with the former Lane Seminary students in the Black section of Cincinnati, but we wanted to see a successful farming community like yours. We may move somewhere nearby someday."

Willis did not exactly let down his guard, but he did smile.

Allen, seeing an opening, then spoke. "Yes, I went to Cincinnati from nearby Lindale, our hometown, to speak with the ex-Lane students who worked there with the Black residents in the center of the city. A couple of them even came to a meeting we'd arranged for the purpose in Lindale, to speak with us about their decision to leave Lane and about their current work."

Willis warmed to the conversation adding, "Lane, yes, I've a friend who gets the newspaper, the Liberator; sent me a note about those students. Oh, heard that Richmond has one of those new anti-slavery societies, too. Seems Quakers were involved as they have been here. Heard the name Coffin as one of the Quakers in Richmond, Indiana. Come, I'll show you around."

So, John and Allen got a tour of Beech—cleared lands with some stumps still evident, well-tended fields of crops and meticulously maintained vegetable gardens near the homes, along with fruit trees promising Fall abundance. Far from a 'dumping ground', they saw what industrious farmers had created. Willis pointed out the site where the community hoped to build a church. They did not see anything in the way of stores or other places of business, but Willis assured them some had made a start, and more were contemplated.

At that point Allen and John decided to part company with Willis and head back to Jeffersonville on their way home. Willis, quite helpfully, mentioned that if they went just a bit north, following the river, they could pick up the National Road, and if they headed east on it, they could then take the Michigan Road south. Somewhat slyly, he added, "We know these routes for sure." Goodbyes were sincere, and John and Allen headed north along the river as instructed.

As they traveled along, mostly in comfortable silence, John did say, "I know exactly what Willis meant about these two roads. Think of it—from the Ohio River to Lake Michigan or from central Ohio to Lake Michigan. Sounds perfect for getting run-aways to Canada; once they reach the lake, they go by boat. Help from Coffin in Richmond and the anti-slavery society thereabouts or in Beech along the way. I'm liking it."

Heading back along the National Road and then the Michigan Road was the easiest that their trip had been so far. Supplies were plentiful along such a main route, and the horses took to the roads with ease. They returned the horses, crossed below the falls this time, and took the first Steamboat back home that they could get. Not the Moselle for sure, but good enough.

Chapter Ten

Society Business

The Mundane

For the rest of 1837 and the first half of 1838, Allen busied himself with his family, his law practice, the church, and Lindale's Gilead Anti-Slavery Society. Rumors and then newspapers reached him about the financial crash that hit the East and then the South, but Ohio and Indiana, with economies mostly depending on small to mid-size farming, were largely spared. Still funds that Indiana counties used to build their sections of the Michigan Road did dry up, delaying further construction and hindering marketing to some extent. But those with farm products to sell had the National Road heading East through central Ohio and on East, or they could head south from the National Road to Cincinnati. From Cincinnati, the Queen of the West, or Porkopolis, they could ship their products east or west as far as they needed to find buyers. Farm economies and the marketing of farm products, as well as the growing lumber businesses in the West, remained viable. Nonetheless, Allen, cautious fellow that he was, worried enough about the crash in the East and South to exchange unbacked paper currencies of any kind for tangible assets—silver, gold, and eventually land.

Elizabeth, born in June of 1837, was Allen and Sophina's fourth child and their first girl. Luckily for him, Allen had waited for the birth before beginning his Indiana escapades. Sophina would have been even more expressive about his absence during such times had he missed the event. Of course, he wasn't needed. Sophina had her friend Susanna and many helpful ladies from the church; much more useful than a 'man', as Sophina pointed out several times. For a while Allen responded by attempting to be extra helpful, even, perhaps, annoyingly so. Fairly soon he settled down and got back to his proper place as father but not one of the hovering sort, before he left for Indiana.

Now that he was back, family life, church, and his law practice filled good portions of Allen's time and energy as they had in the past, but the relatively new activities related to his participation in the Gilead Anti-Slavery Society occupied his thoughts to an increasing degree. Its members took responsibility for reading, reviewing, and reporting on anti-slavery literature, and there was a lot of it. They tackled all they could manage from newspapers, magazines, and tracts, anything that would keep them up to date and could be passed along to update anyone in the wider community who would listen.

They filled much of Lindale's Gilead Anti-Slavery Society's minutes with mundane matters. They recorded who was responsible for what, when the next meeting would occur, and if, as well as when, a speaker was scheduled. The minutes specified in detail which specific works each member was assigned to study and report upon. Allen took on three well-known writings—Channing's Letter to Birney, The Bible Vindicated, and Mrs. Child's Appeal. As noted in the minutes, several members shared coverage of these works.

Allen and John happened to be assigned one work in common, Channing's letter, and the minutes were quite explicit about which letter; Channing's Letter to James G. Birney recorded in two newspapers, Cincinnati's 'Philanthropist' and Boston's 'Liberator'. Both papers were available to them in 1838.

Allen was comfortable with Channing's support of moral persuasion to convert slave owners and, along with Channing, opposed to out and out slave violence and the slave owner retaliation which he still felt would inevitably follow. But Channing went further by expressing the idea that slaves needed to be trained to work for themselves and to express love of family in a more nurturing way. By now Allen clearly knew these thoughts were quite simply nonsense. In talking with John about it, he said, "I know better. I've seen caring slaves; I've seen their love of family. They feel and care as we do, and this Bostonian needs to see them, too. John, think of it. He should see Beech as we have. Not able to work for themselves? Nonsense."

And John added, "He should hear the story of the ex-Lane student James Bradley as we did. Working for himself at night after his work as a slave all day. Making horse collars, raising pigs, farming—all for himself, when he could manage, despite the burden of slavery. Maybe we should send Channing a summary of what we heard from Bradley. He might ask himself if he could do that? What would drive him to do it? A slavery-inspired longing for freedom deeper than any I can imagine, for sure."

Allen, "Did you read Birney's response to Channing in the same edition? What was the line? Something about a rude and ruffian-like shake. I think he was talking about the nation sleeping through the horrors of slavery. I'm guessing, John, you'd like that line."

John, "You know me well. I'm with Birney and with Garrison. Garrison is also a Bostonian. But Garrison is a Bostonian who sees that full emancipation needs to be done now. I see, too, and I will do whatever it takes."

The following is a partial list of the members of the Gilead Slavery Society and their individual assignments as it appears in the society minutes. Note 'Channing's letter' assigned to Allen Miner and John Tibbets and the assignment to Allen of "The Bible Vindicated".

1831		Names		Books
April	21	C Dillingham	x	Mrs Childs Appeal
"		Wm Doan	x	Cabinet of Freedom
"		Mrs Doan	x	Third Annual Report
"		John Tibbets	x	Channings letter
"		Delphy Humes	x	Channings letter
"	22	Enoch Tracy	x	Enemies Constitution Disc
"		Henry Temple	x	Third Report Am. Society
"		A Miner	x	Channings letter
"		E J Tibbets	x	Anti slavery record
"		Betsy Hilton	x	Third Annual report
"		Martha Hubbard	x	Narrative of the R.R. Cin
"		Wm Hayford	x	O. A. S. convention
"		"	x	N. of the R.R. at Cincinnati
"		L D Dunham		Quartily Magazine
"		Elizabeth Lewis	x	Phillis Wheatly
"		C Butler		3 Annual Report
"		A Miner	x	The Bible Vindicated

154

Chapter Eleven

Indiana

An Ally

By mid-1838 Allen was getting anxious about the possibility of making the move to Indiana as he watched currency issues become more and more complex. In 1836 President Jackson had insisted that purchases of federal land would require gold/silver specie. Allen understood that banks in Indiana were experiencing issues over currency backed only by the banks themselves. Land prices were falling, but few could afford paying in gold/silver, as Allen could. It was time to take advantage of his currency foresight. John had listened to Allen on the subject but did not have resources equivalent to Allen's. He had taken Allen's advice and accumulated some gold and silver, enough he thought to purchase the land he wanted in Indiana.

Sophina was pregnant again, so they had yet another reason to get their plan underway soon. Even though he was leaving again while she was at home with the children, her resistance was minimal. She remained enthusiastic about the more relaxed farm life in Indiana she envisioned. At the end of July, Allen and John left by stagecoach that headed north to the National Road and then headed west. They knew just how troublesome stagecoach travel could be, so they chose a coach that used a route they thought would be best. Even so the coach got mud bound once, then stuck at a stream crossing for two days. Allen and John worked away alongside the other passengers pushing and pulling, muddied or drenched or both depending on the locale. What a relief when they reached the National Road, portions recently covered with the new miracle, macadam, no less.

They reached Richmond, Indiana a couple of days later than expected due to the delays and then went a few miles further to Newport where the Coffins lived. John had notified Levi Coffin that he wanted to meet him, mentioning in general their common anti-slavery activities. Fortunately, John left the date approximate, and he left detailed discussion of his more radical thoughts for their personal meeting.

Allen and John arrived at Levi's mid-morning in time to talk before the midday dinner. Levi owned a local pork processing business, so his wife, Catherine, had no problem preparing for guests, even given little notice. There was pork sausage, baked potatoes, and garden salad. Their 13-year-old son, Jesse, helped some, picking in the garden and preparing the salad in the kitchen. Their 5-year-old son, David, slept on Levi's lap while the men talked as softly as three men full of exciting ideas and news could manage.

John, who had arranged the meeting, began the conversation by introducing Allen as his good friend and as an active member of the Gilead Anti-Slavery Society back in Lindale. He added a brief summary of their recent conversation about Channing's Letter. "Both of us had Channing's letter, the one published recently in the Liberator, as one of our assigned works. I don't know if your members are assigned works to study and distribute, but it's one thing we do to spread the word. Allen found Channing's attitude toward slaves condescending, annoyingly so."

That introduction gave Allen a chance to repeat his Cumberland gap experience once again. He gave the account of the chain gang and the old man helped so kindly by his fellow slaves. As he was now thoroughly accustomed to doing, he added, "I spent time in

Kentucky with slave owners and saw their slaves one night. Another old man played on a single stringed, bow-like instrument while children danced; then the dancing stopped, and the mood turned solemn. He sang of freedom; I was moved by these instances of human compassion and emotion, and I could not possibly feel anything but sorrow for Channing's—what should I say? The kindest I can say is his lack of understanding."

Levi responded, "When I was very young, my father and I saw chained slaves being driven by slave traders, just like you describe. In my case the slave driver was far enough behind so that my father got to ask one of the slaves why they were chained. The slave had an answer Channing should hear. He said something like 'they have taken away our wives and children, and they are afraid we will escape and return to them.' All I could think at the time, young as I was, 'what if my father were taken away.' And then a few years later—I could go on and on, but no; I'll spare you."

Allen and John stumbled over themselves saying, "No, no, please tell us more."

"Alright, here's the one from a few years later. My father and I visited a fishing camp. The owner had slaves, but at least he let them fish at night and then sell the fish for their own profit. Channing would like that. My father bought one, and the next day the slave who sold the fish arrived at my father's campsite wondering if he might want to buy more at the same price. Unfortunately, a young nephew of the owner, I'm thinking in his late teens, heard that and took offense swearing he would allow 'no such impudence from a nigger' and struck the slave over the head with a fagot from my father's fire. Blood and burns were severe. I was so moved that I left my breakfast untouched and went off alone to cry."

Just then Catherine, having heard 'breakfast untouched' interrupted with, "About time to touch and perhaps eat dinner. Come along you three. Hope you don't leave Levi's pork sausage untouched."

That brought smiles all around followed by a question from John, "Levi's pork sausage?"

Levi responded, "Yes, indeed, it's my business here. Even sell some salt pork, or smoked, down your way in Porkopolis. Dock workers pack it up in barrels and ship it wherever there's a market. Heading south I take the rivers where I can and rough it on what passes for roads when I can't."

They washed up at the well outside and then made their way back in, sitting at a dining table near the kitchen but not too near the warm stove. It didn't take them long to follow Catherine's instructions; they went right to that sausage. Allen then heaped on the praise. "Mighty good sausage it is, thanks to Catherine's preparation and Levi's business. When you're down our way next time, let us know. We could put you up and sell some sausage in Lindale for sure."

"Thanks for the offer; I'll sell wherever I can. Lindale, with advance advertising from you two; sounds good."

Catherine smiled as they stopped talking long enough to eat more.

As they sat after dinner, Allen asked if Levi knew the stagecoach schedule headed west. "I need to get to Versailles then head down toward Jeffersonville to register for land I want. I'm on a bit of a tight schedule. Wife's pregnant, as she was last time John and I visited Jeffersonville to check availability. Being away so long before the birth didn't go well then; don't want a repeat. Caused a bit of friction I'd like to at least minimize this time."

"I take the stagecoach occasionally, and I know one heads west in the evening. You could get it this evening if you wish. Course you could stay here and pick it up tomorrow; I'm at least going to try to get John to stay for a while, if he doesn't have similar pressing concerns."

John took that offer up. "Would love to stay and talk some more. I know that Allen is anxious; I'm not."

So, Allen left after thanking all for the hospitality shown and for the offer to stay longer. Even son Jesse received Allen's thanks for his help preparing the meal.

John, Levi, and Catherine were now free to talk about their thoughts and activities without having to worry about such conversations in front of Allen. In his letter John had let the Coffins know that Allen was still unwilling to break the law and that he might become uncomfortable if the conversation included the subject.

John began by asking Levi and Catherine what happened in Newport, Indiana, that convinced them to aid runaway slaves.

The question got Levi started on a somewhat lengthy response. "We got involved soon after we arrived here in Indiana and settled in Newport—1826 or so. We found out that several Underground Railroad routes went through here, including the one from Cincinnati, incidentally. There are many former slaves in their own neighborhood of Newport, some freed by their owners but many run-aways. The Quakers from back in North Carolina brought many of the original residents with them when they came here. As Friends ourselves from North Carolina, we simply knew from others about what was happening in this area. Descendants of the original freed slaves became, quite naturally, the place for new runaways to seek help. Unfortunately, slave hunters know that, too. So too many of those seeking help ended up being captured.

"Those attempting to aid them early on simply couldn't hide them well enough, and they didn't have good connections with those who could send them to safety, to Canada for instance. Catherine and I could hide them better in our home, and the 'law' is a lot less likely to question us. We can help with flight to Canada, too. We even began to convince others, those who sympathized but remained nervous, to join us. Our effort became a community effort. In fact, eventually our area became central, receiving runaways from well-known Underground Railroad routes from Cincinnati, as I mentioned, and from Madison, Indiana, down on the

Ohio river. All have large Black communities like ours here with the need for help in hiding and transport."

John added, "And Beech to the west, but I suspect they just head north along the Michigan road." Levi nodded agreement.

Catherine then spoke up. "I remember one case, can't forget it, though there were so many others. A mother feared that her two young daughters would be sold. It happens all too often. She managed to escape with them and somehow make it across the Ohio River. Never did hear how she did that. Then she did what she had been told to do—followed the North star. She and her children avoided roads, traveling across fields and through the woods, eating green corn and fruits when she could find them and going without when there was nothing or only enough for the children. She finally reached our neighborhood. She was taken in by Blacks living in a cabin nearby. She had managed to keep the children relatively healthy, but she was so sick by then that she needed medical help desperately. Dr. Way was called, and he took care of her, as he often did when called upon to help those fleeing to freedom. Others provided clothing for the three of them, so badly needed, before they were guided on their way to Canada. Yes, it has become a community effort, makes all of us feel as though we are better than we would have been without these efforts to aid our fellow human beings."

John, moved by what he heard, as he had been over the years by so many stories of run-aways' heroism, enthusiastically expressed his own hopes. "I've been thinking for some time now of becoming involved, more actively. Andrew Coombs, as you know, is active and has been for some time. He'll help me back in Lindale and Cincinnati. I'm young and could do some of the transporting, I think. There's certainly much of it to do, I've heard."

Catherine replied, "Well, if you do, we look forward to seeing you often or at least hearing about what you're doing. Our connections in Cincinnati are many, as we've mentioned."

Talk continued well into the evening; John stayed overnight as planned and left refreshed in the morning after another iteration of sausage, this time with eggs and toast. He took the same route as Allen before him making use of the morning stagecoach and taking his time. He arrived in Jeffersonville several days later, after stopping off for a few days in Versailles to look around. He really wasn't in a hurry.

Indiana Plans - Jeffersonville Meeting

Allen arrived in Jeffersonville, Indiana, after a smooth stagecoach ride. The National Road followed by the Michigan road and southern Indiana roads made the trip a lot easier than the beginning of the Ohio experience—no mud and no impassable streams this time. He stayed overnight at a conveniently located Inn before arriving at the land office as soon as it opened in the morning; he was in a hurry.

The same, somewhat surly character as before was still in charge, though this time sensing a purchase perhaps, he was quite open and friendly in his greeting. And he was right. Allen knew what he wanted from all the careful searching he had done with John on their previous trip. So, on August 10, 1838, Allen purchased 200 acres of land in Otter Creek, Ripley Township, Indiana, quite a bit more than the 80 acres minimum. Payment in gold specie sealed the deal to the satisfaction of the clerk, the government of Indiana, the US government, and Allen himself.

Allen returned home by the fastest method available, taking a locally rented skiff across to Kentucky and a steamer back to Cincinnati. He arrived home; and when he divulged his good news, he was met by a much happier wife this time around. Good news but followed by a sad event. Later that day, not long after Allen had delivered his good news, Ichabod Temple, long ill, died. It was as if Sophina, having lost her mother at a young age and now her father, really was making a life-changing transition by leaving her family ties to Lindale, Ohio behind and setting out on a new life in a new state.

Meanwhile, John arrived a few days later in Jeffersonville and ended up staying at the same inn; it was convenient after all. In the evening, as he entered the dining area for supper, he chanced to meet David Johnson, who intended to buy land, too. In the course of their discussion, John mentioned that his friend Allen had been to the land office a few days earlier. John wanted to see if Allen made a purchase and if so, where.

John didn't have the one hundred dollars in specie backed currency necessary to purchase what he believed was the 80-acre minimum set by the 1820 Land Act. At $1.25 an acre, though, he wanted to take advantage of such an incredible bargain. As they were talking, mention of the land office caught the ear of another man about to sit down for his supper. He introduced himself as Isaac Jones and asked if he might join their discussion. He explained that he, too, intended to visit the land office the next day with hopes of purchase. As the talking progressed, John and Isaac found that they had similar issues, one not shared by David Johnson, a slight shortage of funds. John then suggested, "Maybe we, Issac, could split an 80-acre purchase in half. Let's all go together in the morning. We can check on the 40-acre split then."

John, David, and Isaac agreed to go together in the morning to see what was still available since John's last visit. Discussion then turned to farming, family, and other familiar topics before they retired for the evening.

They visited the land office the next day, August 15, as planned. After talking to the land office manager, John was pleased to find that splitting the 80-acre minimum, or what the Land Act called ½ quarter plots, was common practice. It was a done deal on the spot. John and Issac each got their 40 acres at the incredible price advertised.

David Johnson went ahead with his plans, too but first John, as he had intended, looked to see if his friend Allen had gone ahead with his purchase and if so, where. And there it was. He had gone ahead and purchased 200 acres, no less, in Ripley County, and the land office manager told them it was near the town of Otter Creek, just as Allen had wished.

David Johnson was impressed by the 200-acre size and thought he'd see if something might be available in the same area. It must be decent land, he thought, if the close friend of John's had made such a large purchase; and besides, John was right there supporting that thought, assuring him that the land was good. He looked around at what was available, found something close enough to Allen's 200 acres, and purchased his own 80 acres. With business completed, they left, heading back to the Inn to celebrate. They parted the next day but agreed to keep in touch. John promised to pass along the news of David's purchase to his soon to be new neighbor, Allen. John returned to Lindale, taking the skiff and then the steamboat out of Louisville, using up portions of his cash doing so. On the way, thoughts of his conversation with Levi and Catherine Coffin occupied him. He was determined to take on Underground Railroad assignments as he had promised the Coffins. Speaking with Andrew Coombs about what he could do was at least close to the top of his list once he reached home.

Risky Business - Ride through the Night

John's opportunity to fulfill his promise to the Coffins came up almost immediately upon his arrival home. He and Andrew Coombs, Jr.'s younger brother, Thomas, saw a young runaway from slavery hiding in the woods and led him to a man named Mr. Hoover living near Brownstown in Clermont County, Ohio. They traveled the 15 miles at night and returned the same night knowing full well that it was very risky business. John, barely 20 years of age, and Thomas about 16 took their chances anyway.

About two years later a man named John Oliver Butler, knowing John and his father were abolitionists, came to John's father's house seeking help, "There's a man and his wife at my house, fugitives from slavery. They'd been hiding in the woods but eventually hunger drove them to risk coming to our house. I don't know what to do."

John thought a moment then said, "I can get them to a safe place, but I would have a problem transporting them with my own team and wagon. I've got workers I don't trust; they'd be suspicious if I just took the team out of the fields; they might well report their suspicions to the authorities."

Mr. Butler immediately responded with a solution. "I have a fine mare and light carriage. I'd be more than willing to risk the mare, not a field horse for sure, if you are willing to risk aiding these two in their escape." They agreed to meet at 9:00 o'clock that night.

Left to consider what lay ahead John thought about the risks in more detail. "Let's see, I'll need to get them to Deacon Barwood's in Cincinnati, the only underground stop I know right now. That's about 22 miles, and I've got to do it before dawn for sure. Nothing like this can be done in daylight. There are three gates on the way, manned by anti-abolitionists, no doubt. Almost everyone opposes helping slaves escape to freedom, and their opposition could well become a great risk to me and my passengers. How am I going to get past those gates? Have to get inventive, I guess."

That evening Mr. Butler hitched the rather spooky mare to the carriage, secured the runaways behind closed curtains, and then drove to John's, arriving at 9:00 as planned. He held the mare while John boarded the carriage and took the reins. "She's a spirited one, for sure," John remarked. Not too far along the so-called Ohio Turnpike John approached the first gate in Amelia, Clermont County. He recognized Gorham Peas, the toll man. "No problem here; he'll recognize me, too, and let me through, I think." John was right; there was no problem.

The next gate was John's greatest fear. It was further along on the same road at Withamsville, and he knew it was usually manned by a keeper he didn't like. "Oh, there he is but a ways back, near where he lives. I've got to get us to the toll booth and gate before him."

The toll keeper, as if reading John's mind, shouted, "Not letting you through until I take a look behind those curtains."

It flashed through John's mind, "He's got a lantern, if he looks into the carriage, we are in real trouble." Time for inventive action and it came to him. He tugged on the reins and the mare, skittish as she was, thankfully this time, knocked against the keeper hard enough to send him running toward the gate to let them through before that beast, as he called her, did real damage.

The third gate proved as trouble free as the first, and they reached the underground Barwood station well before dawn; that mare was as fast as she was skittish. First their "guests" needed care. They hustled them inside. The deacon showed them where they could hide before they proceeded on to the next station. They were treated to a quick breakfast, the one that the deacon and his wife had intended to eat themselves, and then were set up in the hiding place before dawn turned dangerously to sunrise. Deacon Barwood and his wife were more than used to such interruptions in their routines; interruptions happened often and usually at inconvenient times like just before dawn or at some late hour when they were falling asleep or even past midnight when they were asleep.

Once the "guests" were hidden, John had a chance to relate his tale to Deacon Barwood. He gave the mare lots of credit, a heap of praise in fact. He did want to know where his two rescued runaways would head next, but that kind of information was usually kept tightly concealed to avoid any risk to those managing railroad stops. They'd heard of enough problems and could imagine more given the general climate of antagonism toward what was, after all, a completely illegal activity. To avoid asking, John phrased the question in terms of an answer he hoped might be true. "You know, I got going on my desire to help in this way after talking to the Coffins a couple of years ago. This husband and wife would certainly be welcome there."

The Barwood's played right along. The lady of the house simply said, "Can't think of a more welcoming family, if they should happen to end up there."

The deacon added, "Of course we have no way of knowing. But great that you know the Coffins. I've heard nothing but praise for their efforts and influence in Newport, over the line in Indiana."

John added, "Yes, I've purchased land in Indiana near Madison; hope to end up living there. The Coffins mentioned Madison down on the Ohio River as a place like Cincinnati or Newport itself in terms of the kinds of activity that I want to continue."

Conversation continued for a short while before they all began to realize that they were hungry. John was offered a late breakfast and accepted. After breakfast he excused himself, mentioning the need to get the mare and carriage back to their owner. The 22 miles back was a joy—a fine mare, a colorful fall day, and no dangerous cargo. He did leave the curtains closed so the suspicious gate keeper would have reason to pull them aside if he decided to look again. He did and, much to John's carefully concealed glee, showed obvious disappointment at finding nothing.

Chapter Twelve

On Their Way

New Friends

While John Tibbets was busy with his early Underground Railroad activities in Ohio, Allen and family were busy moving to Indiana. In the fall of 1838, shortly after Allen returned from purchasing the land in Otter Creek, Sophina was 3 months pregnant, so moving west from Lindale, Ohio to Otter Creek, Indiana took some careful planning. Despite the pregnancy, Sophina was anxious to get going. She really became quite excited about her dream of getting her family settled into a larger farm life more reminiscent of her childhood in Maine than the somewhat frenzied life they had been living in Lindale. She seemed quite willing and able to ignore the inconvenient timing.

First, Allen wrote a letter to Ichabod Sheldon, the traveling preacher he had met when he visited Otter Creek with John on their initial, exploratory visit to Indiana. The letter simply recalled the earlier discussion they had and explained that he, his wife, and his two youngest children (one nearly 2 and the other 5) would be on their way to occupy the land they now owned nearby. He had already let his two oldest boys, Jacob 11 and Ichabod 9, know that they would remain to take care of the Lindale property with help from Sophina's friend Susanna and other church members, and then join their family in the Spring. He did mention his wife's condition to Ichabod Sheldon but suggested that she would stop off with the young children in Versailles on the way and remain there with appropriate care while he went ahead and made whatever arrangements that he could manage in Otter Creek.

As Allen no doubt hoped, he received as prompt a response as the mails allowed making clear that Ichabod and the church community would welcome them and make all necessary arrangements for them. Ichabod added that several women in the church had volunteered to aid Sophina with the birth and with childcare. Other church members offered housing until Allen could build a home on his new farm. Allen's return letter flowed with appropriate thanks, mentioning specifically that, with such thorough arrangements as his new community had made, his wife and family would come with him directly, skipping the proposed stopover in Versailles.

Toward the end of August, he prepared their two farm wagons by modifying them with a cover of canvas and hickory bows to support it, making one as comfortable as possible for his wife and the young children. In the second wagon he placed tools and supplies, hiring Walter, a farm hand he occasionally employed, to drive it. They took only what he and Sophina thought they would need initially, leaving their Lindale home and remaining goods in the care of their two boys under the watchful eye of Susanna Tibbets. Sophina and Susanna pledged to keep in touch, not that a pledge was necessary.

The trip, with two solid wagons and two strong horses each, went well, much better than Allen's earlier stagecoach ride with John. It was a clear and dry Fall week, not too cold, a break for once, and the stream crossing that had caused such problems earlier did not even slow them down this time. Allen had also let Levi Coffin know that he, his wife, their two youngest children, and Walter would be passing through Richmond and asked if they could stop by at his Newport home. Again, he got the welcoming reply he hoped he would.

They stopped overnight by the road on the way. The family slept comfortably in the wagon Allen had prepared for them while Walter made room for himself in the other wagon. They reached the Coffin home before noon the next day. Allen and Levi sat down to catch up, while Walter cared for the wagons and horses. Catherine welcomed Sophina warmly, leading her and the two young children into the kitchen where the women could talk without the men around to interrupt, as was their want. Catherine began by asking, "How did you and the child-to-be fare on the way here? Any problems? Because, if there were, you are certainly welcome to stay with us. My two-year-old Henry, here, would enjoy the company of your two and might even enjoy seeing a newborn, someone even younger than himself."

Sophina responded with equal warmth, "Well, what a kind offer. But Allen made arrangements with the pastor, Ichabod Sheldon, at the Baptist church near our land in Otter Creek. I'm anxious to see the place and to imagine, more clearly, the beginning of my new life there. I'm a farm girl at heart, grew up on one in Maine, and it has stuck with me. But thank you so much."

Catherine added, "Something just plain good about farm life, the sense of independence, of being on one's own surrounded by newly plowed fields, woods, and streams. Miss it myself. Not exactly what Levi and I have here."

"Yes," Sophina agreed, and then added, "but, Catherine, you and Levi have something here that is so life affirming. I've heard from others how important you two are to the anti-slavery movement. John Tibbets, himself, used the word 'crucial'. He had nothing but praise for your husband, but in particular praise for you."

"Well, yes, we do feel fulfilled in a different way. As Levi is fond of mentioning to potential converts to the cause, the work helps others make their way to freedom, but such work frees our souls, too. We feel Christian action makes us better Christians for sure."

Sophina thought for a moment before responding. "Allen and I continue to support the abolitionist movement in our own way, actively supporting Lindale's Gilead Anti-Slavery Society. We cling to the notion that slave owners will see the sinfulness of their actions. Cling, more and more desperately, we admit to ourselves, as the opposition mounts more and more horrendous responses. Destruction of the Philanthropist Press was a real low blow."

Both women knew to let their different approaches work out over time and said so to each other. They were beginning to feel a real kinship, not only as abolitionists but as strong women with thoughts and feelings of their own to pursue and with husbands sensible enough to let them be. Sophina switched subjects from anti-slavery to her move, "Moving, yes, I leave old friends behind but not forgotten, and I'll be making new ones. In fact, you've been so kind I feel like that's what I'm doing today, making a new friend."

"Yes," Catherine responded, "and it feels good, as it always does. But now, I guess we'd better get on with preparations to feed the hungry mouths around here. If you'd stir that stew, I'll get the bread out of the cellar and heat it up some. That and potatoes will fill them up."

And fill them up it did. After the meal Levi showed Allen and Sophina around town while Catherine kept track of the children and Walter napped in the more comfortable wagon. The walk served them well; they needed to walk off that meal, and Allen and Sophina were able to use the opportunity to resupply, including gifts of sausage by Levi from his shop. Later Allen awakened Walter, and the three men spent time together splitting wood while Sophina and Catherine worked in the vegetable garden and the children napped. The next morning, August 29, the two families, much closer now, parted as Allen and Sophina pursued their new dream and Levi and Catherine continued to live theirs.

Indianapolis - Dreams

Allen decided that, given Sophina's condition, he'd stick with the best roads Indiana had to offer, even if more direct routes were possible. Sophina agreed; she did not relish a rough ride. They took the National Road west to Indianapolis and then the Michigan Road south-east to Versailles. Indianapolis and Versailles allowed for whatever resupply they needed on the way, and they got to see Indianapolis, central Indiana's largest town. They intended to live in Indiana, so it was good to see what the state had to offer, Allen thought.

Allen planned on about five days to reach Indianapolis, and all had gone worry free for the first three. On the fourth, just after they headed off following the morning meal that included good helpings of Levi's smoked sausage, they approached a man limping along in the opposite direction. They noticed that the horse he was leading limped too; clearly, they thought, a man in need of help. The road was good enough for them, but for an aging man, weathered, thin, bedraggled, and clearly tired already, with miles to go before reaching the next possible source of help, walking any road posed serious problems. They stopped alongside him and did what came naturally; they asked if they could help in any way.

The man looked up with an expression that clearly indicated relief and said, "The horse started limping a day back, now I'm doing the same. Thanks for offering; not sure what to do."

Allen secured the reins and jumped down before replying, "Let's look at that horse, maybe just a problem with its hoof. Shoes can go bad in so many ways. And, by the way, what's your name? I'm Allen Miner."

"Hezekiah Hutchins," he replied, "heading back home, Wayne County. Went to Indianapolis; regret it now."

Allen shook his hand, mentioned that he had left Wayne a few days ago, and then moved over to lift the horse's leg, saying, "We just left the Coffin home in Newport. Do you know him?"

Hezekiah, a Quaker and formerly from North Carolina like Levi, had certainly heard of him but lived in Perry, a good distance from Newport. He simply said, "Certainly heard about him but don't live nearby and don't know him personally."

Allen attended to the horse. "Look, seems like the shoe is simply off a bit and quite loose. I've got a hammer, some nails, and a clincher—all we should need. Figured I might have similar problems along the way."

So, Allen went back to the supply wagon, let Walter know what was happening and retrieved his tools. As he started back toward Hezekiah and the horse, his son, David, full of five-year-old curiosity, climbed out. Hezekiah had moved the horse over to a rock by the side of the road. He braced the bad hoof against the rock, while Allen re-positioned the shoe and nailed it back firmly into place.

David jumped up and down shouting out, "Dad, the nails, they're coming out the side!"

They did, but Allen assured his son that they should. "Watch what I do." At least two of the nails needed bending up against the hoof. Allen had seen the local farrier do this, with clinchers, and Allen was handy; he did it well. He used the clincher to grab the offending nails and bend them upward out of harm's way. "See, now they aren't going to snag anything."

Hezekiah thanked him more than once and then went on to say, "Look, if you're headed for Indianapolis, I want to let you know about the rumors I heard there. Made me decide to leave earlier than I intended. It seems the army and some volunteers, I think, have encircled and captured the remaining Indians that were supposed to leave for the West. Several hundred didn't and now they'll be 'force marched' out of there. When I heard they were being driven down the Michigan Road I figured I didn't want to be anywhere near Indianapolis if they went through there."

David jumped right in after hearing that. "Dad, will we get to see the Indians? I want to see Indians."

"Well, son, we'll know when we get there. If we do see them, I suspect we will not see them dancing and celebrating, as you might like to. Clearly, they don't want to leave their homes if it takes an army to move them, as Mr. Hutchins has told us. I suspect it's a very sad time for them."

David pouted a bit but jumped up into the wagon, ready to go see them anyway. Allen and Hezekiah exchanged farewells, but not before exchanging addresses. Allen simply gave the address of the church, not yet sure what his own Otter Creek address might be when they got settled in.

During the next two days, the Miners and Walter settled back into their travel routine except that they stopped and hailed any travelers heading east, hoping for any news from Indianapolis but getting little in the way of specifics. Finally, getting near enough to make Allen a bit nervous, they did run across a couple, traveling in a wagon much like theirs, who had some concrete news. They reported that the army was driving the Indians west to Kansas, leaving the Michigan Road well north of Indianapolis. Relief for Allen and Sophina, disappointment for David.

As they approached Indianapolis, Allen couldn't help turning over in his mind just what the trek to Kansas for a defeated Indian population might be like. Hezekiah had said there were several hundred men, women, and children. Some might be wounded from skirmishes that quite probably had occurred as they were rounded up. Some might be sick; some would be too old and some too young to walk. Were wagons provided? He hadn't heard. He knew next to nothing about the Kansas territory except that it would be a long trip under the best of circumstances. As they neared Indianapolis, he had to let those thoughts rest; his own family's plans needed his attention now.

If Allen or Sophina had thought that Indianapolis, the largest town in central Indiana, was a city in the sense they were used to after experiencing Cincinnati for so many years, they would have been shocked. They didn't really have such thoughts, but still, just how small it was surprised them. The main road, the National

Highway, was hardly crowded at all. They saw a few wagons carrying goods for the market, wherever that was, several men on horseback, and even a few folks walking, chipper as if they didn't have far to go, not limping in distress like poor Hezekiah. Had they been entering Cincinnati they'd have seen the bustle of real city life; people hurrying back and forth from work, banks, and businesses, carriages, many other types of conveyance, construction, law offices, and so much more. Cincinnati was a city of over 40,000, Indianapolis had barely 2,000. It seemed their life in Indiana was going to be of a new and unhurried sort, just as Sophina had hoped.

As they entered the 'city' itself, they began to see houses at least, with more than one that welcomed travelers for a price. Allen stopped at the largest one he saw that welcomed travelers, and, while taking a quick look inside, he asked if there was a market where they could get some fresh provisions. They were directed to Washington Street where they found a decent market. Small as it was, Indianapolis served as the center of Marion County commerce, and a large portion of that commerce came from surrounding farms. Farms—that pleased Sophina, not at all a fan of cities in anyway. And Allen was pleased to see that all the provisions they needed to make the next 5-day trip to Versailles were available.

Sophina did the purchasing. She got out of the wagon, handed the two-year-old to Allen, grabbed David, and enjoyed herself walking from stall to stall talking and bargaining, even haggling with the merchants, skills she had honed over the years. David came alive too. After enduring mile after mile of nothingness, this was exciting to a five-year-old. Allen, watching from a distance, smiled; he hadn't seen his wife quite this content since leaving Lindale. Maybe, he thought, they should stay overnight in one of the nearby houses welcoming travelers they had seen. He had heard that such places often provided good suppers. A meal, a comfortable night's sleep, a leisurely start in the morning all sounded good to him, and Sophina deserved a break. David would enjoy it for sure and so would Walter. Maybe two days. He'd see how Sophina felt.

When Sophina finally returned to the wagon with all the provisions they needed for the next leg of their trip, Allen suggested a stay at what he chose to call an inn and met with immediate, even relieved agreement from his wife. "What a good idea; I could use a nice meal, a warm bath, and a comfortable bed. Don't mind the cooking along the way, but food at an inn, yes, I'd like that." Even David joined in, jumping up and down with obvious delight. When he told Walter about the plans, he could see obvious relief as a broad smile appeared.

The warmth of their response caused Allen to immediately pack up the purchased goods and head back to the closest house open to travelers. Fortunately, it was large enough to accommodate his family on one side and the family of one of the owners, Samuel Merrill, on the other. There was even a separate room for Walter. Samuel shared ownership with Calvin Fletcher who had just moved to his newly purchased farm. Samuel decided to accept visitors until he decided what might be best for a more permanent arrangement; maybe he'd just take over the whole place. With a growing family, 5 children so far, they could certainly use the room.

Supper, even without guests to feed, was something of a production. Sophina offered to help, an offer much appreciated by Merrill's wife, Lydia Jane. The two women, along with David, bustled off to the kitchen. Allen and Samuel settled into a couple of comfortable chairs to talk, with Elizabeth in Allen's lap. Once again, Walter took care of the wagons and horses. Allen started off his conversation with Samuel by mentioning their trip and destination and then got to what still occupied his mind. "I heard, on the way, that the Indians who refused to leave and resettle in the Kansas territory, had been rounded up and were being force marched to Kansas. I initially heard they might come all the way down to Indianapolis; not so, I found out. Just wondered if you'd heard anything more?"

Samuel Merrill, one of the most informed men around, had. "Not a good trip for the old or the young or anyone force marched. Initially the army hadn't even planned to arrange for wagons, but a local Catholic missionary straightened that out. The elders, who needed to ride in wagons, got to do so. Not sure children did, though. I've heard of deaths along the way, and you can be sure there will be more before they reach Kansas. Even heard rumors of typhoid. Real trouble if true."

It all sounded worse than Allen had imagined, and he said so.

Samuel agreed and then went on to another topic he might not have introduced if Allen hadn't shown such sympathy for the Indians. "Sounds to me like you might have some sympathy for runaway slaves, too. Any connections with the anti-slavery movement?"

"Many," Allen replied. "Our trip here included a stop-over at the Coffins' in Newport, outside of Richmond. Do you know of them?"

Samuel sat further back in his chair, as he focused on recollecting old stories. He let his head fall back until he was looking at the ceiling before slowly saying, "Yes, a Quaker, I believe, one with strong moral objections to slavery, so strong that they cause him to ignore any possible legal liabilities. I've spent a number of years here backing our local Colonization Society, anti-slavery for sure but not a solution that folks like the Coffins support. But even I'm beginning to wonder about sending slaves back to places they may know nothing about. Lots of opposition developing among the freed slave communities. I guess I can understand why."

Allen, not wanting to offend, took advantage of that last statement saying, "Yes, freed slaves and run-aways, there aren't many alive that have any memory of Africa. Home is here. Africa is a story passed down but never lived, and even the story is not all that great. But, you know, I have misgivings about the out and out illegal activities like aiding escapees despite stronger and stronger laws forbidding it. I lean toward making the moral argument to slave owners. You know, I've followed the emphasis of anti-slavery societies, like the one I was active in back in Ohio. Like you, though, I'm having doubts about my own approach. Hard to convince folks that some moral argument should over-ride what they consider an economic necessity and a family tradition, right?"

A welcomed call to supper interrupted further discussion except for a question posed by Samuel, "I wonder, sometimes, what I would do if a run-away suddenly appeared at my door desperately begging for help. Unlikely here, but my co-owner, Calvin, settling into his new farm might face such a choice. I think he would help. Like to think I would, too."

"Like to think I would, too, and like your friend, heading for farm life myself, I might face such a choice."

Supper conversation turned to other topics. Sophina and Lydia Jane, while preparing supper and caring for their children, had managed to talk about their lives a bit. Sophina had gushed about the Maine farm life she remembered and hoped to imitate in Otter Creek. Sophina added, "You know I just want a simple farm life. Our farm in Lindale was fine, but we had so much else going on there we could hardly call our life 'simple'."

Lydia mentioned she'd like a much smaller change to her life, just a bit more room in this home she shared with her husband and children. Sophina started the supper conversation by talking again about her early life on a farm and how she so often dreamed of such a life for her own children. Even Walter got to express his agreement with such thoughts. Allen and Samuel let the dream play out without mentioning their earlier musings; no clouds they thought. The Miner family would be on their way soon enough, after that bath Lydia Jane kindly offered Sophina and a good night's sleep.

Otter Creek, Indiana - A New Life

The Miner family and Walter left in the morning and headed down the Michigan Highway toward Otter Creek, skipping the idea of staying a second day at Merrill's and anxious to be on their way to their new life. They had no immediate Indian removal to worry about and had a smooth ride. Allen figured on another five days to Versailles where they would stock up for the final leg to Otter Creek. Early September weather made the journey even better than they had hoped. They arrived in Versailles mid-morning of the fifth day and stocked up as planned. Otter Creek was only a few more miles down a side road; so close they figured they'd push on. Besides, clouds were beginning to form; best to beat any storm, they thought.

About a mile down that side road, they hit a snag. A sizable tree had fallen blocking their way. There was nothing to do but spend the time necessary to saw through it and then use the horses to remove the section blocking the trail. Once again, Allen was prepared; he had known he'd need a good saw to build their new home. In fact, he had a couple of saws, one a crosscut, two-person saw perfect for this job. All he needed was the second person. Allen was about to go back and ask Walter, but David jumped out of the wagon so anxious to help that Allen couldn't bring himself to deny his son. David managed for the first half hour or so to keep his end straight while Allen did the pushing and pulling. They got down toward the end of the first cut when Allen stopped and removed the saw. David was plenty tired by this time but objected to stopping anyway. "Come on Dad, I can do it."

Allen responded, "Son, look at the way the log is lying across the trail. Both sides of the trail are higher than the trail itself. If we continue sawing this way, the tree is likely to snap just enough to bind the saw. No, we need to get the smaller saw and back cut up from the bottom the rest of the way, so that when it cracks, the break will widen where the small saw is. No binding, do you see?" David didn't quite understand but went to get the small saw anyway. Sophina, seeing how tired her young son had become, came down from the wagon, handed the baby to David with a reminder to sit while holding her, and grabbed the small saw saying, "Come on, man, I can do it."

And, despite a bit of worry on Allen's part, she did—small saw, back cut and all. Once his mom so expertly performed the back cut, and David saw with his own eyes, he understood, and he said so. Now all they had to do was cut through with the crosscut saw on the other side of the road—no back cut with the section hanging conveniently from only one side—and remove the cut section to free up the trail. First Allen, with Walter's help, positioned the wagon out of the way, slightly off the road on one side, so that when they were ready to go, they could get around the portion of the tree that still blocked about a foot on the other side of the road. It took some coaxing; the horses didn't seem to think that leaving the trail even by a little bit was a good idea. Then Allen and Walter unhitched them and fastened the wagon end of the harness to the tree. The horses didn't seem to like this plan much either, but at least they were used to pulling logs out of the way; they'd done plenty of that sort of work at home. They did it and did it well. Hitched up to the wagon again, the horses were back in their comfort zone, ready to go.

After inching past what was left of the tree, the road became worse, narrower and full of ruts. Then the rain they had hoped to beat started. Allen began to think they might not make it all the way to Otter Creek that day. Losing about three hours removing the tree, the worsening road, and now rain; he started looking for some place to pull off the road, figuring they'd just stop and stay the night. About 15 to 20 minutes after these thoughts crossed his mind, he saw a small clearing up ahead. It looked like someone had cleared it on purpose; hacking out a wagon-width space long enough for both of their wagons, clearing all the trees and brush that were otherwise unbroken on both sides of the road. He turned to Sophina and let her know his thoughts saying, "I think the way this is going we won't make it to Otter Creek today. We're lucky, though, there's a clearing up ahead, probably the only one we'll find. I'm pulling over, we'll stay the night, start again in the morning."

Sophina, though disappointed, could see for herself that pulling over was the right move, especially since this clearing would probably be their only chance to get off the road safely. Walter fed the horses some hay Allen had purchased along with the other supplies and tied the horses to trees. The horses weren't happy and by this time Walter and Allen weren't either; the rain had started, and both were drenched. Allen and Walter took turns changing clothes in the portion of the wagon that could be curtained off for that purpose and felt better. They all made do, ate some of the fresh supplies, and settled in for the night, Walter retiring to the other wagon. The horses, though, suffered through the rainy night. Not happy they were.

By morning the rain had dropped to a drizzle. They ate a quick breakfast, and the horses finished up the last of the hay. With only a mile or so left to go, all were anxious to be on their way, and though the ruts along the trail were now filled with water, they proceeded without incident. As they approached Otter Creek the trail widened, and woods gave way to cultivated fields. They even passed a small cabin or two as they headed first for the church, hoping to meet Ichabod Sheldon himself, but, if not, they had been assured of meeting church members who knew all about their plans.

Ichabod was not there when they arrived, but John Miller Brown was, working outside the church cleaning up what was left of garden plants, and he introduced himself as they pulled up. Allen introduced himself, Sophina, and the rest of his family, as well as Walter. He got an immediate friendly response from John. "Yes, great to see you all. Ichabod Sheldon mentioned that you were coming and asked us all to be on the lookout. Come on down to my place, down the road a ways, and meet my wife; she'll be inside straightening up some."

The Brown's house was only a short distance down the road. No need to turn off onto another road as Allen noted; there weren't any other roads and hadn't been on the way into Otter Creek. Allen reined in the horses of the lead wagon as John indicated they had reached his homestead. It was the largest they'd seen since they reached the outskirts of Otter Creek—well-kept and, by all appearances, well built. Allen jumped down, took the baby from Sophina, and helped her down while David hopped out the back. Walter took charge of the wagons and horses as usual. John led the Miners inside and introduced them to his wife, Patsy Ruby. John explained that the newcomers were the family Ichabod had mentioned, and Allen introduced his family, including the always curious David and baby Elizabeth. He did remember to let her know that their hired hand, Walter, was out caring for the wagons and horses. Patsy had heard, as had all the church members, that Sophina had a child on the way, and now, into her fourth month, she was beginning to show.

Patsy responded to the introduction with smiles for all, and then turning to Sophina said, "Bet you could use a more comfortable place to sit than you probably had in your wagon. John, these folks will need a place to stay and some dinner. We've got room; I'm sure pleased to have some new people around here, and I sure would like to hear some new stories."

Sophina took the lead in thanking Patsy and showed just how right she was by hurrying Allen out to help do some chores. Not exactly shoving him but close enough. Allen took the hint. He excused himself by saying he needed to help Walter care for the horses and wagons. He even took David with him, and John showed them to the barn out back where the horses were already secured and fed.

The horses seemed pleased, John was pleasant to be around, Allen was feeling almost comfortable, David bubbled with excitement as usual, and Walter was glad to have some help. Once inside the house again, Allen, John, and Walter sat down, and David headed out to the kitchen where the ladies had settled in. A solicitous Patsy had insisted that Sophina sit, saying, "Now you've got enough on your hands with that young'un in your arms and one on the way; my kitchen, easy for me to get dinner ready." Sophina didn't object, as she normally would. She did note one difference from other friendly homes they had stayed at along the way; there were no children around. Maybe they were somewhere else, out playing perhaps.

Meanwhile the men laughed and talked about whatever came to mind. Allen mentioned life back in Lindale and his older sons and friends there. He even threw in a mention of the Lindale Anti-Slavery Society, knowing full well from his earlier conversations with the minister that he was among folks of roughly the same mind. Eventually John got down to asking about the trip. Allen filled him in with some details before getting to what had been circling around in his brain since leaving Versailles. The road to Otter Creek was just plain strange and he said so. "That road from Versailles, I must say it puzzles me. We spent about three hours cutting up and removing a large tree that had fallen and blocked it. No one came along from either direction. No one came along while we traveled and while we were pulled over and slept for the night. Just wondering if it is always so deserted?"

"I've been trying to get folks here to do something about that. We're isolated, no doubt about that. Need to open up that road. We did do a little work; that's why you found that clearing, but it needs lots more effort."

"I'd guess getting goods to market more conveniently would require improving that road, unless you have some other creative way I haven't imagined?"

John, laughing now, came back with, "Creative is what we have to be out here in our patch of wilderness. You'll see. And we do need new people. In fact, new people like you bring us all out to help, more than some other places maybe. We'll be showing you. You all can just stay here until we get your place cleared and built. Patsy and I have already discussed it, and I've put together a crew, if three or four can be considered a crew, to help you out on your place. Lots of clearing and building to do before you all can leave us and take to living out there alone."

"Taking us in, offering help—think I'm going to like it here. Are you sure you have room for the four of us? Walter will be heading back to Lindale with one of the wagons."

"Plenty. Built this place just before we got married, about six years ago. Built with family in mind, but that hasn't happened. It's great to have you and yours around; Patsy and I will enjoy it."

Allen didn't know what to say, so he just nodded and then said something about how thankful they were to be greeted so warmly.

John saved him from any embarrassment by standing up and offering to show him the rooms where his family could stay. "We might even have some time before dinner to unload that wagon of yours and put your things in the barn, so Walter can take the empty wagon back."

And so, they did just that after John yelled in to let Patsy and Sophina know what they were doing.

Madison, Indiana - A Young Man's Dream

While Allen and his family were enjoying the hospitality of John and Patsy Brown, meeting other church members, making new friends, and settling into their new life in Otter Creek, Allen's young friend and companion, John Tibbets, was working on a different path. When John returned to Lindale after his Indiana land purchase, he found out that his older brother, Joshua, had been in Madison, Indiana at about the same time. John knew that his brother often visited Madison, but not that Joshua was there while he himself was quite close by in Jeffersonville. Not only had they missed each other, but Madison was the very location the Coffins had mentioned as a prime site for Underground Railroad activity. That's where John wanted to be, and his brother had already been welcomed there at the home of James and Lucy Nelson. John sent a letter to Joshua immediately, at the address of James and Lucy where he knew his brother had been invited to stay. He wrote asking Joshua and the Nelson's if he might visit, letting them know he was interested in moving to Madison someday. Knowing full well that his brother's anti-slavery opinions mirrored his own, he mentioned the Coffins, describing his visit and conversations with them.

Joshua was busy working with the Nelson family and other abolitionists in the area, including the enthusiastic participation of Sara Ann, the Nelson's 19-year-old daughter. Late in 1838 Joshua, the Nelsons, and Elijah Anderson held one of many meetings in their kitchen. Elijah joined them from Georgetown, the Black section of Madison. He was a key figure in the Black-led Underground Railroad of Georgetown, a primary Ohio River crossing point, located at a particularly shallow and narrow section of the river. An imposing figure, he dominated the kitchen, burly as blacksmiths like himself tend to be, dressed quite formally; black bow tie, white shirt, stylish jacket. He was light skinned, and when dressed formally, he was able to pass as a White man legally transporting Blacks while in fact he was aiding escapees, even in Kentucky. Slave catchers seldom questioned him, and, if they did, given his size, they did so cautiously, even respectfully.

James Nelson began the meeting by asking Elijah, "How's your work going these days? I've heard stories and the newspapers have some coverage, such as it is, but you can provide details to set us straight."

"Well, knowing what you do know about the larger effort, you can probably guess. Georgetown attracts escaped slaves like few other places. If you're running and you need help and you're black, your first instinct is to trust Blacks, right? We're a whole community of Blacks, a largely commercially successful community. Word does get around. Besides, there are times when you can almost walk across the river to us from Kentucky. That's all good. The bad? Well, the bounty hunters know all this, too. We are overwhelmed with them. And, as anti-slavery Whites, they have the law on their side; we certainly don't."

Joshua responded, "Right, you've no doubt got problems aiding runaways; bounty hunters know details, right, who to suspect and where they live. Best to get runaways out of Georgetown and on their way quickly."

Sarah Ann was about to say, "That's where we help out", but James and Lucy stumbled over each other jumping in to respond. "No details need to be mentioned; Elijah knows what he needs to know."

Elijah agreed saying, "No details, that's what we all know is best. Talk gets around too easily, silent and efficient, that's the way."

So, no names or locations were mentioned about those who did the dangerous work in Georgetown or Madison or further north. Instead, Joshua turned the conversation to John. "My younger brother, John, hopes to visit us here. Got his letter to me and to the Nelsons; James and Lucy have extended their invitation to him. Knowing how ardently he feels about what we just discussed, I suspect he'll be here any day now. Sarah Ann, he's about your age; you'll like him." If Sarah Ann had been the blushing type, she might have blushed at such a remark. Instead, she just turned her head down and away and allowed herself a slight grimace, saying nothing.

As the conversation waned, all heard a knock at the front door. James rose to answer and Sarah Ann, always curious, followed. James opened the door cautiously, "John?" It was John, arriving even sooner than his brother had expected. John responded, "Yes, you must be James; I'd hoped my brother shared my letter. I am his brother John, indeed." It was not the law or worse. Sarah Ann took a quick look and retreated thinking, "well, he is at least handsome".

James, smiling, led him in and introduced him, jokingly starting with Joshua. "This is Joshua, claims to know you."

John laughed outright. "What that fellow knows about me should, perhaps, remain unmentioned. But perhaps you could introduce me to the two young ladies and your friend here."

Lucy responded, "A flatterer for sure. I like that. I'm Lucy, and let me introduce this young lady, our daughter, Sarah Ann." This time Sarah Ann actually smiled and nodded.

James then turned to Elijah. "Elijah, this is John. His brother, Joshua, tells us John knows lots of folks involved in our cause. If so, it's quite possible, John, that you've heard of Elijah Anderson—our burly friend here."

"What an honor", John responded, "I certainly have. Some people like the Coffins and the Rankins just stand out as ardent supporters of the cause, hard not to know them. And, though I'd guess that Mr. Anderson would prefer to be less well known, given the extreme danger of his work, he certainly stands out, too."

Elijah responded, "We were just discussing the need to avoid broadcasting any details of our activity, but you're right, the word is out on me and yes, the more people know the worse it is for me and for those who have become or will become connected with me, like you all. In coming here today, I dressed like I think a gentleman would, took a carriage, and didn't stop on the way. Slave hunters are unlikely to suspect me dressed and traveling in style. No sense in leading them to you, exposing people so willing to help us out."

"Well, now that we're all here", James, changing the subject somewhat abruptly said, "we can talk over something my wife and my daughter and I, along with others we trust, have discussed often, establishing an anti-slavery society here in Madison. Our friends from Lindale can help here, active as they've been in their local chapter. Joshua provided a copy of the Lindale Statement of Purpose a while ago and John can bring us up to date. In previous meetings we've decided that the Lindale Anti-Slavery Society constitution is acceptable almost as is, for our society. We've agreed on the basic points; Joshua why don't you just go ahead and read Article 2, the core statement, to refresh our memory."

Joshua retrieved the document from his jacket pocket with a bit of a flourish, and slowly, with appropriate emphasis, read article 2. "The object of this society is the entire abolition of slavery in the United States. While it admits that each slaveholding state has by the Constitution of the United States, the exclusive right to legislate in regard to the abolition of slavery within its own bounds, this society will endeavor, by arguments, addressed to the understanding and conscience to convince our fellow citizens that slave holding is a heinous sin in the sight of God, and that the safety and best interests of all concerned require its immediate abandonment without expatriation. This society will aim to influence Congress in a constitutional way to abolish slavery in the district of Columbia and in the territories of the United States, and to prevent it from extending to any state that may hereafter be admitted into the union."

James then added, "So, that's almost exactly what we decided to accept here. We did add a phrase that is certainly implied but not specifically stated, 'to influence Congress to put an end to the domestic slave-trade.' Both constitutions contain a separate article, article 3, with a necessary warning, 'This society shall endeavour to elevate the character and condition of the coloured people by encouraging their intellectual, moral, and religious improvement. But this society will never encourage the coloured people to assert their rights by force.' We did add the following to article 3. We wanted to make sure we noted that improvement was needed more generally, so we added to that statement on colored people the following phrase, 'and by removing public prejudice.' Obvious, I guess, but worth noting, I think."

John jumped in just as Sarah Ann was about to speak and she let him. "Right, 'public prejudice', so central, changing minds about just how human Blacks really are already. Learn that lesson and slavery becomes impossible to support."

Sarah Ann limited her response to a nod in agreement.

Elijah then summed up, "Yes, anti-slavery societies are all about changing minds within the legal framework and changing that framework through political action. People acting as members must work within the law and, as important, be seen as working within the law. Of course, secretly some act otherwise, as we all know."

This time all nodded in agreement and seemed ready for the final note James provided. "We had been thinking of holding an official meeting soon. Let's make it in the new year, January 5th, maybe, and we should meet in a more formal place. The 5th will give us time to inform others and arrange an appropriate time and place."

Chapter Thirteen

Farm Life

Community Effort

In the Fall of 1838, while several likely members of the future Neil's Creek Anti-Slavery Society held their preliminary meetings in Madison, Allen and Sophina were beginning their new farm life in Otter Creek. Walter had headed back to Lindale as planned. And, though their old Lindale community was far away, the new one, small as it was, proved able to provide all the help Allen and Sophina needed. John Miller Brown came through with the 'crew' he had promised, and his wife, Patsy, had more help from church women than she needed to help care for Sophina and the children. Knowing time was short before winter set in and halted the outdoor work, John and his crew started on the new homestead-to-be within days of the Miner's arrival. Allen was able to get the wagon near enough to the work site so that Sophina decided to go along with 5-year-old David and 1-year-old Elizabeth. The women packed food, cooking supplies, tables, and chairs—all they would need to turn the first day into an event equivalent to a barn raising party. Once there, young David spent the first hour or so helping with setup and eyeing the apple pies, baked the previous evening.

Clearing the land and building the log cabin took weeks, but the women took care of their men along with Sophina and Allen throughout the Fall months, whenever, and as long as, weather permitted work to proceed. Fortunately, the building site wasn't far from John and Patsy's home or the homes of the other volunteers. They simply returned to their respective homes and did whatever needed doing there whenever necessary.

Clearing trees for the cabin and for the beginnings of a farm kept the men busy. It was a lot of hard work, even for men used to working hard. The trees were sawed or axed down and, depending on their size, either prepared for cabin construction or a wood pile, but the stumps, they needed to just go. Stump removal required clearing the sod around the roots and then cutting the roots; the smaller roots with a grub ax and the larger with a two headed pickaxe. Once the roots were cut, some stumps came out with manual heft, some required herculean efforts by Allen's horses with lines wrapped around the stumps and attached to the horses. Others, usually pines, just wouldn't budge, so they were burned in place. Hard work indeed, but these men had all done it often before and knew what they were doing. Allen kept David busy gathering kindling and piling it up. Sometimes he allowed his young son to help lead the horses, but, at Sophina's insistence, Allen kept him clear of the burning stumps.

By the time winter weather moved in and halted further outside work, enough land was cleared for Spring planting, and two rooms of the cabin were completed and roofed over. The very first building erected, the outhouse, stood ready within roughly twenty steps of the front door. But the new home was not ready for winter weather, so the Miners stayed on with John and Patsy. Scarcely a day had passed by without at least one of John's crew stopping by to help Allen. The first Sunday after the weather forced them to stop, Allen rose in church to thank his new community for their efforts, and Sophina added just how much she appreciated the women who helped her and were still caring for them.

As the new year arrived and the Otter Creek community endured the winter weather, events back in Madison progressed as planned. Sophina received a letter from her Lindale friend, Susanna, that included news passed along by Susanna's sons, Joshua and John Tibbets. The Neil's Creek Anti-Slavery Society was formally established, and its constitution was approved on January 5th, 1839. Both of her sons were active members and Joshua was Secretary. One month later Sophina and Allen had news of their own to share; Lucinda Amelia Miner was born on February 4th.

Sophina's next letter to Susanna, announcing Lucinda's birth, was meant to be shared with family and friends, and it included her usual inquiry about her own two eldest sons, Jacob and Ichabod. This one, though, layed out a plan for their reunion. Sometime in early Spring, once she and Allen moved from the comfort of the Brown's home into their own new home, Allen planned to travel back to Lindale to pick them up along with whatever else they had left behind that they thought they would need. What to do with their home in Lindale would need to be decided, but, given that Sophina's brother, Cyrus Temple, and his family were there, they figured there was not any need to handle that issue immediately.

Good plan but not what happened. As it turned out Cyrus and his wife, Sarah, had their own birth announcement in February; their son, Andrew, had arrived. With Sarah and Andrew in the care of the always helpful church women, Cyrus thought he might consider doing what he had often contemplated. He wanted to see what lay further west like many other Ohio men, and he wanted to see his sister Sophina again. He was thirty-one and figured he'd better take this chance before he got much older. He'd take Jacob and Ichabod and whatever Allen and Sophina might need and make an adventure of it. Off went a letter to Sophina and Allen making the offer. Allen, busy as he was, felt luck had struck again, and Sophina certainly liked the idea. Her return letter set up the details including a list of what Allen felt he would need and what she would need along with vague thoughts about disposing of the property sometime in the future. Allen included detailed directions and suggested a stop at the Coffins'. Then he wrote a letter to the Coffins setting up that possibility.

The letters back and forth and preparations at the Lindale end took time, but by late March Cyrus was ready to go. Jacob age 11 and Ichabod age 9 could hardly contain their excitement. A trip west with Uncle Cyrus, joining their family again, well it doesn't get better than that for young folk. Cyrus followed Allen's directions, including the stop at the Coffin Newport home as they passed through Richmond, and then on to Indianapolis and Versailles. The trip went smoothly without any problems, even the late March/early April weather cooperated. In fact, seldom had the region experienced late winter/early spring weather more favorable for travel by wagon. Even the stream in Ohio they needed to cross did not cause any problem, as it had when John Tibbets and Allen had run afoul of it; the 1838 drought had left it nearly dry. And, given the time of year, traveling the inadequate semi-road into Otter Creek was easy; they met no one else on it.

Once in Otter Creek, their first stop was John Miller Brown's house. It was so prominent that everyone new to Otter Creek stopped there first. And, as in Allen and Sophina's case, the greeting was warm and sincere. John, understanding how anxious they were to see their family, quickly offered to lead the way to the Miner's. Slightly off the main road as it was, a guide was helpful. Their arrival was one joyful scene. Cyrus hugged his sister, greeted Allen, and then asked to hold their new baby. Even Lucinda seemed pleased; she accepted the hand off with a gurgle or two. Jacob and Ichabod looked on for a bit before ogling the baby and then giving their mom a hug and their dad what they took to be an appropriate greeting for gentlemen—a subdued handshake. Allen would have none of that, though; he picked them up one at a time and spun around swinging them until their feet were well off the ground. It took a second or two, but the boys ended up laughing and accepting this show of affection. What they really wanted next was to tell their family all about the trip, but those tales would have to wait until later.

Sophina excused herself and headed toward the stove after inviting John to their early dinner. Fortunately for her, he declined saying that Patsy had dinner plans underway. Sophina already had the three extra mouths to feed; two sons she knew ate like there was no tomorrow and a brother who would clean up whatever they left. It was root cellar time of year, so she sent Jacob and David to retrieve the potatoes and beets, now in her own root cellar but provided by Patsy. She had quite a few eggs, also from the Brown family. She had planned an omelet with beets on the side. More beets and a second omelet would do it; adding more day-old bread to the omelet than she would normally, ought to help fill them up. She decided to skip the potatoes.

Dinner went as expected. The young ones ate fast, too fast really; but that meant Jacob and Ichabod got to tell the tales of the trip sooner. They had wanted to tell those tales from the minute they arrived. Ichabod started it off. "We saw buffalo, lots of buffalo, big, bigger than I ever thought they would be."

Jacob added, "Must have been a hundred, crossed right in front of us. Scary. We looked for Indians hunting them, none. Wanted to see that."

Allen then let his sons in on the story of his trip and how they had missed crossing paths with the Potawatomie, as those Indians were being forcefully removed. "I told David, at the time, that these were Indians you wouldn't want to see; sad, sick, driven from their homes, and treated badly."

Sophina, seeing her boys suddenly slowed in their enthusiasm, did what she could to revive it. "Bet Indianapolis was a treat."

Both boys smiled. "It was", Jacob said and then let Ichabod speak. "Treat, that's exactly what it was. Good food finally. And Uncle Cyrus bought a pie. Finished that up quick, a special treat."

"Well," Sophina replied, "no pie today, but let's make one this afternoon, for tomorrow. You two can help. Patsy and I dried apples from the fall we'll use."

Smiles from the boys again, including David this time. "I'll help too."

And that's what they did later that afternoon. Meanwhile Cyrus and Allen busied themselves with some work on the cabin that needed doing, including beginning the addition of the new room, sorely needed now with the extra residents. Cyrus stayed for a few weeks helping Allen and his two elder sons with the new room and with preparation for planting. By the time he left, the cleared areas were ready for Spring planting which Allen started in late April. Initially he had plans to purchase a milking cow and later thought about starting beef production, so part of the cleared area was left as forage for those animals. He'd plant corn, for sure, and oats. With his two eldest sons there to help and with the favorable late April weather, quite warm and not too wet, the work went smoothly; even that new room got completed.

Chapter Fourteen

Neil's Creek Anti-Slavery Society

Developments

While the Miners were settling into their Otter Creek life, the Tibbett brothers and their fellow members of the Neil's Creek Anti-Slavery Society continued their discussions. A week or so after the January 5th, 1839 meeting formally establishing the society and approving the constitution, they were already considering additional resolutions. Joshua Tibbets, Lyman Hoyt, and Lyman's brother, Benajah, had been appointed at the first meeting to draft those resolutions with hope of passing them at a January 26th meeting.

Once again Elijah Anderson visited disguised, as usual, as a White man of stature, his carriage and dress as well as his light skin allowing him to pass easily. This time, though, he had a slightly darker skinned driver, ostensibly his slave but actually his brother William Anderson. William had heard from Elijah and others about the new society and decided, like his brother, that he wanted to become involved in shaping it. Both brothers also knew full well the advantages of making Underground Railroad friends to the north of their Georgetown Black enclave.

After William was introduced, they were both heartily welcomed and joined the discussion. Joshua Tibbets brought them up to date on what was discussed before their arrival; several resolutions had been suggested. They struggled with the somewhat broad phrase in the constitution that "slave holding is a heinous sin in the sight of God"; they wanted to express more clearly just how morally corrupting it was.

Joshua explained, "My brother, John, has even suggested calling American slavery 'the vilest sin on earth.'"

John added, "Yes, and it crushes the souls of victims as well as perpetrators. It's a stain on our nation that we need to wipe away immediately."

William, a recognized religious leader in the Black community of Georgetown, added, "That emphasis in the society's constitution and in this proposed resolution on the sin against God as well as the effect on the souls of the victims can't be stressed enough." He continued, anger rising in his voice, "As a slave myself for what seemed like endless years, I can attest to what it costs the souls of victims. None of the slave holders I suffered under would allow me to read anything, let alone the bible. Religious instruction and worship were not for slaves in my experience, ever. It was a set policy to destroy our souls or to not even recognize that we have souls."

John hearing the anger and knowing just how moving these personal stories were, asked William, "Would you be willing to tell us some of your experiences as a slave? The more we hear from those with real experience the clearer it becomes just what we are up against. We need to understand."

All present nodded encouragement and William began. "Just a list of my slave experiences says a lot—sold many times, jailed often, handcuffed, chained, whipped, starved. My experiences got worse and worse until I was sold south to Mississippi. Think of it,

Mississippi; all hope of escape from that distant hell hole, dashed. It was the low point. Add in attempting to simply exist under the worst owner I ever experienced, a woman without a soul, yes, as a religious man I can't help thinking such creatures exist, a she-devil. I had to struggle to find my way back to hope, and I did, but from what I saw around me and from tales I heard, hope seemed like some desperate fantasy most of the time. My only consolation was my hard-fought night-time success at secretly learning to read and write. And that was the only light in my upbringing as a child with no mother. No bringing up; I was whipped up, starved up; kicked up and clubbed up. I had no schooling except what I stole by fire and moon light, or what little I could glean on the Sabbath, when Sabbath was available to me. Yes, one or two owners allowed a Sabbath, gone for good with the she-devil."

William seemed to be ready to stop, but John had gotten too far into the story. "But you did escape and here you are. How?"

Looking around William couldn't help seeing just how involved others had become. So, he continued. "Well, let's just say I failed to escape twice. After my first attempt, I was stripped naked, stretched out on the ground with feet and hands secured to pegs driven into the earth, and then whipped some 500 times with a large ox whip. My blood soaked the earth. When he was done with the whipping, he had me thoroughly washed. Sound like just a touch of mercy? No, washed with the harshest salt brine his merciless mind could devise. Hard labor followed in chains, and fed? Well, only if small amounts of corn and water can pass as fed."

John reacted with astonishment in his voice. "After this, you tried again? I don't even know what to call it—the word horror sounds mild."

"Well, certainly not right away. Took time and the exceptional cruelty of the she-devil. Finally, I just kept repeating Patrick Henry to myself, 'give me liberty or give me death.' I was miles from the river, miles full of Whites and treacherous Blacks who would be only too happy to betray me. But I still thought writing a pass and getting on a river boat heading north might give me some slim chance. Why did I still think that? Because it was the only idea that could get me out of there. Write a pass? The she-devil wouldn't let me near paper or pen. Got them from a house servant I trusted, and for once I was right. Use a pass on a river boat headed from Mississippi to Louisville with no White man to vouch for me? Crazy, but it worked. One crew member did ask what I was going to Louisville to do, others flatly said the pass looked fake. I told them I was going to Louisville to cook a 4th of July dinner. Don't ask where that thought came from. I was told to show the pass to a clerk. That would have been the end. But God provided cover in the form of 60 or so slaves who were boarded just then. I simply sneaked in with them and never saw the clerk."

"Home free you say? No, not hardly. The slaves got off in Arkansas, no longer providing cover. Even worse, after several days the captain noticed that I hadn't gotten off. He asked for the pass. Then he asked for a letter backing my claim about a master waiting for me. I'd thought far enough ahead to have written one and got it, but the captain just threw the pass and letter on the deck and had me watched day and night as we headed north. We were approaching the Ohio River—Louisville, Kentucky and jail on one side, Indiana and freedom on the other. I did have a knife I'd thought to bring with me; something to protect me, I guess. I thought, 'just give me a moment'. I lay down and snored loudly. It worked, my guard, figuring I wasn't going anywhere, walked off, giving me that moment. And it came to me, from God, I truly believe. There was a yawl, tied to the side of the boat. I threw my ragged belongings in, got in, and cut the ropes securing the yawl. The boat kept going and the yawl fell behind. Minutes later I was ashore in Indiana. And as you said, John, here I am."

After that story, getting back to the meeting agenda took a while. Folks expressed relief, some even clapped William on the back. Others remarked as best they could, all inadequate to express the astonishment they felt.

Somehow Joshua managed to bring the meeting back to order. "That story will serve to inspire us to word our resolutions strongly.

As most of you know, I, along with Lyman and Benajah, have been asked to formulate the resolutions for our next meeting. We need to get on with discussing just what we want to include."

John helped by adding, "Slave souls crushed, slave owners turned into devils; Joshua, Lyman and Benajah should have what they need to inspire strong wording for sure. But there's a whole other area of activity to discuss, political action. We can't let slavery spread to new territories or states; we can't let Southern representatives lead weak kneed Northern representatives to just go along. Lots of work to do and again strong words needed. The use, in our constitution, of the word 'influence' in reference to congressional representatives, seems to me like one of the weaker words we might use. Certainly, we can be more specific."

Lyman responded, "We'll invoke the Declaration of Independence, 'all men are created equal, endowed with certain inalienable rights, such as life, liberty, and the pursuit of happiness.' When they fail to further that noble goal and, instead, cower before Southern evil, we will hit them hard at the ballot box."

Elijah took opposition to slavery a step farther by cunningly suggesting that they add, in somewhat ambiguous wording, something other than a weak purpose, "Should we say something like 'citizens of the free states are morally bound to interfere with slavery in any part of the United States.' Let them say what we know they will about that word 'interfere'; we've covered ourselves in our constitution by acknowledging state's rights and discouraging slave violence. But, some of us might well appreciate the thought of interference. My brother's escape certainly qualified as interference, and after he escaped, Northerners, myself included, interfered by not sending him back. 'Interfere', yes, though we don't want to say explicitly that we intend to break laws."

Benajah responded, "That is clever, and I think I like it. We'll do some more thinking about that."

The others were willing to just let it go at that for the time being.

Lyman suggested being even more specific. "Look, congress passed the Pinckney resolution a couple of years ago and keeps supporting it. Think of this, that resolution contains a clause about petitions against slavery like the ones we might decide to send to congress. The clause specifies that such petitions will not even be considered. 'Laid on the table' and no further action taken, or something like that. We need to send the petitions anyway and then let people know, as widely as we can, just what happens to them. First, let's just add a resolution protesting the Pinckney resolution clause as a cowardly yielding to Southern interests."

Others agreed and then Joshua brought the meeting to a close by telling all that the committee assigned to draft the resolutions would work hard with the material provided to finish in time for the next official society meeting on January 26th.

At that meeting the committee presented nine resolutions with phrases like "We view American Slavery as the vilest sin on earth" and that citizens of free states "are morally bound to interfere in the acceptance of slavery in any part of the United States, and especially in the District of Columbia". There was a passage condemning abridgments to the freedom of the press, abridged particularly in the South and a reference to "life, liberty, and the pursuit of happiness", grounding the society's beliefs in the Declaration of Independence.

All nine resolutions were passed. Then Rev. Louis Hicklin, the Society's chairman, rose to propose two more, including "that we view the late proceedings in Congress as uncalled for and subversive of the sacred right of petition, and that it shows the servile corruption of these false sentinels of liberty." The second said simply that we will not support such candidates for office at the ballot box, candidates "who betray the rights and liberties of Northern freeman in order to win the courtesy and smile of the South." Those two resolutions also passed, and the meeting ended with a short address from Rev. Hicklin. Five more society meetings were held in 1839, dealing with more mundane issues like the purchase of books for a library, financing for various other needs, proposals for speakers, society publications particularly in the

Philanthropist, and relations with the Indiana State Anti-Slavery Society.

Early in 1840 one striking addition was added to their list of concerns, inserted in long passages addressed against the doings of Congress. Congress "has waged war against some of the Indian tribes within our borders who if unmolested would have been peaceable and unoffending." Though the battles in Florida were specifically mentioned, the phrasing left open the possibility of wider concerns. In fact, John Tibbets mentioned one of those concerns. "If my good friend, Allen Miner, had been here instead of managing his farm life in Otter Creek, certainly he would have mentioned the Potawatomie trail of death. He would have pointed out the Potawatomie as such an apt example of those 'who if unmolested would have been peaceable and unoffending'".

"Peaceable and Unoffending"

Representatives in Congress and twenty-four more votes in proportion to their free white inhabitants than the free states and these representatives are paid their salaries out of the public treasury — thus subjecting the free states to an expense for which they receive no equivalent, and which amounts to little less than taxation without representation. — Congress has passed laws or resolutions (at slavery's bidding) in open violation of the people's rights viz — the freedom of speech — the freedom of the press — and the right of petition — It has waged unjust and cruel war against some of the Indian tribes within our borders who if unmolested would have been peaceable and unoffending — The Florida war especially has robbed our country of many of its most valuable citizens and cost the people nearly twenty millions of dollars and of all this slavery has been the procuring cause

Chapter Fifteen

Wisconsin?

Why?

While the Neil's Creek Anti-Slavery Society was formed and maturing in 1839 and 1840, the Miner family lived the farming life in remote Otter Creek. Just how remote, it troubled Allen more and more as the years passed. He was never able to purchase the milk cow they wanted, and thoughts of the beef enterprise faded, too. There just weren't any animals for sale anywhere nearby. Weather was favorable enough in the early planting months of 1839 but worsened in the Summer and early Fall. Drought and heat ruined his corn crop; only other grains—rye and oats—survived along with hay and straw. Getting any crops he did raise to a market required traveling the far less than ideal road into Versailles, and prices there as elsewhere in the mid-west were low. The 1837 financial panic in the East and South had finally reached the mid-western agricultural economy in 1839. The 1840 weather was even worse for farming and no better financially. They didn't even get a Spring planting break as they had in 1839. The winter had produced little snow, and they faced drought right on through the growing season. Prices for crops remained low.

Allen's income was low, too low. There was no law practice for him out there in friendly Otter Creek. They survived and that's about as good as this new life of theirs got. Of course, their neighbors, suffering the same problems as they were, proved again and again to be good people, bringing moments of joy and companionship into their lives. Also, Allen and Sophina got to know David Johnson, John Tibbets' friend whom John had met at the Inn and accompanied to the land office back when John had made his own Indiana purchase. John had followed through with his promise to David, letting Allen know that he had spoken with David about Otter Creek and about the Miner's purchase. He added that, based largely on that purchase and his own encouragement, David had purchased land nearby.

The Miner's new friendship with David led to others, including Peter Aller and his older brother, Jessie, as well as David's older brother Daniel. The Miners, Allers, and Johnsons got together several times and talked at length. Along with the usual topics of farm life—weather, crop failures, prices, mishaps—talk of just plain leaving began to come up as farming profits worsened or disappeared altogether. Most, including the Miners and the Johnsons, had purchased their land at the enticing price of $1.25 an acre, and even though the financial downturn continued, land speculators, often from the East, still expected to make money when they later sold any farms they could buy in communities like Otter Creek, even if they paid a good price initially. Landowners like the Miners and their friends stood to make back their investment and more should they choose to sell.

The Johnsons became the first to act on the sell and move option, selling their land and buildings to one of those Eastern speculators. News had reached them from a friend, Samuel Lewis, of fertile lands to the north in Wisconsin. That news came with an offer David and Daniel just couldn't resist. Samuel offered a place to stay while the Johnsons looked into where they would settle. They arrived in June of 1840, lived in the small, crowded Lewis home with as many as 24 people at a time and looked around.

Exploring in the area took them along Indian trails that had seldom been traveled even by the earliest settlers.

Samuel told tales of those early settlers who arrived less than a year before him in the summer of 1839. He enjoyed telling how they made the first wagon tracks to Evansville, in Union, where they settled. He described those trails as Native American, and related how those settlers were visited by large numbers of quite friendly Winnebagoes, led by Chief Little Thunder. No harm was done to the settlers; the Winnebagos seemed merely curious, and they broke camp without incident moving on to, well, no one, not even Samuel, knew where.

The Johnsons didn't inconvenience the Lewis household for long. Having arrived June 25th of 1840, they'd built their own places by July 2nd with help from local men. They were squatters like others in the area. David would make his purchase of 80 acres 3 years later, and Daniel would end up with 320 acres years later. The nature of the land made building and clearing much easier than what Allen and Sophina had experienced back in Otter Creek. The land was part high, dry, rolling prairie with deep, rich black loam and sand, along with stands of burr oak. Excellent conditions, available lumber, and fertile clear land—what took weeks in Otter Creek to accomplish was done in days. Besides, they could live off the land; clear springs provided the purest water, game abounded, streams were ideal for fishing, wild berries were plentiful, and the grasslands ideal for raising the family milk cow or cattle. Once both Johnson families were settled in, they prepared for gardening and farming and even planted late vegetables to fill the root cellars for the winter months.

News from Wisconsin - Moving On

Early on, one government function existed in Union township, Wisconsin, besides land surveyors—the Post Office. Once the Johnson families settled into their Wisconsin farm life in late summer of 1840, they sent a glowing letter back to their friends in Indiana encouraging them to give the territory serious thought. The Miners and the Allers didn't need much encouragement; they were ready to leave. Sophina talked to her older brother Ebenezer who had shown interest in moving with them if they chose to head for Wisconsin. Ebenezer, his wife Mercy, and six children, William, Charles, James, Eleanor, Mary, and Elmira had followed Sophina to Indiana from Clermont, Ohio after their father, Ichabod, died in 1838, and they moved in close to the Miners' Indiana homestead.

Ebenezer didn't take much convincing either. The Miners, Allers, and Ebenezer's family all left Indiana in early 1841, traveling in covered wagons, and despite snow encumbered roads and trails, they arrived safely in Wisconsin. Once there they all crammed into the farmhouses belonging to the Johnson brothers. The Miners and the Allers stayed with David Johnson and Ebenezer and his family with Daniel Johnson.

Something else transpired during the trip. Ebenezer's daughter, 22-year-old Eleanor, and Peter Aller spent a good deal of their time together, getting as close as courtship allowed with her father close by. On March 28, 1841, they were married before the Justice of the Peace; the first recorded marriage in Union, Wisconsin.

The Miners were able to settle in as fast as the Johnsons had before them. They purchased the land in 1842, but, like the Johnsons and other early settlers, they squatted first and purchased when they got around to it. By April 1842 Allen and the Johnsons were already established members of the community, so established that they became members of the first Union township board of officials. Allen Miner is listed as one of three township Supervisors and David Johnson one of three property Assessors. The three Supervisors, Allen included, were also elected to the position of Fence Viewer.

Fences performed the crucial function of separating the township's two main sources of income—animals and crops. The first source, animals like cattle, often wandered off and then headed straight for the other main income source, crops, eating up both the cash crops and the feed crops. Some of the farmers quarreled loudly when the loose cattle belonged to one farmer and the crops to another. Hard feelings, fights, and sometimes even legal trouble ensued. Many had heard and agreed with what John C. Calhoun said when asked by Federal Government Departmental heads about what products of domestic industries should be assessed and reported on. Calhoun looked over the list he had been handed and exclaimed that they had omitted the most important one—fencing. He went on to state that fences cost more and were more important to farmers than any other domestic product.

So, Fence Viewers were, by necessity, respected members of the community who could talk reasonably to potentially angry and financially distressed fellow citizens, soothing the conflict and seeking just responses. It was the perfect job for the lawyerly Allen Miner, and it had the potential of opening new avenues for his legal talents after his years in Indiana as a farmer with no law practice.

Allen and David Johnson, given their positions, officially attended town meetings. At town meetings the whole community was welcomed, and the meetings developed into party days, a bit of relief from incessant farm labor. The first meeting was held in a local home. After that, meetings were held at Ball Tavern. With a drink or two and a game of baseball or quoits to play and wrestling, young men could show off before young women; those attending thought 'what's not to like?'

The games, if not the drinking, got interrupted at one such meeting when it rained. The barn on the other side of the road from the tavern provided shelter for all, and it was perfect for wrestling. The onlookers formed a circle, and two wrestlers fought in the middle until one lost. The rules allowed the loser to select the next opponent for the winner. In one case the loser called for Jessie Aller.

Jessie must have seemed like the perfect choice; a big, very strong man. But Jessie refused. He said he didn't know anything about wrestling, wasn't interested, complained as best he could, but the crowd had none of it. They chanted "Jessie, Jessie" and wouldn't let up until Jessie realized he'd have to give in. Into the ring he went to face a much smaller man. He quite simply grabbed his opponent by the collar with one hand and by the seat of his pants with the other hand, lifting him off the floor and holding him at arm's length. Then he marched him out of the barn throwing him into a manure pile. Rumor has it that no one ever asked him to wrestle again. Not exactly the way his friends, the Miners or the Johnsons or even his brother wanted to establish their reputations, but effective none-the-less.

A few months after Allen actually purchased his land, Sophina bore another son, Cyrus, in June of 1843. The birth was recorded as occurring in Evansville instead of the larger designation, the township of Union. As a farmer and responsible Fence Viewer, Allen built fences. Rock fences and Osage Orange fences were familiar to him, but rock fences took forever to build, and Osage Oranges took a long time to grow, so he built a split rail fence with the plentiful supply of wood on his own land. He fenced in his animals, pleasing his neighbors and saving his own crops, trusting that his neighbors would do the same. As official Fence Viewer, he was able to bring the matter to their attention, if they didn't follow his lead.

Allen and Sophina remained happy with their move from Otter Creek. They had family and friends close by, Allen was a respected community leader, and township meetings provided entertainment for the whole family. One problem they had experienced in Otter Creek hindered them in Union, also, and may have been even worse; getting goods to market wasn't at all easy. The roads were bad, little more than rutted trails in poor repair. Landowners were supposed to maintain the roads along their property lines, and being good neighbors for the most part, they did their best, but they were unable to do much more than maintain the muddy trails that already existed. Given muddy trails and winter weather that could be severe, wagons loaded down with goods had a hard time. They had a long way to go to reach Lake Michigan where goods were shipped to the best markets in the East. Often winters were so bad that some of those trying to drive to market simply had to return home. Some even had to abandon their goods and wagons before walking home in order to save themselves and their oxen.

Wisconsin Politics - What's Happening?

Political life for Allen and his close friends evolved over the years. Throughout the 40's and 50's they remained active, and by 1854 Allen is listed as the Township Treasurer and his friends Peter Aller and David Johnson as township Supervisors. They attended all the township meetings, often in official capacities or at least as respected attendees with significant voices in proceedings. After one township meeting in 1843, Allen, Sophina, Peter Aller, his wife Eleanor, and the family of Sophina's brother, Ebenezer, as well as the Johnson brothers stayed behind instead of attending the games to hold their own private meeting. They were all strong anti-slavery supporters, and they wanted a chance to discuss local efforts more privately with those they knew were like-minded.

Ebenezer began the meeting saying, "We know each other well and we know where we stand on slavery. We ought to take a public stand. Some of us belonged to Anti-Slavery Societies elsewhere; why not here?"

Allen added, "The Gilead Anti-Slavery Society, back in Lindale, helped clarify issues for me. We read, we talked, we supported local efforts and spread the word as best we could. But we ended up somewhat disappointed. Always felt it wasn't enough."

"Right," Sophina added. "My friends, the Tibbets brothers, helped start the Neil's Creek Anti-Slavery Society in Indiana. It was different though. They got active in politics, supporting candidates and petitioning Congress. Of course they were just north of Georgetown, the Black community along the Ohio River, and were able to work closely with prominent Blacks there. And we all know just what sort of help was needed that they could offer."

David Johnson doubled down on Sophina's last thought. "We do indeed."

Ebenezer's son Charles wanted to know more. "What help?"

Ebenezer's wife Mercy answered with a warning. "The Georgetown Blacks couldn't safely transport those seeking freedom further north without help from Whites like the Tibbets. But, and this is important, we must never mention names of those who help except when talking with those we know and trust. It's illegal to offer such aid."

Brother Daniel added, "But I don't know of any such activity here, political or otherwise. Anyone else hear anything?"

Peter Aller answered, "I've spoken with a few folks, Jacob West for one. Jacob let me know of his support and of his interest in the anti-slavery Whig Party."

"Exactly," Sophina responded. "Politics, like Neil's Creek was involved in; we need to get more involved."

"But", Mercy noted, "we can't do all they did. There's no Georgetown here, right?"

Ebenezer added, "If there is such a community here, I haven't heard of it, and given how newly developed this area is, what would it be—one or two folks?"

Peter had an answer. "No, we can't expect a community, but we are well placed to help folks on their way to freedom, on to lake Michigan and from there to Canada, where truly free Black communities do exist."

Allen changed the subject adding a nagging concern of his own. "We've all probably heard about the friendly visit of Little Thunder during an early settlement year. He was a Winnebago, I think, but I can't help thinking some Potawatomie might have returned here after they were removed. That removal, so brutal, sticks with me. I'd like to check it out here and add it to anti-slavery concerns. Neil's Creek did."

Ebenezer responded, "Right, so, maybe it's time for plans. Who will do what? Allen, looks like you already have one assignment, checking on the Potawatomie and maybe Little Thunder's tribe, too. Anyone else?"

Daniel Johnson spoke up. "We've been here longest, and we've relied on lots of helpful folks we've come to know closely, like the Lewis family. They might well be interested. I think David and I could look into just how wide support might be here for anti-slavery activity of any kind, and we can add pro-Native American support to our inquires when responses seem positive."

Sophina added, "Daniel, David—maybe Mercy, Eleanor and I could help by talking to wives and daughters of anyone you might add to the sympathetic list. You know, woman to woman talk. Wives and daughters don't always agree with the men folk, as you no doubt know."

"Got that right, too." Daniel replied, grinning. "We'll pass on the names we get to you all."

Peter had an offer too. "I'm interested in following up on the Whig Party. As I mentioned earlier, I've already spoken with Jacob West. He'll let me know of others who might be interested."

Allen offered to help. "I'm interested in the Whigs, too. I'd like to join you in finding out more."

"Well, that leaves me with nothing to do", Ebenezer chuckled. "I'll invent something. Why don't I travel on up to Lake Michigan and see what I can find out about getting runaways and even freed slaves to Canada. I'll take a little time off or maybe carry along some goods to sell and call it business."

Peter brought the meeting to a close. "Seems like we all know what we want to do. Shall we meet again, maybe after the next township meeting?"

"Or some Sunday after church." Ebenezer suggested. "Let's just see how long it takes to get the information. We see each other often enough to decide on a date later."

Nods all around. They headed out just as the wrestling was nearing an end. All the wrestlers seemed joyfully engaged and relatively at ease; Jessie hadn't shown up.

Chapter Sixteen

Getting Involved

Support

Discussions of the Anti-Slavery cause spread in Union and surrounding communities over the next few months and on into the next year as each member of that private anti-slavery discussion group gathered information, took note of allies, and spread the word. Peter Aller and Allen Miner were particularly busy campaigning for the Whig Party anti-slavery candidate for president, Henry Clay. They spoke often with Jacob West, the confirmed anti-slavery Whig Peter had mentioned, and generally allied themselves with Jacob's campaign efforts.

The discussion group had asked the Johnson brothers to talk with the base of friends they had built since arriving, and the Johnsons got back confirming the solid sentiment in the area. Rock county citizens, like most in Southeastern Wisconsin, were anti-slavery. They did not find anyone who defended slavery, not even anyone with reservations. Some backed gradual emancipation and the American Colonization Society that would send freed slaves to Liberia. At times even Clay supported that idea, so unacceptable to the two anti-slavery societies that members of the group had followed in Ohio and Indiana.

Sophina and Eleanor found anti-slavery support among wives and daughters strong. Send freed slaves to Africa? They did not find one woman that could stomach such nonsense. They couldn't help adding that quite a few women they talked to were interested in adding their votes to the cause, once they were allowed the right to vote.

Meanwhile Ebenezer planned his trip to Lake Michigan. He'd take along non-perishable products to sell, partly because he had extra but mostly to make the trip look legitimate to anyone who might cause him problems. Even in such an anti-slavery area, there were those who spread negative rumors about anyone showing an interest in transporting slaves illegally. An empty wagon on a long trip would be odd; a full wagon would pass unnoticed. Trying to figure out just how the highly secret transfer of slaves worked, without raising suspicion was tricky; it would not be easy. He had heard a few rumors about slave routes, and he could speculate, but that's all.

One rumor suggested that there was anti-slavery activity in Milton, to the east of Union. So, before leaving he thought hard about what sort of route runaway slaves might take, if that rumor turned out to be true. There was little doubt that, if they made it to Wisconsin from Kentucky, Ohio, Indiana, or Illinois, they would be headed for Canada. So, the issue evolved in his mind to figuring out how they might best reach Milton and then reach Canada from Milton. He considered the old stagecoach road through Janesville, an obvious route to Milton, or maybe they just followed Rock River, a bit less obvious and therefore safer. Once they reached Milton, could they somehow cross Lake Koshkonong? If so, would they keep following the Rock River at the Eastern end of the Lake all the way to Lake Michigan or find some other route? He thought to himself, "All sounds plausible, I'll fill in details as I go."

Ebenezer decided that he'd check out the Rock River route to Milton on horseback first. He didn't expect any path along Rock River to allow the easy passage of a wagon; he left his wagon home to be picked up later. He was right about the path. He had to pick his way carefully, leading his horse at times and even wading once or twice, but he did make it to Milton. Ebenezer and most abolitionists knew one name in particular, Reverend Edward Mathews, an ardent and outspoken abolitionist from Milton who spoke often to both hostile and sympathetic audiences, risking his life in doing so.

First Ebenezer asked a passer-by for the local Baptist church, figuring no one would find that question suspicious. He was right; the first person he asked smiled saying, "Well, as a Baptist myself, I'm pleased you asked. Just follow this road to Henry Crandall's house, third house on the left. We hold our Sunday services there and welcome all who might wish to join us or to just learn about our Seventh Day Baptist beliefs."

Ebenezer replied, smiling in return. "Henry Crandall, thanks, I'll enjoy meeting him. I'll be back in a week or so, maybe stay for a service."

They parted practically friends—a good start for Ebenezer. He went on down to the Crandall house and met Henry, introducing himself as a fellow Baptist and asked about the services in Milton.

Henry answered, glad to meet anyone interested in his church, "Welcome, yes, we're a small church meeting here for now. One of our most energetic members, Joseph Goodrich, has plans to build an academy near here. Hope he does, we could meet there instead of in my house. I'd like that. And, somehow 'academy' sounds more appropriate for church services than someone's house, right?"

Ebenezer responded as a Christian should but hedged so as not to offend. "I guess anywhere people meet to praise the Lord is a good place but you're right, academy sounds fine, elevates the occasion, perhaps we might say." He dropped the thought quickly and got on to what he hoped might lead a bit closer to the information he wanted. Feeling more confident, after positive responses to his questions about the church, he pushed a step further. "I did want to ask you about affiliation with anti-slavery societies. Some of my friends have heard Reverend Edward Mathews speak passionately about establishing them in Wisconsin. Wondered if you might introduce me to him, to discuss what steps we, back in Union, might take to, perhaps, join an existing anti-slavery society or eventually even to start one of our own."

Henry, glad to discuss a subject so close to his own heart, replied, "Reverend Mathews, such a courageous and fiery speaker. Few have spent as much time—shall I say—in the lion's den. Lucky more than once to have survived speaking, as he insists on doing before pro-slavery audiences. Unfortunately, he doesn't stay in one place long. All I can say is that he'll be sure to make the anti-slavery conference in Racine, coming up fairly soon, I think. I suspect that will keep him in Racine for a while at least."

Ebenezer jumped at that opening. "Racine, well, my plan was to go back to Union, pick up my wagon and goods and head to Racine as a good place to sell. Right on Lake Michigan with ample shipping. Guess all I need is a good way to get there."

"Well," Henry replied, "there is a ferry that crosses Lake Koshkonong run by Joseph Goodrich's brother, William, an avid anti-slavery man you might want to meet. But, with a wagon you might want to avoid the ferry fee and go by road, such as it is, along the southern border of the lake toward Whitewater and then on to Racine."

"Sounds good," Ebenezer responded, "thanks for the information. Sure hope to see you again, if not on my return with the wagon, then some other time."

With that final exchange they parted, and Ebenezer headed back to Union for his wagon.

Racine - Anti-Slavery Society Meeting

Ebenezer returned home and spent a few days catching up with family and friends. He had much to tell them all about his Rock River adventure, meeting Henry Crandell, and his hopes of meeting the Reverend Edward Matthews in Racine. He expressed his newfound confidence that he was onto the right route for former slaves fleeing to Canada, supporting his view by talking at some length about the Lake Koshkonong ferry run by Joseph Goodrich's brother, William, an avid anti-slavery man he hoped to meet. Several days later he loaded his wagon and headed back to Milton by road this time. He had one important stop to make on the Madison-Janesville stage road on the way to Milton. Allen Miner lived along the road, and his wife, Sophina, had just given birth to a son, Cyrus, their sixth child. As Sophina's older brother, he was anxious to stop in, check up on his sister, and offer his congratulations. When he got there, he stayed for a couple of days, giving them plenty of time to celebrate together.

The rest of the trip to Milton went smoothly enough; the stage road was a lot better for traveling than he'd experienced during his Rock River escapade. This time he went directly to Henry Crandell's house and again struck up a friendly conversation. He asked once more about the Reverend Mathews and got the same response. Best bet was still Racine. But this time Henry offered to introduce him to Joseph Goodrich, the well-known abolitionist he had mentioned earlier as considering the building of an academy in Milton. And since Goodrich happened to be visiting Henry, he did so without delay.

Henry introduced his new friend to Joseph, "Joseph, I want you to meet Ebenezer Temple. This is his second visit here in a week or so. An abolitionist like us, he asked about our plans. I told him you were the person with plans."

Joseph greeted Ebenezer and then took up Henry's comment. "Plans, yes, lots of plans, we'll see what comes of them. You've probably heard from Henry that I want to build an academy. We'll have a good place for church services, our ongoing anti-slavery meetings and discussions, and a school to teach young people math, their ABC's and, yes, about their responsibilities to help others, like the former slaves seeking freedom."

Ebenezer returned the greeting saying, "Henry, here, tells me you have a brother with similar anti-slavery interests and that he operates a ferry that crosses Lake Koshkonong. Thought I might see if I could meet him, too, on my way to Racine. I'm trying to meet as many abolitionists along the way as I can; my friends back in Union want to make as many connections of the sort as we can."

Joseph stumbled a bit over the word 'connections' and ended up just repeating it, "Yes, connections, good for the cause, for sure."

They didn't go any further; they all knew they were touching the subject they weren't ready to discuss openly. 'Connections' might well be interpreted as the Underground Railroad sort. Ebenezer would have to wait. He did ask Joseph for a note to his brother, William, hoping it would help ease the conversation once they met. Ebenezer was getting more and more sure that the ferryman played a part in getting runaways to Canada. As politely as possible he suggested he'd be on his way, anxious to see what William might reveal.

That evening he approached William Goodrich's ferry at the south mouth of Lake Koshkonong, the so-called Goodrich crossing. Instead of visiting William immediately he decided to seek out a site where he might spend the night watching the area, thinking he might luck out and see Underground Railroad activity. He thought it unlikely but decided to give it a go anyway.

As he'd suspected, not even on a very dark night did anything of the sort occur. In the morning, he saw that the ferry had remained docked. He thought it probably would have moved on under the cover of darkness if a runaway transfer had occurred. He did not hesitate further before going on down to meet William. He introduced himself, and after some pleasantries produced the letter from William's brother Joseph. It served well as an introduction to the anti-slavery interests he wished to explore.

After scanning the letter, William asked Ebenezer about his past involvement in anti-slavery causes. Ebenezer responded, sounding quite a bit like Allen, "Back in Ohio I belonged to the Gilead Anti-Slavery Society of Lindale along with a number of friends and family. We studied, we lectured, we spread the word. We hoped we made a difference, but we ended up feeling something more needed to be done. So, now that some of us are up here, including members of my family and many of my friends, we are ready to get involved again. Just how best to help is what we need to know. I'm taking the goods in that wagon up to Racine for sale. On the way I decided to talk to folks with similar feelings and see what I can find out about the activities up here in Wisconsin."

William took that in and seemed to be thinking over a response. Finally, he simply said, "My brother probably talked some about Anti-Slavery Societies springing up around here. Heading to Racine? Well, you may catch the meeting of the Delavan Anti-Slavery Society coming up soon, I think. Good source of ideas to help for sure."

Ebenezer affirmed that he hoped to attend the meeting. "Others have mentioned the meeting and even suggested that the Reverend Mathews would be there. I want very much to meet him and talk about our interest in and around Union."

That brought an encouraging response, "No one could tell you more; no one would be willing to tell you more; he's one courageous fellow. He talked to me. My ferry seemed to interest him. Speaking of watercraft, you'll want to speak to A. P. Dutton, another avid abolitionist. He knows all about steamships out of Racine. He'll be at the conference, too."

That was the closest Ebenezer had gotten so far to confirming thoughts he had about the Underground Railroad route. He stayed cautious though and simply said, "Well, sure hope I'm in time for the conference. But if I miss it, I'd guess I could look up Dutton, right?"

William confirmed that thought saying, "Everyone there knows him. Just ask anyone about steamships, and they'll send you to him."

"Good," Ebenezer responded, "but I do hope to make the conference. In fact, think I'll say goodbye and be on my way as quickly as possible. Thanks for the guidance, much appreciated."

"Right, stop by on the way back, if you want. If I'm here, you could stay, maybe even overnight and we could talk at greater length. Good luck selling your goods."

With a thanks for the invitation, Ebenezer climbed aboard his wagon and headed for Racine. He pushed the horses as hard as he could and made the trip in four days, arriving late in the evening. He did inquire about where conferences might be held from a young man traveling in the same direction, not mentioning which conference might interest him. He got a better answer than he had any right to hope for. Good directions and a question, with an encouraging smile, asking if he was going to attend the upcoming Delavan meeting, starting in a couple of days. Ebenezer smiled and simply said "yes", receiving a cheery "see you there," in response.

He gave some thought to visiting A. P. Dutton before the meeting but decided against it. Better to meet in the right sort of environment—the anti-slavery conference. Instead, he set up camp and spent the time resting up, checking out the general area, and even staying up one night again hoping he might see transported runaways. Again, no such luck.

While checking around he found out the Delavan meeting would begin mid-morning; he decided to arrive at the conference site at least an hour early. That turned out to be a good decision; people were there already mixing and talking, so he joined right in. He saw his young friend, the one who had given him directions. Another cheery hello helped him feel less alone than he might have otherwise. He talked to quite a few of the attendees, and he was glad to find out that many, like himself, were not from Delavan but simply there to add support or gather information. In fact, it seemed that though the Territorial Anti-Slavery Society began in Delavan, the meeting had become much more general and was known as a meeting of the Wisconsin Territorial Anti-Slavery Society. By the time the meeting got underway, Ebenezer felt quite comfortable. He had hoped to meet Dutton at the meeting, but for some reason the steamboat person, as he was called, wasn't there. Maybe later, he thought.

Finally, the meeting came to order, and the Reverend Edward Mathews, who founded the organization in 1842, took the podium to lead the proceedings. He thanked those in attendance, praising his friends from Delavan especially, and then got right down to business. He introduced Reverend William Allan, currently a representative of the Illinois Anti-Slavery Society. Reverend Allan was a tall commanding figure, well known as an inspiring speaker and as a former Lane Seminary student. The attendees were clearly pleased that such a prominent man had come such a long way to be there with them.

Reverend Allan began with a short history of his early involvement. "Many of you may have heard of the Lane Seminary students who left the Seminary risking our theological careers because the Seminary leaders refused to let us debate anti-slavery notions like abolition vs. colonization. I was a young fellow back then, let's see, 1834, guess I'm not that old right now." That elicited laughter from some in the audience. "Those discussions, held despite the opposition of those in power, led to our leaving, the best event in my life, as it turned out. From there many of us went to Cincinnati's Black community, a thriving Black community I should say, where we lived, studied, taught, and preached, learning more and more from members of the community just what 'humane' meant from those who lived it every day against odds we found hard to believe."

Ebenezer sat there listening to what he already knew about the Lane students, thinking that if ever there was an opportunity for him to break into Wisconsin's inner circle of abolitionists, talking to

Rev. Allan about his own experiences with the Lane students would be it.

Reverend Allan continued, "I found my calling there in Cincinnati, not immediately; no lightning bolt revelation, but a change that would guide my life from then on. I went on to Illinois and joined anti-slavery advocates and became a traveling representative for the Illinois Anti-Slavery Society. Those travels bring me here today to share what we have done in hopes we can assist your efforts.

"First, you need to know that I come from the South and from a slave-owning family. My father was about as kind a slave owner as one could find, and he supported the colonization solution to slavery, to be gradually implemented. I, too, shared that view for a while, but my time at Lane brought me in touch with one of the most influential of abolitionists and a leader of the student movement, Theodore Weld. I suspect his reputation as a leader is known to most of you. It did not take him long to convince me of the error of my ways. Just how thorough my conversion became in a very short time I might illustrate by reading from a speech I gave before we were forced by our convictions to leave the seminary. I hope that the passion I expressed then will serve as a way of confirming your convictions. Here it is, I'll read from it.

"'What is slavery? Before we can prescribe a remedy, we must understand the disease. We must know what we are attempting to cure, before we give the medicine...

"'At our house it is so common to hear slaves screaming from a neighboring plantation, that we think nothing of it. The overseer of that plantation told me one day, he once laid a young woman over a log, and beat her so severely that she was soon after delivered of a dead child. A bricklayer, a neighbor of ours, owned a very smart young negro man, who ran away, but was caught. When his master got him home, he stripped him naked, tied him up by his hands, in plain sight and hearing of the academy and the public green, so high that his feet could not touch the ground; then tied them together, and put a long board between his legs, to keep him steady. After preparing him in this way, he took a paddle, bored it full of holes, and commenced beating him with it. He continued it leisurely all day. By night the young man's flesh was literally pounded to a jelly. It was two weeks before he was able to walk. No one took any notice of it; no one thought any wrong was done.

"And lest anyone should think that in general the slaves are well treated, and these are the exceptions, let me be distinctly understood, cruelty is the rule, and kindness the exception.

"I think I will leave you with those images and with that thought, 'cruelty is the rule, and kindness the exception.' We are engaged in a fight against unimaginable cruelty directed at our fellow humankind; keep up the fight, keep up the fight however you chose to wage it." That final call to action led to a standing ovation, a fitting end to Reverend Allan's speech.

Ebenezer stayed through the day until the end of the conference. He waited his chance and then managed to work his way into what became a three-way conversation with Reverend Mathews and Reverend Allan. Ebenezer began by telling them about his experiences with the Lane students. "Just to introduce myself, I'm Ebenezer Temple from Lindale just outside of Cincinnati. My Lindale friends and I became well acquainted with the former Lane students' efforts in Cincinnati, visiting them where they were doing the work you described and convincing them to help us form our own notions of the anti-slavery society we wished to establish. They sent James Thome and James Bradley to Lindale...".

Reverend Allan raised his hand in a gesture to interrupt and excitedly exclaimed, "Two better members of our group would be hard to find. James Thome and I were as close as brothers, he, too, grew up in the South in a slave holding family and came to abhor it as I did. James Bradley, a former slave, I know just how passionately he can tell his story."

Reverend Mathews simply nodded his head in agreement and then shook Ebenezer's hand. "Welcome to the movement. After you heard Thome and Bradley speak, I don't doubt your passion rose, and I'm more than pleased that such passion brought you here to our conference."

Ebenezer was anxious to respond. In his excitement he may have pushed further than intended. "Yes, we were and are inspired. We took our time trying to get it right and to bring along as many members as possible, and eventually we established Lindale's chapter of the Gilead Anti-Slavery Society. We kept notes, we read widely, we provided others with information, we lectured, we preached, we informed the media. But, though I'd like to think that we inspired some slave owners to give up their sin or inspired a slave or two to escape, I can't site one example. There has to be more we can do."

Reverend Allan just nodded his head in agreement, but Reverend Mathews, always the forward one, responded more directly. "Of course there is more to do, and we, here in Wisconsin, are blessed to have some willing to risk all to do what we know needs to be done. Any former slave who reaches us will get any help they need; of that, I can assure you."

Ebenezer had finally reached the connections he had so ardently sought. His response was simple and to the point, "Just let us, back in Union, know when and how we can help, and we will. Just send the request to me, and I will provide supplies and members dedicated to helping."

This time both Reverend Mathews and Reverend Allan agreed as one. Reverend Mathews assured Ebenezer he'd be in touch. Ebenezer then asked one more question, "There was another abolitionist I'd heard about often; folks suggested I talk to him, Achas Dutton, described to me as A. P. Dutton, the Steamboat man. Wondered why he wasn't here."

Reverend Mathews answered more guardedly this time, "A busy man for sure, yes, talk to him and let him know you have spoken to us."

With that final recommendation they parted. It was clear to Ebenezer the steamboat link, that he was now quite sure existed, was highly protected, indicating just how important a link it was. He'd certainly talk to Dutton and maybe even spend time seeing what he could see, but, even if he got the chance, he would not ask direct questions. He already knew what he needed to know to be part of Reverend Mathews' work, he had no need to understand every detail of a route and certainly did not need to know, any more explicitly, this carefully protected steamboat link on the way to Canada. In fact, not knowing was safer. If asked under duress, should it come to that, he could honestly deny knowledge. Just the right frame of mind when involved in this sort of highly dangerous undertaking.

So, he remained overnight back where he had stayed earlier, but didn't watch the steamboat docks for 'activity'. Instead, he got a good night's sleep and went on down to the dock with his wagon full of goods to sell, in the morning. Dutton was there, and at first, he and Ebenezer took care of business. Dutton helped Ebenezer unload the grains, stored them temporarily on the dock next to a steamship, and paid Ebenezer the going price in Racine. Ebenezer did note the name of the steamship, the Chespeake, but thought nothing of it at the time. Years later he found out just how important a link to Canada the Chespeake was.

Ebenezer did express his regret at not seeing Achas at the meeting, using Dutton's first name as a sign of their newly forming friendship. He talked about his friends in Union, his discussion with Reverends Mathews and Allan, and his associations with the Lane students, but he did not press at all, and they simply parted as two people who had shared a friendly conversation on matters of interest to both of them.

Time to Meet - Plans

Ebenezer's trip to Racine and his discussions with participants at the anti-slavery conference had yielded all the information he needed and more. He had contacted Reverend Matthews and arranged with him to become a conduit for further local 'activity' whenever the opportunity came up. It was time to return to Union and talk over with his friends about all he now knew. On the way, though, he intended to stop back at Goodrich Crossing and talk to William Goodrich, taking up the offer to stop by and stay overnight to allow for further discussion. He did not really need any further discussion, but he didn't want to be rude by ignoring the invitation. So, after about five days of relatively easy travel, he arrived at Goodrich Crossing only to find that William was, in fact, away crossing the lake on his ferry. Ebenezer simply left a note of regret that they hadn't been able to meet as planned, promising to stop in another time.

Once Ebenezer returned home, the original group (Allen and Sophina Miner, Peter and Eleanor Aller, David and Daniel Johnson, as well as Ebenezer and Mercy) decided they'd meet as soon as possible. This time they invited Jacob West to join them. He was so supportive and so well known in their small community that they thought his presence would be important. They met a week later at Ebenezer's home, and all wanted to hear from Ebenezer first.

Ebenezer obliged, clearly pleased to tell his story. "Well, good to start at the beginning. I wanted to try to meet as many Wisconsin anti-slavery leaders as I could, just to try to figure out how we might fit into the larger effort. I pretended I was headed to Lake Michigan to sell my farm goods. In the back of my mind, not too far back, you understand, I thought that I might follow a path that I imagined runaway slaves might follow if they were headed to Canada. I had no idea even if runaways made it to Wisconsin, so this was all conjecture. My first thought was that they'd avoid major roads, so instead of taking the wagon initially, I went by horseback attempting to follow the Rock River east. Sure would have been a fine secret route, but what an effort. Thought I wouldn't make it at times. Ended up in Milton, well known as an active anti-slavery center.

"Then I returned here by the main road and visited Milton a second time with the wagon full of goods, traveling the far more comfortable Madison-Janesville stage road. Both times I spoke with Henry Crandall. His house acts as the local meeting place for

Baptists and, as I eventually found out, the local meeting place for anti-slavery supporters. I met Joseph Goodrich, too, on my second visit. He talked quite openly about his anti-slavery stance and planned to build an academy in Milton for meetings, church services, and education of the young. He gave me a letter of introduction to his brother, William, who operates a ferry on Lake Koshkonong. A ferry: perfect way to transport runaways, I thought, but of course nothing of the sort came up in our discussions.

"I did hear along the way that a major anti-slavery conference was going to take place in Racine, right there conveniently located on Lake Michigan, perfect for transporting goods east or even north to Canada, right? I had heard the conference was sponsored by The Delavan Anti-Slavery Society, apparently the first established in Wisconsin. But I soon found out that it was, in fact, a more general Wisconsin Territorial Anti-Slavery Society meeting. Met important contacts there including the Reverend Edward Mathews and Reverend William Allan. Imagine my surprise when Reverend Allan mentioned his involvement with the Lane students those of us from Lindale know so well. That connection got me into a discussion with the two reverends and finally led to an agreement that Reverend Mathews would keep in touch with me. If they need our help of any kind, they will contact me."

Jacob West interrupted. "Just want to be sure that any talk about runaways is conjecture and any help we provide to the movement is legal as far as the public is concerned. I guess, given the laws both in this state and nationally, that's obvious enough."

Ebenezer nodded agreement and then added, "Even Reverend Mathews would agree, and he's by far the most outspoken of advocates. That's why we set up the single point of contact here."

Jacob took over at this point and asked those charged with finding out about local support what they had learned. David and Daniel, Sophina, Eleanor and Mercy reported what they had made clear earlier. This area of Wisconsin strongly supports anti-slavery efforts. Jacob then asked Allen and Peter Aller to report to the group how they thought they might further the group's beliefs through political action.

Peter took the lead. "Allen and I have allied ourselves with Jacob by campaigning for Clay and the Whigs here in Union. Jacob is particularly concerned about talk of annexing Texas fearing, as Clay made clear he did, that if Texas became a state, it would most certainly be a slave state, and slave state expansionists would get the boost nationally they desired so fervently. Allen and I are becoming known as Whigs around here, not as well-known as Jacob but clearly identified to the public as party members."

Jacob agreed and added an explanation. "The national Whig party has far too strong a wing of slave owners and slave state supporters. We all know their argument. Without slaves they could not support family farms, let alone plantations—could not survive financially."

Allen added, "This argument has infected some Whigs in the Northeast, too. Without cheap cotton from the South, the northern textile industry would suffer, they claim. Not many in the Southeastern Wisconsin Territory support such views. I suppose that financial argument may have lingered in some minds, left over thoughts, perhaps, from back when they lived in the Northeast and their industries depended on cotton. As anti-slavery Wisconsin Whigs, we feel compelled to answer arguments like these, even if they aren't all that prevalent locally. Besides, Southwestern Wisconsin still uses slaves in iron mining operations, despite the territorial law against slavery, and they get away with it; unfortunately, it seems, nobody enforces the law where finances dictate behavior."

"Good" Jacob responded. "We seem to have come to quite similar observations about where we stand. Now I think we need to be sure we agree on what's next and how to present our efforts to others. I'd say it's obvious that we don't discuss any of Ebenezer's 'conjectures'; that's for Ebenezer to handle as the single point of access. What we can discuss publicly is what we want to do in terms of an anti-slavery society and what we can do politically. Just wondering if we want to form our own society. Any ideas?"

Ebenezer, smiling broadly, agreed on the 'conjectures' issue. Then added a thought that had occurred to him at the meeting in Racine. "Seems to me that we might create our own anti-slavery society but perhaps not now. We could only create a small society given the current size of our community; we might be able to do more if we simply added our support to a larger, existing society—maybe the one with my friends in Milton."

Allen added, "Given what I've come to think about the limits of these societies, I'm not for starting a small one. I'm all for joining an existing one and putting most of my efforts into political action."

Jacob then took charge of the meeting again. "Let's figure out when to address a wider group of supporters and figure out where, too. The church would be best, I think. I'll contact the pastor and see when he thinks we could hold a meeting. Meantime, why don't you all figure out what you would want to say, write it down, even. We'll give it a final look and chose a presenter."

Ebenezer added what he figured would meet with the agreement of the others. "Sounds good. There's no doubt in my mind who the presenter should be; I vote for Jacob West." Hands went up to a chorus of ayes. All agreed to write down what they would want included and the meeting came to an end.

Private Lives, Public Lives - Sad Days

1844 was an election year, and public life—meetings, travel, politics—sometimes obscured private lives. For Allen and Sophina there was still the farm to run and children to raise, friends to help and trips to the market with goods to sell and items to buy. Two months before the election, in early September, Sophina lost her good friend and mentor Susanna Tibbets back in Lindale. All she could do was send their sincere regrets to Susanna's daughter Elizabeth (Tibbets) Duncan and the rest of the family; not the kind of sendoff she would have wished to give her oldest and dearest friend. In February of 1844 their eldest son, Jacob, turned 17 years old, one year older than Allen had been when he left home in Steuben County, NY for Kentucky, never to return as it turned out. Would his son show similar signs of restlessness? Allen had stopped repeating the Kentucky stories, at home at least, several years ago. There was no sense in encouraging Jacob or his brother Ichabod, two years younger, to imitate such recklessness.

Allen, Jacob West, and Peter Aller continued to support Henry Clay's Whig campaign for the presidency, and the local Whig candidates. The three of them, along with other local Whigs, continued to strongly oppose the Texas annexation that was likely to give pro-slavery advocates two more Senators and serious political leverage nationally. Along with Clay, they made a consequential political mistake, focused so exclusively as they were on the anti-slavery issue. In December 1844 Clay's defeat was finalized and the major reason for it was largely recognized; concerns over the Texas pro-slavery issue were overshadowed by the overall national enthusiasm for expansion. Locked in as they were by their own enthusiasm for the anti-slavery cause, they downplayed the public's more general feelings.

Allen's notes for the long-postponed community-wide presentation summarized the issue succinctly. "Along with Clay, himself, we misjudged just how popular expansion itself was despite any misgivings about the slavery issue. We believe this issue was central in Clay's loss. Since the election, we have firmly supported 'Conscience Whigs', those opposed to slavery anywhere, period. We are seeing the Whig party begin to splinter, certainly after the 1844 election and even before, into northern 'Conscience Whigs' like us and the aptly named 'Cotton Whigs', the Southern Whigs and their supporters in the East where industry remains all too dependent on southern cotton."

That meeting finally took place early in 1845 with Jacob West speaking before a larger than expected turnout. The township had grown, as had Jacob's reputation; many anti-slavery advocates and some just curious from surrounding townships attended. Among the advocates from another township was Jesse Saunders, an anti-slavery activist from the newly formed Baptist Church in nearby Albion. Jacob stuck to the points as planned, though the large audience weakened the argument that the area had too few interested citizens to start up their own anti-slavery society. He simply modified the argument slightly by suggesting that given the growth and interest shown, a new society might be worth trying sooner than they had thought. He added a suggestion based on an earlier conversation with Saunders that in the meantime they might consider joining with the already established society in Albion. Then he quickly shifted to politics and laid out the work to be done now that Clay had lost the election. He concentrated on the Wisconsin movement for statehood, arguing that they should all support it as one more counter to Southern slavery interests in the Senate. For once they were successful. That movement took a few years, but by May 29, 1848, Wisconsin became the 30th state, one established as a free state in its constitution.

Wisconsin anti-slavery supporters strongly backed a clause in the Wilmot Proviso that would have prevented slavery in any new state, including Texas. It was initially introduced by David Wilmot from Pennsylvania in 1846 and passed in the House where sheer numbers gave the North an advantage. But it failed several times in the Senate where the even split in states, and therefore Senators, meant nothing of that sort could pass. The proviso would have been a significant victory, but instead it led some northern Whigs to waffle; they began to express varying degrees of concern about the anti-slavery cause when debates about the Wilmot Proviso brought the anti-slavery issue back into focus. Beyond the backing of the Wilmot Proviso, there was little the Wisconsin anti-slavery contingent could do as the Mexican War dragged on and Texas went from being part of Mexico to an independent country anxious to become a state.

For Allen the political turmoil gave way to personal turmoil in 1846. On November 16, his wife, so strong and resourceful, so critical to their life in all its aspects, died giving birth to their seventh child, Mary Amanda. As Allen struggled, he tried to imagine life without her; he couldn't. A newborn, three children under 10, and three teenagers to raise or at least guide, a farm, his political, legal, and religious life; he couldn't see how he could handle it all alone. So, he didn't. Less than three months later, on February 7, 1847, he married Emeline Wolcott Caldwell, daughter of Nathaniel and Abigail Wolcott and widow of Henry Caldwell, another strong woman to help with Allen's offspring along with her own four children by her previous marriage, and, yes, to guide Allen himself as Sophina had. Eleven months later, at age 37, Emeline gave birth to the first of their four children. Allen's personal life flourished again, though night after night he would wake up from dreams of his 21 years with Sophina.

Allen continued his political life with help from Emeline. By October 1848, he had worked his way up to the point of representing Union at a Rock County Whig Convention held in the town of Janesville. Representatives from Union included Jacob West, along with the earliest of settlers, Samuel Lewis, who had taken in the Johnsons when they first arrived, and Alanson B. Vaughan who was a Whig Representative in the Wisconsin Legislature. Not bad company for Allen; he really was now part of the local political inner circle.

The 1848 Rock County Whig Convention firmly supported the Free-Soil Party Buffalo Convention's strongly worded anti-slavery platform as well as its US presidential candidate Martin Van Buren and its vice-presidential candidate Charles Francis Adams, a son of John Quincy Adams. The Whig Party nominated war hero Zachary Taylor for president, but, horrifying to Allen and his friends, he was also a Southern slave owner from Louisiana. Whigs who managed to stomach a slave owner for a presidential candidate tried to balance the ticket by choosing a New York Whig, Millard Fillmore for Vice President. The Buffalo Platform made clear just how reprehensible Free-Soil members found the Whig ticket headed by a slave owner, despite the attempt to appease them by picking an acceptable Vice President. The Rock County Convention, echoed in

Newspaper accounts and at their own convention, how firmly they, too, now stood against their former Whig allies.

But again Allen and his friends chose the losing side, this time by a large margin—the Whig Party's Taylor earned 163 electoral votes, the Democratic Party's Cass earned 127, the Free-Soil Party's Martin Van Buren earned none. Still the Rock County Free-Soil party members remained active locally through the following years of the party's existence. In 1854 the party finally gave up as a separate entity and merged with the Republican party. Allen Miner, Jacob West, Daniel Johnson, Peter Aller, and a member of the Vaughan family still served in various capacities. They strongly opposed the misnamed compromise of 1850, a pivotal, pro-slavery piece of national legislation.

Allen, his lawyerly instincts intact, actively followed events. One evening, after the 1850 compromise passed, he sat down and layed out his thoughts to his wife, Emeline, who had quickly learned to just sit and listen to him when he needed to work out what he was thinking. "That 1850 'compromise', you know, mimicked the 1820 Missouri Compromise but even worse it amended and supplemented the 1793 act 'respecting fugitives from justice, and persons escaping from the service of their masters', as the wording goes. That 1793 act provided the means for slave owners to recover slaves and even provided a penalty to anyone aiding escape. The constitution had not gone that far. It simply stated that slave owners had the right to recover but avoided specifying any means or penalties."

Allen went on, "The 1850 so called 'compromise' increased the penalties, increased them and then some. Those new penalties included fines of $1000.00 for marshals and deputy marshals who failed to execute warrants, and when slaves were in custody if the marshal failed to keep them in custody for any reason, even if an escape was not the marshal's fault, they became liable for the cost of the lost slave. An additional section of the 1850 'Compromise', provided similar penalties to anyone aiding in escapes, even going so far as to add possible jail time on top of financial penalties."

Emeline added, "All these 'Fugitive Slave Laws' are so offensive. I can't even tolerate the constitutional clause itself; though, as you have said, it is the least explicit."

"Right, you know, in fact, William Lloyd Garrison took your point about the US constitution so far as to refuse to participate in politics altogether, because, he argued, all politics are based on the constitution, a constitution containing the Southern inspired clause he saw as an insult to humanity."

Allen and his friends did not go that far, but nonetheless the original clause and the escalating harshness of the penalties were impossible for them to accept. They increasingly shared the growing outrage against Southern immorality. They did not realize it at the time, but eventually they came to understand that if there was a single moment when the Civil War became inevitable, passage of the 1850 'compromise' was it.

Chapter Seventeen

Different Opportunities Different Places

California Ho - Gold - Yes. Ice?

Jacob, Allen's eldest son, took his time leaving the family; not at 16 like his father, not even at 20 after his mother died, but at 22, Jacob set out for Marysville, Yuba County in Eastern California. Allen and Jacob discussed plans for the trip and what Jacob intended to do once he got there. Jacob wanted to start a business. He had heard from Martin Pease, the JP who had married Allen and Sophina and remained friends of the family though he still lived in Ohio, that the ice business was booming in Cincinnati. Some shipped goods need to be kept cold to be safe and fresh, like meats, fish, fruits, and vegetables. Now with ice, shipping them longer distances became practical and profitable.

Allen asked, surprise was clear from expression and gesture, "Ice? In California? That's odd."

"True," Jacob agreed but then quickly added, "I've looked into Marysville, up in the mountains. Two rivers merge there and form a lake. That lake interests me; from what I can gather it's just right for providing lots of ice. The rivers are where gold is found. Not interested in gold digging, but people with gold and money will want the best, and ice is part of getting them the best things to eat. I'll sell plenty of ice to the local merchants, once the gold diggers sell their gold and look around town for places to spend their money. Merchants will buy the ice, for sure, with newly enriched customers lining up for their goods. That's my hope, anyway."

Allen then asked, "What will you need to get started? Will you need money from an investor, like me?"

Jacob answered quickly; he had asked Martin all about what he would need. "I'll need a couple of good plow horses, a sturdy wagon for hauling, and a horse drawn ice saw; it's sort of like a plow with a large saw attached, or so Martin says. Not sure where to get one; guess I'll figure it out when I get there, or maybe I'll just make one."

"Make one if you can. You are good at making things, and I'm guessing it will come at a hefty price if you have to buy one," Allen replied. "We can get the wagon and horses here, and I'll help with costs once you get to California. Got to say lots of people talking about heading there, crossed my mind even. Course the big draw is gold—reports of big strikes, so everybody says. Even hear that Marysville is involved. That saw, though, that's up to you."

Jacob jumped in, "I'm going to ask Martin for more details; I'll ask him to draw one and send it to me."

Jacob had already received several other details from Martin that he somehow forgot to mention to his father. Martin reported that he'd heard of cases where the weight of horses and men broke the ice plunging them into the ice-cold water; lives were lost that way. Others were lost crushed by the sheer size of the blocks sliding and slipping into them. It was cold, hard work, in fact just plain exhausting. Jacob knew all this, but he was strong and healthy and figured he'd be fine.

While Jacob waited for Martin's drawing of the ice plow, he began to put together whatever else he and his father thought he would need for his trip and his business. Meanwhile another adventurous soul, later to marry into the Miner family, caught the gold fever itself. Lewis Cummins set out from nearby Rock County for what would become Placerville, CA but at the time went by the far more colorful names of Dry Diggins or Hangtown. Whatever its name, the place was wild west rough. Hard working gold miners, isolated along the river, were murdered and robbed as they took the gold from the river bottom. The robbers were simply hung when caught. Actual legal trials were rare or brief; 'citizen' trials followed by lynchings were the rule.

Hangtown was an all too appropriate name, as was Dry Diggins. Some gold miners had to lug loads of 'dry' earth down to the river to wash out the gold nuggets. Eventually folks decided neither name was all that appealing and changed it to Placerville after the so-called 'placer gold'. Placer gold came mostly from the river bottom; the miners scraped the river bottom mud up with short handle shovels that earned the name placer shovels and then panned for whatever flakes of gold they might be fortunate enough to retrieve that had been washed down from far richer veins upstream in the mountains.

To face the multiple dangers of mining above Placerville, Lewis Cummings, unlike Jacob, had family with him; his father and two brothers old enough to stand guard. They arrived in 1850, less than a year after the most famous of Hangtown cases, one worth a quotation from a current Placerville historical page. "...an impromptu citizen's jury met to consider the fate of the three accused. The jury wasted little time reaching a verdict, guilty of robbery. Then the question was asked, what shall be done with them? Someone shouted, 'Hang them!' The majority agreed. And so it was that the first and most famous hanging in the Mother Lode town was carried out. The site was a giant white oak in the corner of Hay Yard near the center of town... Today, only the tree stump remains, hidden in the cellar of a bar on Main Street in Placerville named—quite aptly—The Hangman's Tree Bar."

Kansas?

The gold discovery of January 1848 at Sutter's Mill near Placerville became well known with as many as 1000 miners working up-stream along the American River by the summer of that year. Lewis Cummins, his father and brothers were a bit late to the rush, but they did find a camp site and they did find gold. Better yet they survived their wild west experience. Lewis returned to Janesville, Rock County, Wisconsin in 1852, and courted, then married Allen and Sophina's 16-year-old daughter Elizabeth on November 20, 1853.

Meanwhile Jacob's ice business plans matured. Begun in 1850 in Marysville, CA, as planned, his business prospered, and by 1860 his ice business and a complimentary teaming business were described as extensive. He had several horse-drawn wagons making deliveries, and the teaming/Ice business was very successful with $4000.00 worth of property plus the $1,500.00 cash Jacob had on hand. Jacob's business prospered by 1860 and so did his personal life; he married Cavy Ann Johnston, daughter of Charles and Catherine Johnston. At age 14 Cavy had crossed the plains with her family to nearby Yuba City, taught school for a few years and then married Jacob. So, yes, ice, as well as gold, seems to have favored the younger members of the Miner family as they sought out different opportunities in different places.

Lewis Cummings and Elizabeth (Miner) Cummings were typical members of the Miner family's younger generation. They were restless folk, not of the sort to settle down in one place for long for sure. In a July 1856 census, they are listed as having lived in Mitchell, Mitchell County, Iowa for two years. During those years Lewis started and ran a successful mercantile business and purchased $1600.00 in real estate. An 1860 census has them living in Potosi Township, Linn County, Kansas, though they had moved there four years earlier. Lewis' father and his brothers made the same journey from Michell, Iowa to Linn, Kansas. By 1862 we find them leaving Kansas headed across the plains with ox teams in a wagon train along with Elizabeth's brother Cyrus ending up in Walla Walla, Washington where they stayed for a year before Lewis and Elizabeth moved on to the Marysville area of Yuba County, California.

Cyrus? Well, he was even more restless. He left home at a younger age than Allen himself had; not at 16 but at 14 he left Rock County, Wisconsin for Linn County, Kansas and initially stayed with his sister Elizabeth. Lewis Cummings and his wife Elizabeth along with Lewis' father and two brothers had gone to Kansas to aid the newly forming Kansas Free State movement. Cyrus became more involved in the free Kansas movement than his sister or brother-in-law and their families could have imagined. He voluntarily enlisted in the militia and then later was drafted into the union army under General Lane. During his time in the militia, he experienced the first of his military career shocks. It was early evening toward the end of May 1856, just before the militia intended to set up camp for the night near Lawrence Kansas, when a scout returned running, out of breath, and clearly alarmed. "It's gone, completely gone. Burned to the ground."

Cyrus, standing nearby, tried to understand. "Gone, what's gone? Calm down, tell us what you saw."

The scout, whom Cyrus scarcely knew except that his friends called him Tom, got himself under control and described exactly what he saw. "Standing safely above Lawrence, I could see that The Free State Hotel had burned, it's gone. A couple of other houses had been burned, too, and the town was nearly empty. I know Lawrence; it had a couple of newspaper offices, and it looks like they're gone, too."

Cyrus and others listening chimed in with various versions of "who would do this" and "why?"

Tom was sure he knew. "Got to be that sheriff, Jones, figured he'd seek revenge after he got shot there trying to arrest us Free State Kansans. More trouble coming, I figure."

Cyrus was the first to respond with the obvious question. "Should we go on down there and see what we can do?"

Tom, not so sure now, stumbled a bit in response. "Umm, we need to be careful. Jones, well, he's devilish, quick tempered. Just guessing, I'm, well, I don't want to face him and his followers; we'd need a strong force. I'll report to our commanders, see what they think. They make the decisions anyway. Going to let them know how I feel, though."

Tom left to report while the others continued talking among themselves. Several who wanted to go take a look for themselves were convinced to wait until they got orders. None had been in the militia for long, so waiting for orders didn't come naturally. But they did respect their well-known commanders, Brigadier General of the Free State Militia James Henry Lane and Colonel Samuel Walker of the 4th Kansas Calvary, regardless of what they may have thought of other leaders of the various forces that had come together to defend free Kansas but at present were stationed a safe distance from Lawrence. General Lane and Colonel Walker would know what to do, they agreed.

Tom's report was concise; he'd rehearsed it as he rode over. He included his desire to go on down and investigate further with a sufficient force, but Lane and Walker had even more up-to-date information. The sack had actually occurred a couple of weeks ago, and several citizens had since returned, though they kept a low profile. The problem now was different. Pro-slavery forces had established three "forts" blocking all supply routes into Lawrence, forts that were just log cabins with slots for rifles. Primitive forts, yes, but effective at warding off gun shots from any attack they might face and effective at creating severe shortages of supplies causing near starvation in Lawrence.

Col. Walker figured that the more Tom knew and communicated to his fellow militia members the better and Gen. Lane agreed, so they provided him with a newspaper account of the May 21st sack of Lawrence by raiders from Missouri. That account, as well as similar accounts in papers throughout the North, linked the sack with the caning of abolitionist Republican Senator Charles Sumner by pro-slavery South Carolina Congressman Preston Brooks that had occurred the next day, after Sumner's remarkable speech condemning that Missourian attack. Taken together, as they were, these two events inflamed abolitionists and made the title "Bloody Kansas" real to many. Throughout the summer, attacks increased from both sides, including a John Brown raid only three days after the sack of Lawrence at Dutch Henry's Crossing along the Pottawatomie and Mosquito Creeks. John Brown and his sons had intended simply to capture pro-slavery men there, but instead they killed four or five who tried to escape. Nothing like four or five killings seen as murders to inflame tensions, leading to more murders on both sides of the slavery issue.

Tom was met with eager inquires when he returned from the commanders to his group of militia men. Talk had traveled quickly among the forces waiting there, and Tom was forced to turn his remarks into what amounted to a speech rather than simply exchanging comments as he had before he left to report to the commanders. He had a flare for it, quoting Sumner's speech at its most dramatic. Sumner had called the attackers "murderous robbers from Missouri, hirelings, picked from the drunken spew and vomit of an uneasy civilization." Cheers of support rose from all as Tom read that spicy quotation with a voice dripping with disdain.

Meanwhile, Gen. Lane, Col. Walker, and other commanders continued to discuss just how to respond to their present situation most effectively. Clearly, they needed to eliminate those forts surrounding and cutting off supplies to Lawrence. Captain Bickerton wanted to attack Fort Franklin first, the only one of the three forts that had a cannon. He knew just how useful that canon would be to them. If they could capture it, the other forts would be easier to breach. General Lane liked the idea, but Colonel Walker questioned it, pointing out one obvious objection; their attack might well itself come under cannon fire.

No decision was reached that day nor in the following weeks. In early June, Captain Bickerton and General Lane convinced Colonel Walker that Fort Franklin should be first, despite the added risk of cannon fire. Captain Bickerton wanted that cannon; General Lane was used to risk, known for raids into Missouri with limited resources and considerable success. He had carried off more than his share of pro-slavery "possessions" including firearms, ammunition, and, most notably, slaves later freed in Free Kansas. He earned his reputation as commander of the Kansas Free State Army, known colloquially as Jayhawkers or Red Legs. Jayhawker—a combination of hawk for predatory and blue jay for noisy. The Red Legs were known as a secretive group that scouted the Kansas border aiding troops but never officially recognized. Buffalo Bill Cody admitted that as a member of the Red Legs, "We were the biggest thieves on record."

The attack in June on Fort Franklin took place but failed. That cannon was just too much to face, and their gunfire failed to hit the pro-slavery forces in the fort. They decided to try again in August, hoping that a larger force would yield a better result, but, like the first one in June, initially they failed. Bullets still bounced off the fort's logs and the return fire was withering. One young man, a Quaker so enraged by Bloody Kansas that he defied his pacifist religion, took up arms for the anti-slavery forces, but got off just one shot before further engagement became impossible. What he experienced was reported by Rev. Richard Cordley, an early resident of Lawrence, "At the command to fire he emptied his gun in the direction of the fort, but he said the enemy's bullets so pelted the ground about him, that he could not reload without running the risk of catching one of them. He lay still, therefore. He said the bullets struck all around him, and threw the dirt in his face, and splintered his protecting fence post, but spared his head. He said, 'It was the most careless shooting I ever witnessed.'"

Finally, the anti-slavery commanders came up with an idea. They saw a wagon loaded with hay nearby. Ten militia men, hiding behind it, pushed it toward the fort. When they got it close, they set it ablaze and pushed it right up against the fort. The raging fire spread to the fort's logs, and as the fort began to burn, those inside panicked, ran out, and surrendered. Their weapons were recovered along with the cannon, so well-known that it had a name—Old Sacramento.

The anti-slavery forces now had Old Sacramento that they had fought so hard for, but no cannon balls. Several days later Captain Bickerton came up with a brilliant solution; typeface from the destroyed printing presses had been scattered all over Lawrence. Lead type was perfect for melting and molding into cannon balls. Now, with Old Sacramento and plenty of cannon balls, they were more than ready to attack the next two forts. First, they went to Fort Saunders and battered it with those cannon balls, shouting a salute at each round, "here's another issue of the Herald of Freedom", in honor of the destroyed free Kansas newspaper, the odd source of those very cannon balls. Fort Saunders and then Fort Titus fell to Old Sacramento, the Freedom Herald salute, the Jayhawkers, and all the other anti-slavery troops.

As the forts fell and afterwords through April 1862 when Cyrus left Kansas for Walla Walla Washington with his sister Elizabeth and Lewis Cummings, he followed General Lane. During those years Kansas became a free state, and the Civil War broke out officially at Fort Sumter, as if it hadn't already unofficially in the territories of Kansas and Missouri.

Cyrus followed Lane into the official army and the unofficial Jayhawker battles or skirmishes. During one unofficial Jayhawker incursion into Missouri in September 1861, Lane's forces were defeated and forced to retreat at the battle of Dry Wood Creek, near Fort Scott, Kansas, by forces led by Missouri secessionist Sterling Price. But, Lane in retreat simply waited until Price moved north, and then took his Jayhawkers over the line into Missouri territory and attacked several villages ending with the sack of Osceola. Plundering hawks that they were, Lane's men freed 200 slaves and stole 350 horses, 400 heads of cattle, 3,000 bags of flour, and quantities of supplies from all the town shops and stores as well as private carriages and wagons. Nine local men were rounded up, given a quick, drumhead court-martial, and immediately executed on the field of battle. All but three of the town's 800 buildings were burned to the ground; the town never fully recovered. Eventually those freed slaves, along with hundreds of others freed in similar raids, became part of the first Civil War Black regiment, organized by General Lane.

The Osceola raid did not go well for Cyrus, though; wounded severely, he was relieved of duty and spent months recovering, first in a hospital but fortunately soon at the home of his sister Elizabeth and Lewis. He described the events to them one evening but left out any reference to the nature of injuries that would result in his remaining single and never having children, facts he was unwilling to face let alone discuss.

Elizabeth tried to point Cyrus' account in a positive direction. "Think of what you helped accomplish, Cyrus, so many blows against slavery, against 'owners' and slave supporters. Kansas, a free state with hundreds of former slaves you helped free. You've done so much of what we all came here to do."

Lewis caught the gist and added, "Yes, we all came here to further the anti-slavery cause and we've succeeded. Kansas is a free state, doing its part to see that the freed slaves you helped release from their cruel bondage stay free. We can all move on now, if we wish, feeling good about our time here."

"Move on?" Cyrus had not heard about any such thoughts.

Elizabeth took the lead in answering as she tended to do when potentially delicate subjects arose. "Lewis and I have been thinking that with Kansas now free, we have helped do what we came here to do; we helped spread the word, advocating for a free Kansas. We were politically active. Lewis went so far as to become a Justice of the Peace, ruling as a justice, in a free state, should. His term as a justice comes to an end this year, so we began to think about what's next."

Lewis furthered her thoughts by adding, "Much of my family, like us, lived in Mitchell, Iowa and Walla Walla, Washington before coming here—thought we might all return. Cyrus, with your dad and his wife, along with your brother Jacob and his wife, in Mitchell, maybe we'll return there after selling what we own in Washington. That would be some family reunion."

Cyrus took several moments before responding, clearly thinking it over. "Well, you know, wounded as I am, I can't rejoin General Lane and besides he's been embroiled in fights with other commanders. Heard even the President was involved. Seems the man I respect so much and followed is losing the squabbles, and I can't help him. I guess I have done all I can here, like you, maybe you two are right. Time to move on."

Moving On
Epic Journey to Walla Walla WA

The move from Kansas to Walla Walla, WA was a classic family event. Cyrus and Elizabeth let their father Allen know, and he was pleased to hear that they would be joining the Cummings family in Walla Walla first, but that Mitchell, Iowa might be their eventual destination. Allen and Emeline had already sold their land in Union Wisconsin and moved on to Mitchell with their younger children Henry, Leander, and Lemuel. Their second child and only daughter, also named Emeline, died prior to their move. Even Cyrus had been there before his trip to Kansas. So, at least the hope that Mitchell just might be their final destination was much better to Allen than thinking of them remaining in far off Kansas. Much later in life Allen wrote a letter to his family that expressed his wish to have them all near him; he held those feelings in for years, encouraging his sons and daughters to seek out their own lives as he had, but he felt the absence of his scattered family, none-the-less.

But first, before Allen and Emeline could see any of their family members living in Kansas again, Cyrus, Elizabeth, Lewis, his father Josiah, and other members of Cummings family took the treacherous journey from Kansas to Walla Walla. They made quite a large party, five horse drawn wagons, but not large enough for the dangers ahead. At the beginning of their journey, they sought protection at forts to avoid possible Bleeding Kansas raiders. Quantrill's Raiders, the most violent of Missouri based, pro-slavery guerrillas, roamed into Kansas often, murdering abolitionists. Their fear was reasonable, so they set up camp their first night in Osawatomie protected by John Brown's so-called fort, actually a cabin belonging to John Brown's brother-in-law, Rev. Samuel Adair. This abolitionist outpost had been attacked before, back in 1856 by another pro-slavery raider, John Reid, in retaliation for John Brown's earlier Pottawatomie Creek raid. Both raids resulted in deaths, including one of John Brown's sons.

The Miner/Cummings families all knew the history and, knowing it, camped the first night as close as they could to the fort, leaving the next morning for Fort Lane, near Lawrence, Kansas. Fort Lane was established by Cyrus' much-admired leader, General James Henry Lane. Like John Brown's fort, it was not much of a fort; just a 4-foot high, rough structure made of limestone. It did have windows called embrasures with the sides slanted out to give its three cannons a wider target range.

Soon after arriving at Fort Lane and after a fire was built and supper begun, Cyrus told the story of his first militia experiences related to destruction of Lawrence, Kansas. He included lots of details and spoke with considerable flair, ending his narration expressing his dedication to Lane, whom he credited with leading the forces freeing Lawrence, voicing with emotion, "I have a deep loyalty to General Lane, and I leave Kansas, as I've mentioned to my sister and Lewis, with regret, regret that I can no longer further help him here. He is our Senator, and I do hope that somehow he comes out of the squabbles in Washington and Kansas with the honor he deserves."

If any of the others held less sanguine opinions of Lane, they didn't speak out. None of them had fought with him, as Cyrus had, and none of them knew him as Cyrus did. Certainly, Lane had his detractors in Kansas including the governor and other high-level government officials and military commanders. Cyrus didn't know what would eventually happen in Kansas regarding Lane; he'd have to wait.

Supper continued quietly for a while as they all settled into eating. Josiah and his sons had managed to bag several rabbits that afternoon, so what might have been a sparse meal had turned into one they would remember fondly as the trip became less and less accommodating. Lewis broke the silence; he wanted to express once again, as he and Elizabeth had when they discussed the Kansas departure with Cyrus, just how successful they had all been in furthering their free Kansas goal. "Think of it, folks, Kansas is a state, a free state, say that again, a free state, and we all helped make it happen. Shall we have a round of applause for ourselves or maybe a drink or two in our honor?" Not much opposition to either suggestion; huzzahs all around and not just a few toasts to the cause.

As they moved on the next day, they got their first hints of what lay ahead. They were entering Indian land and the natives insisted on payment for the intrusion into what was, at the time, theirs. Then, as they approached the Big Blue River, three of their spare horses were stolen. They managed to recapture them, and no one got injured. They moved on and reached what was colloquially called "Dobe Town", because there was nothing to build houses with except adobe. At least there were supplies, and they knew they needed to stock up with food and feed for the animals to prepare for leaner times ahead. Then on to Marysville, Kansas where they had one final chance to stock up before heading across lands with only Indians as inhabitants. As an alert against native attacks, they posted guards every night.

After reaching the Platte River, a courier caught up with them, bringing news that some of their friends, well behind, wanted to join up with them. They stayed and waited a week at Deer Creek, a comfortable place with driftwood to burn and grass for their animals. Once their friends arrived, they allowed a day of rest for the newcomers and then followed the Platte River toward Fort Laramie, now with a party enlarged by four men, three women, and two boys. One of the new wagons measured how far they went each day using an instrument stuck on the front wheel. At the end of a hard day, it raised spirits a bit to know how much progress they had made. The additional people and wagons helped make their journey feel a bit safer, but they did not feel safe enough for dangers they knew might lie ahead. A week later they reached an established trail that much larger groups used, so, fearing the dangers, they waited two more weeks until a sizable wagon train arrived which they joined.

On May 20 they began their wagon train journey west with a total of sixty-five men, eight women, two boys, and a 12-year-old girl. Back at Deer Creek, they had gotten their first news of the Civil War by telegraph; not good news at the time for the North. Not good except for one small item from Kansas that raised Cyrus' spirits considerably. He related his version of the news at supper to his family and to those friends who had joined them at Deer Creek. Even some of the new wagon train folks listened in. "Look, it's not good news for the North, true, but one thing is to the good; our Kansas forces will get a military leader we can count on to pursue our cause aggressively. The telegram says that General James Blunt is in charge now. That's Lane's man, he'll fight like Lane, take the war to Quantrill, Reid, and his kind instead of sitting back and waiting for more disasters in Kansas."

There was general agreement that taking on the war against advocates of slavery in Missouri or even in Kansas or wherever anti-slavery troops found them was good, but several voices were heard expressing caution. This was war; Kansas would suffer attacks, maybe even more ferocious than those they'd experienced so far. Some even still expressed fears that aggression would breed aggression, though most knew that war meant exactly that.

The next day they continued their journey along the South Platte River eventually passing into the Black Hills of the Dakota territory. The road became worse and, of particular concern, narrow. There was no place to circle the wagons or to set them up properly if attacked by any of the Native American tribes in the area. But luck rode with them, and they escaped harm, as they often did under similar circumstances. On leaving the Black Hills, trail conditions improved. They came upon a creek with water and grass for their animals. The area turned out to be a fine place for Elizabeth Cummings to ride her trusty saddle mule, Bettie, around camp, one of her favorite forms of transport.

They crossed the North Platte River and followed the Sweetwater River to Independence Rock, spending a day there inspecting what appeared to be a huge boulder covered with names of previous visitors including one dating back to 1843, the date of Fremont's first trip, and another from 1850 with the name of a Cummings relative. Further up the Sweetwater they reached what is called Devil's Gate, and when a couple of the party explored it, they found out why. They described having to drop down five or six feet in some places, in order to continue on the trail, not knowing how they would get back up. There were sights they described as astounding. The Sweetwater ran through solid rock having cut a gap nearly 400 feet deep. Compared to the depth, the width between the cliffs looked narrow enough for a man to leap across, but only if you looked far enough ahead toward the end of its 1500-foot length. Fortunately, no one tried; the width is actually 50 feet at its narrowest.

The next 1000 miles took them across the bleak prairie lands. There wasn't even fuel to burn to prepare meals so they used buffalo chips, storing them dry so they would burn when needed. They made it across the Rocky Mountains with no trouble, camping on the Western slope at Pacific Springs. Here they had sage brush to burn, better than buffalo chips for sure. Conditions improved; they found grass for grazing, reasonable trails, deer and antelope to eat, and water to drink.

Further on, though, the Green River had risen and blocked their way, preventing attempts to ford. There was a ferry. With so many people now heading west, operating ferries had become quite lucrative or, for travelers, expensive. Just to make matters worse, this ferry was broken; it took days to repair. Once they got across, they found a trading post, which they soon discovered was also quite willing to price gouge all travelers. 30 cents a pound for flour. At the beginning of their journey, a bushel of corn cost 15 cents.

For travelers the term entrepreneur took on a negative meaning. However, the trading post did have one much appreciated item—a guidebook for the rest of their journey.

Most of the wagon trains went on to Idaho; a few split off and headed for California. The guidebook certainly painted a far too rosy picture of the way forward. The roads described as good turned out to be little more than trails a horse might make; Native American passages were not wagon wonderful. Then they faced more problems. They reached Deep Creek, and this time there was no ferry at all. It took them days to fill the creek with rocks, so the wagons had a chance of crossing. The Guidebook? Well, some just wanted to heave that pack of lies into the creek. Traveling did improve for a while and then more crossings tested their ingenuity again. One shallow river crossing with an uneven, rocky bed required pulling wagons and their contents across separately with ropes, another required hefty payments for crossing on a bridge that more of those entrepreneurs had built.

So far the various tribes of Indians had simply watched them or charged them money to pass through their lands, but at this point, one tribe finally attacked. The wagon train was well prepared, having had the full trip to plan, and they easily circled the wagons and thwarted the attack. Other tribes proved helpful when they reached the Snake River. A very busy ferryman agreed to take their wagons across but not the horses. They ended up hiring the Indians to swim the horses across, a difficult task that required several attempts per horse. At $2.00 a head, the final cost of their 'helpfulness' was nearly enough to leave the Miner/Cummings group broke.

As they continued to follow the Snake River they had to cross the High Desert region, a dry, sage brush covered plains with late August temperatures over 100 degrees. It was hot and dry; and, as if extreme heat and dryness were not enough, a wheel on one of the Cummings wagons took the worst of possible moments to break. They managed to get it back on and the next day repaired the spokes with green willow branches they had happened to bring with them.

There were more rivers to cross, entrepreneurs to pay, and potential Indian hostilities to consider. By the time they reached the Bitterroot River, a pound of flour cost 50 cents. For the Miners and Cummings money was so short they needed to find a way to ford the rivers rather than pay a ferryman, and they even spent some time prospecting for gold, but they knew the threat of an Indian attack meant that they needed to stick with the rest of the wagon train as it moved on. At least the Bitterroot, despite its name, provided them with sweet tasting fish, the first salmon and trout they'd caught after crossing so many rivers. Later they traded with the Indians for smoked, dried salmon and vegetables, too, and yet they lost horses to Indian theft at about the same time. The relationship had its ups and downs.

They all made it to the Touching River where the Miners and the Cummings felt comfortable enough to leave the larger wagon train as it continued to move on. Later that day they were invited to dine in a mission building created and maintained by a missionary to the Indians, Rev. H. H. Spaulding. Cyrus noted that September 27, 1862 was the first meal, indoors, since April 12th. They traveled on toward Walla Walla reaching the Columbia River with Steamboats capable of carrying supplies from Portland. They had to get supplies on credit; they were out of money, but they reached Walla Walla, and there they prospered.

Chapter Eighteen

Coming Together?

Mitchell, Iowa

During the years that various members of their family worked to legally prevent slavery in Kansas and then journeyed on to Walla Walla, Allen and Emeline Miner and their children—Henry, Leander, and Lemuel—spent their days in Mitchell Iowa, having sold their land in Union, Wisconsin. Before Allen and Emeline arrived in Mitchell, Allen and Sophina's daughter Lucinda and her husband James Dudley already lived there as did Lewis Cummings, his wife Elizabeth (Miner), and his father, Josiah. Even Cyrus had spent some time in Mitchell before leaving for Kansas. Allen remained hopeful that someday even more of the family would come together in Mitchell.

Years earlier, members of the Miner, Dudley, and the Cummings families had become active members of the area surrounding Mitchell. As early as 1854 Lucinda Miner and Josiah Cummings were founding members of the area's first church, the Free Will

Baptist Church. Even earlier, in 1852, Josiah Cummings was the first to settle in Mitchell township and by 1854 he platted Mitchell. James Dudley, who had married Lucinda Miner late in 1857, platted the appropriately named Cedar Township town of Dudley in Mitchell County in April. Family members continued to be leaders, active in local politics and holding local offices. A few years later James Dudley served a term as Clerk in Cedar township and in 1861 as sheriff of Mitchell township.

Allen was a farmer and a lawyer, but he was also a savvy investor. He bought land at what the federal government, anxious to expand, priced very attractively and then he sold after development in the areas significantly raised the prices. Once an area became 'established', all prices went up, and at that point it became financially sensible to sell and move west yet again as new land opened up, again at cheap prices. Allen and Emeline's sell and move strategy from the Rock County area of Wisconsin to northwest Iowa was imitated by many. News of opening lands spread rapidly, and those who were in the know and prepared acted quickly and prospered.

Allen knew both the good and the bad involved in westward movement. He'd bought and sold at a good profit several times in Ohio, Indiana, and Wisconsin. But he had come to realize just how bad for Native Americans these deals were. The same government that made the land available at attractive prices did so by first clearing out Native Americans, either by bargaining with them and then usually reneging on the bargain or simply by rounding them up, too often with extraordinary brutally, and forcing them further west.

Allen had a history of experience with Native Americans that made him especially sensitive to just how bad these deals were for them. He'd just missed crossing the route taken by the Potawatomie as they were removed from Indiana and Wisconsin during the infamous Trail of Death. He'd talked with his political friends in Wisconsin about that experience and had thought about looking further into it. He'd known from his youthful experience just how compassionate Native Americans could be when, as a 10-year-old, he'd saved a Seneca youth on the way home from his trip with the militia to Niagara and then been aided by what he had thought were fearsome Seneca warriors. Those were warriors who had refused to be rounded up and sent to reservations, the fiercest of the fierce in his young mind before he experienced just how kind they were to him when he needed help so badly. Those moments had become transformational for him as he grew and came to understand those youthful experiences more fully.

Allen had talked often with his friends, Sophina, and their children about his Native American experiences and sympathies, but he had not been as open about those feelings with Emeline and had not pressed the issue with their children. Of course, Emeline, as a smart and sensitive soul, knew how Allen felt about Native Americans and their treatment by the government. But she had reason to avoid the subject, too; her late husband, Henry Caldwell, had served in the US Army in Wisconsin and had been in the conflicts that so troubled Allen. In the Winter of 1857, as they sat one evening warmed by a hearty fire and relaxed by some hard apple cider, the subject finally surfaced.

Three-year-old Lemuel sat on Emeline's lap, while six-year-old Leander and nine-year-old Henry sat on the floor constructing what began to look like a barn out of the blocks of wood that Allen had cut into various shapes for them. Emeline began, as she had so often before when difficult subjects arose, by asking Allen a simple question but couching it carefully. "Here we are, so comfortable, some of our family with us, others nearby, and relatively well-off, too, thanks to your careful planning and hard work. All good, yes, but I know you have thoughts about what we've done, about, well you know. What are you feeling now?"

Allen certainly knew. But he, too, decided to tread lightly. Smiling he sent his wife a kiss, the kiss flying from him to her, saying, "Yes, we are lucky to be here, to have family with us, to be as comfortable as we are. But, you know, you're also right that I have what I can only describe at this point, well, as what? Misgivings? Sounds a bit weak. I wonder, did I ever mention to you the Neil's Creek Anti-Slavery Society's statement about the congressional treatment of Native Americans? It remains so clear in my mind; think I can almost quote it. 'Congress has waged war against Indian tribes within our borders who if unmolested would have been peaceable and unoffending.' Right. Not sure society members had the Potawatomie in mind, but it sure applies to them. They had several agreements with the federal government and congress broke them all. And then, well you know that story, the Trail of Death. They sure were 'molested'."

Emeline sat back attempting to look relaxed and succeeding to some extent, nodded and then, as she was about to respond, Henry jumped up, knocking over the blocks, and exclaimed excitedly, "What story, tell me."

Leander broke in, too, " Poota what?"

Allen responded, not as sternly as he might have. "Henry, Leander, your mother was about to speak; you interrupted. Tell you the short version now, maybe more later, OK? That's Potawatomie, incidentally. They were promised compensation for a right of way, a highway, through their territory; instead, they ended up being forced from their land, forced brutally. Now let's hear what your mother was about to say."

Emeline took the cue. "Well, yes, 'misgivings', as you said, that's a bit weak for me, too. Henry and I, married for years, never talked about his involvement in battles or skirmishes with natives, if there were any. It was as if army life was a separate existence for him. It hurt me that we didn't, I must admit. Makes me glad we are talking now."

Allen, pleased, responded, "I'm glad, too; lots on my mind and no one better to share it with than you. I should have known that. But first, Henry, it's bedtime for your brothers. See them to bed and then you can return."

Allen didn't wait for Henry's return before beginning to bring Emeline up to date on his thinking about what had just happened in nearby Iowa and in land to the north in Minnesota. It all came pouring out. "Anyway, think of this. Pretend you're part of a Sioux tribe. You survive and provide for your people by hunting and fishing over a wide area. Other tribes, well, sometimes you must fight with them. Beats me why, but you do. Maybe because you want to hunt or fish there, and they want to hunt or fish there, too. Then, quite suddenly, compared to the thousands of years your people have lived this way, other people, White people, arrive and set up boundaries completely without meaning, incomprehensible things called territories and states with rules that make no sense. Some of these people don't seem to mind your being around; even seem friendly. Allow the hunting, fishing, and moving about that you do, no objections. Others complain. Something about growing things and ruined crops. They even build enclosures to keep their animals in or to keep the animals you hunt out. Insist that you avoid these enclosures. You can't move around freely anymore. Even the bison you depend on dwindle, over hunted now that these other people are swarming in. Anger escalates; you're angry, they're angry. Accusations escalate, you're stealing, they say; you retaliate, and maybe even do end up stealing. Sounds all too human to me."

Henry got back just in time to hear the line about anger but just sat and waited to hear more.

"So, what happens?" Allen continued, "Spirit Lake happens. Last winter was mighty cold. Hard for hunting and fishing and ranging over wide areas. The Sioux run out of food; they're starving. Several years earlier they'd agreed to a treaty with the US government, having been convinced it would help them through the hard times they saw coming, hard times like this last winter. Well, it didn't help. A chief's brother ends up killed by an angry settler. The chief and a small band of followers retaliate. Lots of settlers in isolated cabins killed. Women were kidnapped. Nothing good came of it, and we live on what had been their hunting and fishing range and we prosper. Just can't quite square it all with my conscience."

David summed it up. "It's not fair."

Emeline agreed and added, "Sure fits with what you've been feeling, darling, but I don't know what we can do about it."

Allen responded, "Not much. All I do is think about what I've heard about the treaty. Got to thinking what I'd have done if I had been advising or representing the Sioux as the treaty was presented to them. Couple of simple thoughts. Did they have a competent translator? Can't imagine how legal language can be translated, even by a good translator. Heard that there were fur traders involved that wanted a cut of the promised payments for the land the Sioux were ceding to the government. Yearly annuities were supposed to be paid to the Sioux. How'd that get funded? In Washington, I suppose. But was it funded? Did anybody check on that? Some land was set aside for Sioux hunters. Was it enough for hunting? Not hardly, I've heard. Were they supposed to become framers? Heard that was the plan. 'Civilize' them, I guess. Who would provide equipment and training? Wonder how that worked out. I'm guessing that the Spirit Lake massacre of settlers is at least part of the answer; it didn't work out."

"Which", Emeline added, "brings up another question. Is Spirit Lake the last of Sioux attacks? Sounds doubtful."

Allen agreed. "Fortunate that we are far enough away from the reservations, far enough so I figure we are not in danger, at least."

Mitchell Reunion 2 - Not to Be

Allen and Emeline had hoped for a complete family reunion in Mitchell County, Iowa. Some of those who traveled from Kansas to Walla Walla, Washington in 1862 had thought of going to Mitchell but either ended up elsewhere or remained in Walla Walla. Even Josiah, who was one of the founders of Mitchell, remained in Walla Walla until he died in 1874. Elizabeth and Lewis didn't return, either, though before their Kansas adventure, in the mid-1850s, they had spent several years in

Mitchell, and Lewis had established a mercantile business, another reason for his family to return.

Cyrus, the rambler, continued his wandering, having started the perfect business for someone who likes to get around and see places and meet people—hauling freight. Working first out of Walla Walla, Washington and then Marysville, California, Cyrus established routes to Idaho and Nevada. The Nevada route took him across the California/Nevada territorial boundary to Washoe County, Nevada and Virginia City. In April 1863, Cyrus, after miles on dusty trails called roads by some, stopped into the local Virginia City tavern. As he always did on such potentially relaxing and congenial occasions, he struck up a conversation with several men seated at a large, rough-hewn table toward the back, enjoying an afternoon of extended leisure.

As the conversation progressed, another man joined the group. He was impeccably dressed; white button-down shirt with a slightly off-white vest and a tan suit jacket topped off with a velvet collar and wide lapel with pants to match. He was bushy haired, neat not tangled; his mustache trimmed. He introduced himself to Cyrus as Samuel Clemens; others there, locals all, knew perfectly well who he was. One of them, though, who couldn't help kidding the well-known jokester, called out, "or Mark Twain, known to us all as a fellow who will sink that low for a story."

Another among the group couldn't help himself either, "'Story'? No, fables from our very own confabulator."

Laughter was general, and even before Samuel could get in a witty word or two, Cyrus had his say; "Can't say I'm too particular—a story, a fable, even the fabulous, I'm delighted to listen. Told a tale or two myself from time to time."

"Good man," Samuel responded, "We'll have to get together and spin a few without these—what shall we call them— 'what really happened' dullards around."

No telling what tales might have been told on the spot, if the clock hadn't chimed reminding Samuel that he was running out of time to finish an article for his paper, the Virginia City Territorial Enterprise. "Got to go, y'all. Say, Cyrus, come along with me; might need some help making a 'story' fabulous."

"I'm with you." Cyrus was up and out of there, delighted with his new acquaintance.

On the way to the newspaper office, Cyrus retold the story of the Indian attack on his wagon train to Walla Walla, adding whatever he thought would enhance the tale, now that he felt so completely free to do so, saying, "The attack was ferocious; Indians on all sides, an arrow struck within inches of my head. I was lucky to escape with my scalp, others not so lucky, even a mother and her child torn away from the wounded father. Still haven't heard from them."

Samuel responded simply by saying, "Well, interesting, lots can happen during an attack like that, and given all the excitement, stories are bound to differ. Got an Indian attack story myself I published recently. We could go over it some when we get to the office. Oh, wait, the Indians die in my story, perhaps we'll make their end a bit more exciting."

Samuel had referred to the piece just written called "Horrible Affair." It told of a report that "a noted desperado" had been seen running into a tunnel up in Gold Hill after killing two police officers. Samuel wrote that several citizens pursued the desperado to the mouth of the tunnel but felt uncomfortable confronting such a man in the dark and narrow space. Instead, they sealed the entrance and waited for someone who was obligated to take on such a dangerous encounter. The next day, when a posse arrived, they unsealed the tunnel and found five dead Indians killed by the foul fumes after the tunnel had been sealed—three men, one woman, and a child dead but no desperado.

Once they reached the office, Samuel dug out the story and Cyrus read it. Cyrus couldn't help feeling concerned about the ending. At the end Samuel speculated that sealing the tunnel suggested good initial intentions but with bad consequences.

The bad consequences? Not the dead Indians according to the article. Samuel ignored the dead Indians and wrote that it would be bad only if the desperado, dead or at least mentally impaired, did not get a fair trial. Cyrus felt the need to respond without offending, "Got to come up with a more exciting ending. Two of the Indians were alive enough to shoot arrows at the posse and wound a couple before being shot to death. The posse, of course, didn't want to let it be known they had been wounded by a couple of enfeebled Indians, so they'd made up a story to cover that embarrassment. What do you think?"

Samuel responded with an outright burst of laughter. "Got to say I like your ingenuity, but I'm thinking that might be a bit much to sell."

With that Samuel told Cyrus he really did have to get back to work. They parted, promising to get together again. That was not to be. Samuel left for San Francisco a month or two later and Cyrus got busier than usual with his hauling.

Chapter Nineteen

Marysville?
Mitchell?

Allen and Emeline enjoyed the company of their family members who were already settled in Mitchell or had moved into the area shortly after their arrival. Allen and Sophina's second son, Ichabod, had arrived a year before Allen and Emeline, settling on land there in 1854 and purchasing it in 1855. Land and census records show that Ichabod married Cordelia in 1855. Sophina's uncle, Ebenezer Temple, and his family along with Mary Amanda Miner, Allen and Sophina's 7th child, moved to nearby Cedar township, Mitchell County, in 1860. Mary (later called Mercy) married Milton Rice Dudley in 1862. So, there they were, Allen and Emeline with their young children Henry, Leander, and Lemuel, Ebenezer Temple and his family, Milton and Mercy Dudley, and David and Lucinda Miner—at least some family living in and around Mitchell to cheer them.

But family life took heart wrenching turns in those same years; Ichabod died in the first half of 1856 at age 27 of an illness that medical experts of the time were unable to diagnose. Ichabod's wife, Cordelia, remarried a year later and moved back to Wisconsin. David also died in Mitchell within a few years of Ichabod's death. Lucinda married James Newton Dudley, brother of Milton Rice Dudley in December 1857, adding another family member, but nothing could alleviate the loss of Ichabod and David.

Far to the west of Mitchell, Iowa, other members of Allen's family began to center their lives in Marysville, in Yuba County, California. Allen and Sophina's oldest son, Jacob, had his ice and teaming businesses there that continued to prosper, and, naturally enough, his success became a draw for relatives. In 1860 Jacob married Cavy Johnston. In 1852 she had traveled to the general area by wagon train from Iowa with her family. Her father Charles B. Johnston captained the train; he was a well-known leader. The Johnston family settled in various locations within Yuba County but ended up in Marysville.

If others in the family decided to make the trip from Mitchell to Marysville, no one could have been better prepared to lead them across the plains, still inhabited by potentially hostile Native Americans, than Charles. Charles had traveled often across the area and knew his way around. Not even Cyrus traveled from here to there as often as Charles did. He also knew well the Sauk tribe that ruled the area; he'd been captured during the Black Hawk War of 1832 and would have lost his life then and there had he not earlier befriended the Sauk chief Black Hawk himself. The chief risked dissension amongst his warriors by providing Charles with a horse so he could escape. The 1852 wagon train trip that brought the captain and his family, including Cavy, eventually to Marysville faced only one attack near the Platte River, only a skirmish really; quite likely only a skirmish because of Captain Johnston's expertise.

Lucinda and James Dudley remained in Mitchell for only a few years before leaving for Marysville in 1865. One would think that a wagon train trip from Iowa to Marysville, CA would have become much easier and safer than the one led by Charles Johnston thirteen years earlier in 1852. Trails would have improved; local tribes would have come to accept western travelers or would have been so beaten back as to hardly pose the level of danger they had previously. Seems reasonable but not correct. James and Lucinda decided that she and their three small children should not endure or risk the wagon train trip. Reports from others who recently made similar trips from Iowa to California were not encouraging. Children still suffered and even died, and Sioux tribes still attacked the wagon trains. Their fears were reasonable.

James and Lucinda discussed the trip often but had difficulty figuring out how they could get their young family to Marysville. Discussions developed into plans late one winter evening in February 1865. It had been one of those fine Winter days, already hinting of Spring, warm enough so that the fire wasn't needed for heat, only for cooking. They tended to keep it going during the day with a few logs added as needed then let it go out. Children were asleep for the night; even the baby didn't need them right away. They were free to plan.

Lucinda began the discussion; she'd heard enough from Jacob's wife Cavy about the 1852 trip across the plains to wonder how she could possibly manage. "You know how much this trip you want to make worries me, trudging along thousands of miles across plains and over mountains. I just can't see how I can manage with one child probably still nursing and the other two so young they need me all the time. Cavy's told me just how rough it was when she made the trip with her father; she was young, fourteen, I think, without children, and yet she suffered from the walking and from the exertion of doing routine camp chores once they camped. You know, those chores expected of women on the trail."

James knew how worried she was and had thought about it for some time. "Right; I don't think you should try to go with me."

That was not the best way to start; he was interrupted immediately. "What, you want me to stay here with your three young children by myself while you go off to golden California?"

"No, no. First, you know I'm not going for gold, just think I'll find opportunities there, maybe a teaming business like Jacob's.

And, land's cheap. But of course, I'll want you and the children there with me. Just how to do it, that's the question."

Lucinda, surprised, wondered. They hadn't discussed other possibilities. She threw up her hands and simply said, "So, how?"

James kept his voice calm and his response brief. "Well, there is another way to get to California; by ship."

Lucinda, a little upset with James' calm tone while she remained annoyed, answered a bit briskly. "By ship? I suppose you've already looked into how that might be done."

James, unable to avoid a slight smile, responded, "Well, yes, I've given it quite a bit of thought, and, well, I have a plan. If you're willing of course." Pursed lips and a nod was all he got.

"We could go by coach down to Council Bluffs where you could board a steamboat for New Orleans and from there pick up a clipper around Cape Horn to San Francisco. Once in San Francisco either I could pick the four of you up and travel with you to Marysville or maybe you and the children could just take a stage couch."

Lucinda, her head now spinning, responded. "Now that's some plan. Sounds like a long trip. Why not cut it down some by going across Panama? I've heard that's possible."

James had his answer ready. "Well, thought about that, too. First, it would mean an uncomfortable transfer from ship to whatever land transportation is available. Heard it isn't all that great. Then the trip across the isthmus on really lousy roads. Or there is a railroad, not sure about the schedule for passengers. Then back on a ship. Would you have to wait around for one at an inn or something? All that trouble and I haven't gotten to the worst part. The area is known for plagues of all sorts; malaria, yellow fever, and more. We just can't chance it. Trying to think of your safety and the children's. The Cape Horn route seems best. I figure it will take you about six months and my trip across the plains about five. Would give me a little time to get set up there."

Lucinda softened, feeling his concern and appreciating the thought he'd given his plan. She simply said, "Give me some time to think this over. There's a lot to consider."

Off to Marysville - Separate Ways

In early April 1865 James and Lucinda's plans were finalized with only a few changes. They decided they'd travel down to Council Bluffs, Iowa together and leave from there on their separate and very different journeys. Council Bluffs was a major steamboat center for travel up and down the Missouri River, especially for those headed to and from the newly discovered gold mines in Montana. It also served as a major departure point for wagon trains headed west on the Mormon Trail. Once there Lucinda and their three small children would stay in a local hotel, along with all they'd need for their trip. James would make steamboat arrangements for one headed to St. Louis, where, as stateroom passengers paying good fees, steamship company personnel would in turn see that Lucinda and the children were transferred safely to a New Orleans bound vessel and eventually to the ship that would carry them around Cape Horn to San Francisco. James would load into his wagon the bulk of what they would need for their new life in Marysville.

Once James and Lucinda finalized their plan, they told the rest of the family. Several family discussions followed, and soon other family members planning on the trip to Marysville decided that leaving from Council Bluffs made sense to them, too. There were so many wagon train convoys leaving from there that they could be assured of joining one in short order. Many pioneers came from the East, so the business of getting wagons and people across the Missouri river at Council Bluffs had become a competitive business; that competition meant prices were reasonable and ferry availability not at all a problem.

For Lucinda, worried as she was about her young children, it seemed the wagon trip to Council Bluffs might well be more uncomfortable than the months traveling by steamboat down the rivers and eventually by ship to California. She was more than happy to have more members of the family with them should any difficulties arise during what would be nearly a month in a wagon jolting its way over what she imagined would be rough and pot filled roads on the way to Council Bluffs. On the other hand, for steamboat passengers like herself, she knew that form of transportation had evolved over the years and developed excellent accommodations with state rooms on the upper deck and even entertainment and childcare options. After all, passengers were now a sought-after source of funds, adding significantly to what the companies derived from freight.

So, in mid-April, James, Lucinda and their children, along with three Dudley brothers, Allen and Cyrus, left Mitchell for Council Bluffs. Not one of the female relatives went with their husbands on this trip, perhaps as leery as Lucinda had become of so many hard months by wagon train and not as willing or able to travel around Cape Horn by ship. Lucinda would certainly miss the women. She'd miss their companionship and the help with her young children they had so often provided. Allen Miner, James, Milton Rice Dudley (husband of Amanda Miner Dudley), along with two other Dudley brothers, Thomas and William, did go. Cyrus had managed to join them after planning a conveniently timed hauling trip over the recently finished Mullan Road between Walla Walla and Fort Benton, followed by a lengthy detour so that he could reach Mitchell in time to share the adventure from its beginning, despite already living in Yuba County, California, the ultimate destination. Cyrus enjoyed travel and adventure, and he couldn't resist this one with his father and brothers-in-law.

Cyrus, as the most experienced traveler, led the way from Mitchell to Council Bluffs as guide and scout. He had a medium sized Conestoga wagon pulled by oxen, the ideal combination for hauling on the trails he often used. Others in the group, mostly farmers as they were, simply modified their farm wagons by adding bent-wood ribbing holding canvas tops to shield supplies and themselves from the weather. Most figured their field horses would serve as draft horses to pull their lighter wagons and the goods, expecting to save on weight by walking themselves or riding spare horses, if they had any.

No one they knew had recently traveled the roads they took to Council Bluffs, so they planned cautiously. If they met with wet or severely gutted roads, they all figured Cyrus would be best prepared to handle the situation and then be able to leave his wagon and come back on foot to guide the rest. As it turned out all this caution was unnecessary, though it was comforting for all. The roads had undergone considerable improvement in recent years as stage couch travel and mail routes became established along them. Early spring rains had caused wet portions, but nothing they couldn't get past with relative ease. They made good time with much less jolting than expected, arriving on the east side of the Missouri River days earlier than expected.

James and Lucinda had decided that she and the children would settle in across the Missouri River in Omaha, Nebraska so they could stay in the Herndon House Hotel, a luxury hotel of the best sort. They all went across together, leaving the wagon with Allen, allowing a comfortable trip across the river without the wagon and all the supplies. Once his family was settled in the hotel, James returned to Council Bluffs to meet with the Captain of the A. J. Majors; Capt. Wright had just returned from his Spring trip north to supply the mining country. Those Spring trips were what James and Lucinda had counted on, knowing that Spring rains swelled the Missouri River far enough north to allow steamboat travel to Fort Benton, the last possible point reachable by steamboats carrying gold seekers, supplies, and mining equipment for Montana. They figured the timing would be right to catch one taking a return trip.

James met with Captain Wright who was eager to make a good impression with his passengers and was more than accommodating. He assured James that Lucinda and the children would get the best of care aboard his steamer. He showed James the upper deck stateroom the family would enjoy with its view of the river and quite comfortable furnishings. He introduced James to the childcare assistant, a mild-mannered young woman who seemed delighted at the prospect of having Lucinda and the young children on board. And he showed James the dining and entertainment areas, more than ample for sure. James returned across the river and told Lucinda about what he'd arranged. Lucinda was delighted, mischievously whispering in his ear, "Sounds pretty fine to me. You enjoy bumping along the trails while I glide to California." James simply smiled with satisfaction.

James saw Captain Wright one more time before leaving on his own journey while Lucinda remained comfortable in the hotel with the children. The captain assured James that he would retrieve his family from the hotel and see them safely to St. Louis. Once there he'd take them to another hotel and arrange passage to New Orleans. That had been the plan, but the reassurance was appreciated.

Before James left, the captain told him a tale or two. He had just passed the wreck of the Bertrand on his way back from Benton. He relayed what he'd seen and learned as news from several other sources spread. The Bertrand had hit a snag and ended up stuck on a sandbar not too far from shore. As the captain put it, "If there's any luck in such cases, you know loss of ship and life happen often up there; if, I say, then near to shore is lucky and a sand bar is lucky. Many swam for shore, others were able to use the ship's yawl, launched quickly by the mighty fine crew. There are any number of ways for steamers to get in trouble up there; that snag that may have done in the Bertrand, logs or trees completely under water; hit one wrong and that's it. Then, if the river doesn't get you, the Sioux might just decide to attack, you know, for whatever reason occurs to them. Happening often enough to warrant caution."

James sent a message to Lucinda assuring her that all the plans were in place. All they needed to do for now was relax and enjoy themselves and wait for Captain Wright to get in touch. Somehow, he did not mention the Bertrand story and certainly not the Sioux, though both concerned him. He figured she didn't need to hear about wrecks, and, since he was also headed into Sioux country, he'd not bring that up either. He might as well have mentioned both; she already knew all there was to know. Some of those Bertrand passengers, after the wreck, had made their way down to the Herndon House, and the story was the talk of the place. There was no lack of Sioux and Crow uprising stories either. In a note back to James she sent her love but did not mention the stories. She did let him know how much the children missed him and how often she had to reassure them that they would see him as soon as they arrived in Marysville. She also failed to mention something else she thought might be true. She'd missed her cycle, usually quite regular. Was she pregnant? She figured he didn't need that thought to add to his worries about her.

James and the rest of those journeying with him left a couple of days later, linking up with a large wagon train headed out along the Mormon trail. Meanwhile, Lucinda discovered that she would have company crossing the Missouri to the steamboat and then on her ride down to St. Louis. Captain Wright had made similar arrangements with others staying at the Herndon Hotel; several were women, two with children. The captain picked them all up, along with their belongings, making a single trip across the Missouri and then seeing that they were comfortably accommodated once on board. For Lucinda, those belongings included one item no one else had—her sewing machine. Sewing machines were expensive and uncommon, having come into mass production only about 10 years prior. Months sitting around on the steamboat with only the children to care for, no meals to prepare and even with some help with the children, she knew she would have lots of time to sew.

One of the women with children, Mary Gilbert, was headed to New Orleans and then on to San Francisco. The common destination and the steamboat and ship trips there meant they had much to discuss and quite naturally became friends as their plans unfolded. Both women had made the same decision for the same reasons; they would take the longer route around Cape Horn rather than risk the shorter Panama crossing. As James had argued when he and Lucinda made their plans, bad transportation across Panama and outbreaks of malaria, yellow fever, and other diseases there made the longer trip the better one. That kind of news got around, and once Lucinda and Mary mentioned their plans at the hotel, they heard many corroborating stories. Both had very young children to consider. Lucinda had William and Mary had Ezra, both nearly one year old. They also had two-year-olds, Lucinda had Abraham, and Mary had Oscar. With the health of the four young ones, Lucinda's five-year-old Jacob, and themselves to consider, they had little doubt that the long way really was the best way.

The A. J. Majors left the next morning on a sunny spring day of the sort that cheers the spirit after the long, cold winter. Lucinda couldn't help thinking of what she had said to James about their separate trips, and as she sat on the deck, watching the shore glide by, she mentioned the conversation to Mary. "So fine here; told my husband, before we parted, 'sounds pretty fine to me. You enjoy bumping along the trails while I glide to California'. And here I am gliding along with good company—you and my five-year-old Jacob. No need to coddle William right now. Don't even need to hold him. He's with little Abraham, in the care of the childcare lady, along with your two. So good. Wonder if James is skinning some just slaughtered rabbit for lunch? What's on the menu here? Forgot to check."

Mary couldn't help laughing and then responded, "Not rabbit for sure, maybe fresh caught fish or, say, whatever specialty the cooks, not us, think up. We might have to get up and check that menu. Or, maybe we just sit here until lunch time and find out then."

"Oh," Lucinda responded, "I do like the way you think. I'm for 'just sit here'. Wait a minute, what's that? An Eagle, right? At that Jacob jumped and exclaimed excitedly, "That's four we've seen just today!"

Lucinda continued, "Right, we'll just sit here and glide on down the river, watching the eagles and whatever else we see."

At roughly the same time, Lucinda's husband, James, was not skinning a rabbit. His chores were not that simple. He was out with the advance hunting party, as he would be often in the days ahead, hoping to down something a lot larger than a rabbit. The whole wagon train needed to eat; deer or even buffalo would be more like what they'd need to feed their own group and as many others as they could. Cyrus joined him, and they got lucky within the first few hours, dodging rattlesnakes and taking down a deer. They gutted it in the field and hauled it back to camp for preparation. They were too busy to watch for an eagle, if there was one, and they did not linger in comfortable chairs. Midday meal? Taking time in the middle of the day to make a fire and cook that deer was not sensible. They would prepare that fire in the cool of the evening when they had time to cook. They settled for what had become the common noon fare, breakfast leftovers of dried pork and bread.

That evening they made the fire, having collected whatever fuel they could find along the way, after the many wagon trains that had preceded them and had taken much of what had been available. Cyrus had added some fuel to his supplies, having remembered how bad the problem had been on his earlier trip from Kansas. So far, though, they had found enough good wood along the way. No need yet for Cyrus' stash or, thank the Lord, buffalo chips. That evening went well. The venison was just fine roasted over a large fire. Several women smiled as their children danced and sang, the children unwinding after a day of having to walk too fast beside the wagons, their short legs making it difficult to keep up. They needed to celebrate; they needed warmth and good food; and once they were done, they needed sleep more than anything else. The animals ate well, too; in early May the grasses that had become available for grazing in April were still plentiful. As the sun went down, James felt almost as good as Lucinda had all day.

Long Way to Go- Through Better or Worse

Days passed, weeks passed, and James and Lucinda continued to experience what they had early on; Lucinda comfort, James hard days eased only around sundown. When Lucinda and the children reached St. Louis, the captain proved as good as his word, perhaps even better. The hotel was fine, but what a surprise he had for them all when he took his charges down to see the steamer accommodations he had arranged. They found this steamer even more extraordinary than the A. J. Majors.

This was the new "Queen of the River", the M. S. Mepham, described as, "A 'no expense spared' boat, with a Pickering grand piano and oil paintings by Mat M. Hastings of St. Louis; chinaware in the buffet with gold design from Landon & White, silverware from Rogers & Smith, other furnishings from A. T. Stewart, all of New York. The Mepham also had an extensive bridal chamber as well as a large spread eagle on the pilot house, carved by T. G. Bering of Philadelphia. Andrew Ackley superintended the outfitting, and the Mepham had crowds of visitors just to look at her as she passed through Pittsburgh and Cincinnati on her way to St. Louis."

They were all introduced to the ship's master, Captain A. St. Clair Thomasson, who pointed out many of the stylish enhancements while emphasizing the amenities. More good news followed. They would leave the next day. One more afternoon and night in the hotel then off to New Orleans. Lucinda whispered to Mary, as the tour ended, "I think I'll just skim over this when I get to talk to James about my trip. Don't want to crow."

Mary responded, smiling, "Right, phrase it gently somehow."

So, while Lucinda and Mary continued traveling with their children basking in the luxury the M. S. Mepham provided, James soldiered on—walking most of the day to save the spare horses from overuse, hunting, dressing deer, and yes, even a rabbit or two or three, and building fires, even when the fuel became scarce, and the use of buffalo chips became too common. Often the children, after their exhausting day of walking, had to stumble out around the campsite looking for dry buffalo chips to be used that night and wet ones to be dried for nightly fires to come. They had to bring the chips, dry and wet, back using whatever bit of cloth that would contain them, often their own outer clothing. That dancing and singing they had managed to enjoy early on in their trip gave way more and more often to simple exhaustion and deep sleep.

The wagon train traveled on average about 10 miles a day, typical for the trails they were taking. Not far into their trek, the route began to follow the Platte River along Native American trails. Cyrus, with his Conestoga and oxen, knew to pace his time on the trail; slow and steady. Others, less experienced, with draft horses and their somewhat lighter, modified field wagons, tended to spring ahead, and sometimes made over 20 miles in a day. Cyrus often warned them such haste might well cost them. He'd seen plenty of exhausted horses, so far gone that they needed to be put down. The remaining horses then tired quickly, unable to handle the effort required of pulling without help from the now dead horses and without help from spares once they had been used up, too. With less horses pulling they slowed down below the average distance. They needed to replace dead horses, using up days finding new ones. The problem was so common that farms along the way made a business of buying exhausted horses, feeding them back to health, and selling the then refreshed horses to those next in need. It was a perfect business for sure; buy exhausted horses at low prices from desperate travelers and sell refreshed horses at a high price, once again to the desperate. Some finally heeded Cyrus' other advice and replaced horses with oxen which were cheaper, more reliable, and, unlike the horses, able to feed on whatever forage was available.

In early July the wagon train approached Fort Laramie. Cyrus, Allen, and the Dudleys were in the lead having followed his 'slow but steady' advice. They'd all switched to oxen for pulling the wagons, too. While waiting for others to catch up and wanting to know whatever news might be of interest or of use, they sent Thomas and William Dudley ahead on their faster spare horses to check with fort personnel and with the telegraph operator to get the very latest. When the men returned, the news they brought quickly spread throughout the train, and it wasn't encouraging.

Cyrus, Allen and the Dudleys—James, Milton, Thomas, and William—chose to make their own fire that evening, instead of joining with any of the larger groups as they often had on other evenings. They wanted to discuss the news more privately and to make their own plans, as necessary, before discussing any decisions more broadly. Cyrus had become somewhat irritated with those outside his close traveling companions who wouldn't listen to the good sense he offered. And those who refused to take his advice didn't care much for him, either. Some were even outspoken about their feelings and one or two were downright nasty. Besides, given the hot days of July, it wasn't the best of times for large gatherings that required a larger cooking fire. They built a small fire, cooked up a duck Cyrus had bagged along the river that morning, and finished their meal with leftovers from breakfast.

They ate, sitting at some distance from the fire on whatever they could find to use for seats. Allen had insisted on bringing his rough wooden chair for such occasions, but the others used whatever came to hand—water buckets, logs or just a pile of prairie grass they would later feed to the oxen or to whatever animals would eat it. Cyrus, often the first to speak, summarized what they all had just heard. "The Sioux and others are attacking along the Northern Platte, not good news. Reminds me of the skirmish we had with them on the trip from Kansas to Washington. Had the best of leaders then, Captain Johnston, and held them off without much trouble. Hope we can do as well if we meet them this time."

Allen, head down, scratched the dusty ground in front of his chair and then spoke hesitantly. "Got to say, I hope we don't meet them at all. Still, I don't know, what if whatever they do just holds us up? We all know we must get over the mountains before winter weather catches us. We started a bit late, April would have been better, grass up by then and we'd have had more time now."

James agreed and added what he meant as encouragement. "Well, true. Glad, though, we'll be breaking off toward California rather than going with those headed for Oregon. We'll all go through the South Pass, not bad at all, really, hear it even has a telegraph now. But then we split, and, well, the California trail, it's better than heading on for Oregon in bad weather, I think."

James's brother, Milton, agreed, adding praise for James' wisdom. "Still, I've got to say, even if all goes well, good we didn't risk women and children. You provided passage for Lucinda and your young ones round the Horn. Good thinking, considering the risks ahead and what we've been through so far."

Easy Ways? - Well...

Lucinda, Mary, and their children enjoyed the trip down the Mississippi as the M. S. Mepham's Captain Thomasson had promised they would. They ate lavishly and enjoyed the entertainment provided. The two friends spent hours just watching the shoreline pass by, sitting comfortably in deck chairs while the children bounced up and down in delight. They spotted eagles, buffalo, ducks, and water loving animals of all sorts. They passed barges, towns, cities, even docked a few times at larger port towns and got to tour and shop. Lucinda managed to buy sewing supplies; cloth she wanted and locally produced shell buttons she found enchanting. The only activity aboard they avoided was gambling; neither could square that sort of thing with their Christian values.

Meanwhile the wagon train proceeded along the Platte River. The general worry about native attacks increased caution causing much slower movement forward, worrying the Miner/Dudley folks even more about the winter weather to come in the mountains. The wagon train widened whenever the plains allowed to add depth in order to thwart any attack from the Crow or Sioux. By mid-July word reached the convoy from travelers headed east that the army had given them warning to move east quickly, citing possible trouble from the Sioux. What that meant to the train heading west troubled them all, and as a result they slowed even further. Slowing did give them more time to hunt, and Cyrus began to think about bigger kills, buffalo maybe.

Cyrus and James, along with Thomas and William Dudley, decided to give that buffalo idea a try, heading out one morning early on horseback with a packhorse to cart the kill back should they be successful, guns ready for buffalo or for possible attack from Crow or Sioux. Under other circumstances they often hunted on foot, but not this time; they needed horses to hunt buffalo and possibly to flee hostile natives. It wasn't long before they stumbled across a single buffalo, separated from the herd and limping as if injured or perhaps wounded. James downed it with a single shot, and, as they hurriedly gutted it and prepared it for the trip back to camp, they noted that in fact it had already been wounded. Even that single shot might have been heard by those they feared. Then, what they feared happened. They spotted at least three natives approaching. Now the wounded buffalo made complete sense, this small hunting party must have done it.

Cyrus, experienced at negotiating with natives, took charge and simply approached them signaling peace. James and his brothers quickly understood and pointed their guns toward the ground. This was a Lakota Sioux hunting party with their own good reason for acting peacefully, other than being outgunned and outnumbered; they'd wandered far into Crow territory, their traditional enemies. They didn't want to attract Crow warriors any more than Cyrus and the Dudleys did.

One of the Sioux, after returning the peace signal, warned the others saying in Lakota, "Careful, we can't win here, and we don't want any noise to reach Crow warriors who might be nearby. Let's just get out of here alive." Much to their surprise, they left with a bit more. Cyrus pointed to them, then to himself, and finally to the buffalo, leaning down and running his finger down the length of the beast, doing his best to indicate that they could split it.

The Lakota hunter who had spoken to the others was clearly the leader. He approached Cyrus slowly copying with his finger the motion Cyrus had used to indicate sharing. He knelt by the buffalo and slowly drew a knife, as clearly as possible signaling his intention to help with preparing for the split. They worked together making short work of the task. Each took their half and managed to hoist their portions onto the extra horses both parties had brought along for the purpose. They signaled peace once again and parted, having experienced one small but wonderful moment of mutual understanding.

By late July, as the wagon train headed for the Platte River Bridge where they intended to cross, they were warned to stop proceeding west entirely by a contingent of soldiers sent for the purpose. A July 26 battle at the North Platte River Bridge left the army unsure about what might happen next, including to wagon trains.

They had to stop entirely. That increased the already widespread fear of the Rocky Mountain winter crossings. The delay could cost them their chance to avoid the serious winter weather quite capable of making portions of the trails impassable. Convoys caught this way, with travelers dying of starvation and some even resorting to cannibalism, made up the legends all knew. The Miner/Dudley families now shared their thoughts and concerns with their fellow travelers but also sat down alone together several times to plan their own next moves. They had heard from the soldiers and from travelers heading east that the Arapaho, the Lakota Sioux, and the Cheyenne had successfully attacked the fort at the Platte River Bridge as well as a nearby wagon train, but that they then headed north.

Several nights into the delay, the Miner/Dudley contingent sat down again over their evening fire and made final plans. Cyrus outlined his thoughts first, "We need to avoid contact with Indians on the warpath; sure would be different from meeting that small hunting party. They're heading north, so we should head south, right? Trouble is, I don't know of any good trails from here south that wouldn't take us too far out of our way."

Allen had a thought. "Why not just head for that Platte River Bridge crossing? It's on our trail anyway and the soldiers seem to have secured it. Far as I can read from what they're saying, aren't they chasing the tribes north of the bridge?"

James added, "Right, that makes the North Platte River Bridge south of the action. Got to say I like that thought." Others agreed.

Cyrus agreed, too, but added, "Just one problem. We've got to convince the soldiers to let us go ahead. I'll talk to them tomorrow morning. As usual, we're in the lead, so we can just split off from the rest. Why don't you all spread out and see if you can get support from others in case the soldiers want larger numbers and won't let us separate from the rest."

Most of Cyrus' plan worked. Though the soldiers were reluctant when Cyrus first spoke to them in the morning, as the day wore on others in the convoy, encouraged after talking amongst themselves and pressed by the Miners and the Dudleys, in turn pressed the soldiers until they relented. Those soldiers, though, thinking of the Miner/Dudley group as leaders, insisted on going with them and on spreading all the wagons out when the landscape allowed, taking every precaution against possible attacks. They certainly weren't about to split the wagon train into two smaller groups, as Cyrus had wanted. But still, Cyrus achieved a lot—a lead position, an army escort and advice, and they were on the move again. Not a bad plan it seemed.

Meanwhile Lucinda, Mary, and the children reached New Orleans without having to plan a thing. Once there, Lucinda did think about promises she had made to keep in touch with her husband. As far as they knew, New Orleans would be the last place before San Francisco to attempt to reach him by telegram. Lucinda and James had discussed that possibility and settled on the South Pass station, well known as a center for telegraph activity, as the best place to send it. She had time in New Orleans before any San

Francisco bound ship arrived, so she took the time to think about what she would say. From the start of her journey, she had suspected that she was with child once again; now she was sure.

She sent the telegram. It was short and to the point, as telegrams needed to be. Just to be sure he knew, even if he missed the telegram, she sent a longer version by mail, assuring him that her care aboard the steamer was excellent and thanking him once again for their decision to have her travel by steamer. She didn't exactly say 'glad I'm not with you hoofing it' but made that point clear enough. She sent the letter to Marysville in care of her brother, Jacob, figuring of all her relatives there, he was the best known locally. Hard to imagine a letter reaching Marysville and not reaching him.

Meanwhile James and his fellow 'hoofers' made good progress to the South Pass. Once they made it through, they pressed on, reaching, faster than they had dared hope, the point where the main California trail split off from the one headed to Oregon. From there some had suggested a shorter route off the main trail, but Cyrus discouraged the thought, having heard that the other trail, though perhaps a time saver, wasn't as easy to travel. Fortunately, all their concerns about winter weather proved just that, concerns not reality. The bad winter came well later in the season. In fact, the only rough part of the journey they encountered was the road to Marysville, once they left the main California trail, simply because the Marysville trail was a side route, not as heavily traveled and therefore not as well maintained.

All felt relief as the much-feared winter trip through the Rocky Mountains came to an end. Just one glitch; no telegram awaited James at the South Pass station. Why? James couldn't imagine that Lucinda wouldn't have sent one from New Orleans as they had planned. Was she OK? The telegraph operators at the pass had mentioned interruptions caused by the Sioux attacks. He clung to that thought. She sent it and it got lost. He just swallowed hard and kept any misgivings to himself.

Chapter Twenty

Welcome to San Francisco

The Emperor

Lucinda, Mary, and their children were alive and well as the ship found its way into San Francisco Bay. They had not caught malaria, yellow fever, or cholera so common in areas they visited, and they were not infected from others who had chosen to take the shorter route across the disease riddled isthmus, several of whom were taken aboard their ship as passengers at Panama City. They did suffer, like many aboard, from various stomach ailments, probably caused by badly preserved meat the ship picked up along the way. A storm around the cape and delays getting to the cape, as they waited to enter small and inefficient ports to pick up scarce supplies, had caused the need for that meat from a source that would have been avoided otherwise. Fortunately, they made up the lost time running up to Panama City and from there to San Francisco. Despite the delays, they made it in the 6 months Lucinda and James had originally calculated, arriving mid-November, now nearly 7 months into Lucinda's fourth pregnancy.

The day they docked was cold for the bay, in the mid-forties, and rainy; not what they would have liked for their much-anticipated arrival, but it was an arrival none-the-less. Lucinda and Mary had anticipated a view of the bay and of other ships in its waters; they didn't get one. But they did get what they wanted way more; a chance to set foot on California land, a state that had become part of their homeland only a few years after their own home state of Iowa. Little did they know what more awaited them. The captain liked surprises, and he had one. Norton I, Emperor of the United States and Defender of Mexico, would be there shortly to meet them and welcome them to his domain.

Mary had heard something of this phenom but not Lucinda. Mary proceeded to explain, "Well, I've heard that San Franciscans have enjoyed encouraging this derelict. He lives on the street, mostly, or sometimes a boarding house for the poor. You'd think after declaring himself Emperor, he'd be living in a mental institution. But no. Instead, citizens support him—feed him and outfit him so he looks the part."

Lucinda smiled enjoying a bit of levity after their leisurely days at sea. "Think I'm going to join in on their fun. Do I bow? Curtsy maybe."

Mary laughed. "As deep a curtsy as you can manage, given your current condition. That's the spirit."

Their levity was interrupted by the captain who sought to prepare his passengers for the arrival of his majesty. He gathered them on the side of the ship facing the dock and repeated the essentials to all, mostly what Mary had told Lucinda with added caution to treat the emperor with exaggerated respect. Most of the passengers reacted by smiling or smirking, but then, within a few minutes or so, they joined in on the spirit of the event.

Just in time as it turned out. The Emperor made his appearance surrounded by an entourage. His outfit was all one could wish. Mary couldn't help commenting, "Look, he's wearing a blue navel jacket, and are those really gold-plated epaulettes? Love the beaver hat with that peacock feather and rosette. I've heard he often wears a sword or walking stick but not today, just an umbrella. Given the weather, that's about the only truly appropriate item. Of course, for an emperor, the whole outfit is so appropriate."

Most passengers managed to control their amusement, some hiding a laugh or two by turning away. Those along the rail, including Lucinda and Mary, curtsied, Lucinda barely but Mary and others quite deeply, as Mary had suggested. The Emperor acknowledged the deference shown with a nod of his regally bedecked head and spoke a few words, "Welcome to my city, center of my empire. Several of my subjects, as you see, join me in inviting you to come ashore and enter our land."

After several moments, once it became clear he would say no more, the captain responded with ample solemnity. "We are privileged to be so royally greeted by the Emperor of the United States and the Protector of Mexico. Long live the Emperor." Cheers erupted from his subjects followed by equally boisterous hurrahs from those aboard the ship. The Emperor then simply turned to leave, executing that turn in what some might have been justified in likening to a pirouette. Subjects followed, and once they were all at a goodly distance, the passengers were free to laugh, snicker, or simply enjoy as they felt appropriate, the crowning moment they had just witnessed.

It was time for the passengers to depart and go their separate ways. The parting, after so many months together, traveling together and enduring together, was difficult for many. Mary and Lucinda would not part, though. Mary's husband, Frank, had reached San Francisco months ago and managed to purchase and set up a home for his family. He was there to greet his wife and their children, but to his surprise and at Mary's insistence, they would be taking in Lucinda and her children until her husband arrived or until the baby arrived. Lucinda tried to convince Mary that she could handle matters herself at the hotel suggested by the captain, the Occidental, but she gave in and went with Mary and Frank saying she expected James to arrive soon.

Meanwhile James had not received the telegram from Lucinda at the South Pass station as they had anticipated. So, when he heard that Jacob had a letter from her for him, the news came as quite a relief. Must have been the Sioux uprising that had caused considerable difficulties with telegram transmissions, and it got lost in the confusion, he thought; the explanation he had hoped was correct. News of a letter was a relief, cut short, though, by reading it. The letter Lucinda had sent him through brother Jacob alarmed him. She had made that whole trip with child, and she was well along by now if she already knew it in New Orleans.

He needed to act quickly, and he did. He decided to go to San Francisco and then take Lucinda and the children back to Marysville by stagecoach as the quickest and gentlest form of transport available. Unfortunately, the stagecoach wouldn't get them from the main road up to Marysville comfortably, and the schedule was quite unreliable, so Jacob arranged to take James's prairie schooner down for that last leg. Elizabeth thought a woman should go along with James to be there to help her younger sister through any complications that might occur, but she couldn't leave her 8-month-old home alone and didn't relish taking him along either. Instead, she thought to ask her sister-in-law, Cavy, Jacob's wife, if she might go. Cavy and Jacob had no children, and all Elizabeth needed to do was ask. Cavy responded on the spot, "Of course I can go and will; we're family and I do love Lucinda. I'm so glad you asked."

Chapter Twenty-One

Marysville

Long Awaited Family Reunion, sort of

Despite their many initial concerns, the stagecoach ride went smoothly, as smoothly as such a trip could go with three small children, a pregnant Lucinda, her fretting husband, and sister-in-law Cavy, all crammed into a stagecoach along with the three other passengers required to fill the coach to capacity. One of the three other passengers added a bit of tension by insisting that the children be quiet. James's scowl quieted him while Lucinda pulled their children more closely to her. One of the other strangers added a slightly subtle jab at the complainer by pointing out that the children's small size meant more room per adult, including the complainer, a hefty fellow who needed that extra room more than anyone else aboard.

As usual on stagecoaches, room for passengers was not the only issue. Baggage took up space, too. Not all that Lucinda had taken with her on the steamers and the ship could go with them by stagecoach. She took as much as the stagecoach would allow; the sewing machine for sure, a few clothes for herself and the kids, favorite toys carefully selected, and some of what she had sewn during those long, pleasant days at sea, including a couple of items for the child to come. Mary had offered to store any excess; Lucinda had gratefully accepted.

The stagecoach got them to the junction of the main road and the less-than-ideal Marysville side road. From there the prairie schooner ride, arranged by brother Jacob, turned out to be especially provident. They would have had to wait four days for the next stagecoach taking that route with enough room for all of them. And the prairie schooner ride itself, carefully navigated by James, was quite bearable; there were no complaints from Lucinda or anyone else. The mood became more and more upbeat as they got closer and closer to Marysville, and when they finally got there, family awaited to cheer their arrival, lifting their spirits to a level that even a word like 'giddy' was inadequate to express.

Nothing ruined the elaborate surprise Lucinda's family had prepared to welcome her more formally. The next day all the relatives now living in and around Marysville would gather and celebrate with a party. But for now, sister Elizabeth took charge reminding all that it was late, Lucinda and her children needed rest, and tomorrow would be the best time for further greetings. James agreed. Back when James and Jacob had discussed the prairie schooner alternative, Jacob, who lived close by in the center of Marysville, had offered his ample home as a place for all to stay initially. It was convenient also because Jacob and Cavy would be hosting the party. Cavy, also tired from the trip, took up the 'let's get them to bed' advice, practically herding Lucinda and the children away. Jacob and James followed, hurried along by Elizabeth.

Fortunately for the party plans, Lucinda and the children took full advantage of their comfortable accommodations, slept soundly and awakened quite late, well rested for the first time after five days and nights of uncomfortable travel. By the time they washed up and dressed, almost all the guests had arrived. Lucinda and the children, expecting to find only James, Jacob, and Cavy, were greeted by quite a crowd. Cavy's family included her father, Charles Johnston, her siblings—William, Mary Ellen, Samuel, Richard, Charles, 10-year-old Laura Sophia, and 8-year-old Francis—along with Mary Ellen's husband, William Dayton Smith. Cyrus Miner and Elizabeth's husband, Lewis Cummings, were a part of the early crowd, too.

In fact, the only late comer was Allen Miner. He woke a bit later than usual, took time for a leisurely breakfast, and spent more time just sitting thinking about how good it was going to be surrounded by so much family. He thought, too, about those who weren't there. He'd taken the 1865 wagon train trip to Marysville, but knowing the dangers, he'd left his younger sons—Henry, Leander, and Lemuel—with their mother, Emeline, back in Mitchell. Though news was sketchy at best, he had heard that dangers from the Crow and even the Sioux were now worse for travelers than what he'd faced. He would enjoy what family he could and patiently await a reunion with his wife and young children once travel became safer.

With his thoughts of this day as one of joy, he arrived late but smiling. The greeting he received met and even surpassed his expectations. Jacob had already set out a chair for him; others crowded around and filled him with talk of Lucinda's journey. All he needed to do was sit and take it all in. Lucinda went over and greeted her father warmly and repeated the accounts she had already given the others.

First, she assured her father that she had rested well and was feeling fine; then she began, "Got to tell you first about our San Francisco arrival. Can you believe we met the Emperor of the United States and the Defender of Mexico? What fun. We curtsied, cheered, and kept from laughing as Himself welcomed us to his dominion, cheered on by his adoring entourage."

Allen laughed and responded, "Heard all about him. Get the San Francisco papers from time to time, and he's mentioned often enough to make one wonder what they drink in that city."

"Well," Lucinda responded with a smile bordering on laughter, "saw more flasks there than I see around here, that's for sure. They must have a water shortage, right?"

"Right."

Lucinda continued, "My traveling friend Mary offered us rooming at her place, but I could see that came as a surprise to her husband. She stood up strong though and insisted; he accepted us and treated us most kindly. Mary even suggested later that she'd help me with the traveling, but James and Cavy arrived the next day, so I didn't need any other help, except to store some things. Someday we'll have to get to San Francisco and retrieve what I left and, for sure, take the opportunity to thank them in some appropriate way. Maybe arrange a personal meeting for them with the Emperor; that would do it, don't you think?"

Allen, enjoying himself, responded, "Can't think of a better way to thank San Franciscans, maybe add in a flask with some home brewed—uh, water."

"Now that's my dad, just the right touch. So, on to the stagecoach ride and the end of the journey, thanks to Jacob. Got to admit that I had my concerns, crowded in a stagecoach—two adults, three children, me with child, and three other passengers; but all bad thoughts melted as we traveled on, and here we are, safe and well, ready to party. Bring on the flasks. Oh, should a lady be saying that?"

All Allen could think at that moment was that if hugging a daughter were appropriate, this would be the time. Instead, he just said, "On with the party; James, please bring me a flask, filled with—you know what."

James responded, "Definitely, and one for me, too. Why don't we pull that chair of yours closer to the spread Jacob and Cavy have laid out on the table. It's all the best we could put together from around here. And, there's a surprise at the end of the table, right where we'll put your chair. I managed to pack some oysters from San Francisco Bay in ice, and they made it just fine."

And quite a spread it was. There were those oysters, but hearty local goods too: roasted wild turkey with cranberry sauce, boiled mutton, smoked meats, soused calves' feet, lots of fish, canned vegetables along with the cold hardy varieties still available fresh in late November before the coming winter weather, turnip salad, corn bread, and desserts—stewed fruit and pies and puddings, plenty for the nearly thirty people there. A number of close friends rounded out the crowd.

Most had been prepared by those attending the day before or several days before. Elizabeth had made her favorite pumpkin pies usually reserved for Thanksgiving but quite right for this event, a true thanksgiving of a special sort. She'd stewed a pumpkin and rubbed it through a sieve, then mixed it with eggs, butter, and milk. For flavoring she added ginger and nutmeg along with a dash of something in the spirit of the event—a glass of brandy. Sugar was added, too, of course. Generally, she followed her favorite recipe from Mary Randolph's, The Virginia Housewife cookbook, placing the mixture in a bottom crust with decorative crust on top, as the cookbook instructed.

Jacob himself had bagged turkeys two days before and spent the time necessary to pull out all the pin feathers, scalding and picking for hours, a task that left his hands chapped. They were oven ready the morning of the party, and that oven helped heat the house. Others labored in the days before and on party day. Lucinda was spared all this planning, preparation, and cooking, as she had been on her trip around the Cape.

Food, flasks, and fun with friends and family—Allen enjoyed, all enjoyed, right on through the afternoon. Lucinda got to joke with this joyful audience about her comfortable trip around the horn, pointing out as many of the jokes she could remember about James's trip compared to her own. She saved her favorite for when

James joined the group around her. "Mary and I sat on the deck as the steamer headed on down toward New Orleans. Watched buffalo, eagles, all sorts of animals. Wondered about what's for lunch. Decided we'd just wait and find out what the chefs had cooked up for us. I believe about the same time, you, James, were hoofing it along in hot July sun, or maybe out trying to get a rabbit or something along with some firewood to cook it up in the evening, if you had any energy left. About right?"

James managed a somewhat smug smile saying, "Oh, no, we ended the day dancing around the fire joyfully eating up that rabbit along with just wonderful breakfast leftovers. That's my story, and I'm going to cling to thinking that's how it was."

Gentle chuckles from those around him. An outright laugh from Lucinda. So it went, an afternoon Allen and those close to him thought of as the best of times. For Allen, though, the memory would become somewhat dulled as days, weeks and months passed with only letters connecting him to his wife and sons he'd left behind. What to do about that pressed heavily on his mind more and more often.

Chapter Twenty-Two

Home

Marysville, Mitchell, Mattole?

Allen's thoughts about his split family—many here in Marysville, California, many back in Mitchell, Iowa—continued to trouble him. His wife, Emeline, and their three youngest children remained in Iowa; letters helped, but still, he was missing so much. Besides, those in Marysville were restless and within a few years several had left. His daughter Elizabeth and her husband Lewis Cummings left quite soon after Lucinda's 1865 "homecoming" party, moving all the way to the Pacific Ocean, settling in the Mattole valley. By 1866 Lucinda and James joined Elizabeth and Lewis in Mattole, and by 1867 Lewis took a preemption claim on some fine farming land there, allowing him a claim to buy that land at a low federal price once he developed it. He began right away improving it to solidify his claim. Even Jacob and Cyrus, though still living in Marysville, were away often, pursuing their teaming and freighting businesses. Marysville just wasn't feeling like home to Allen anymore; he needed to return to Iowa and ground himself in the family he'd left for far too long.

Allen kept up with the evolving transportation options, so he knew that returning to Mitchell, the place he now found himself calling home, wouldn't be anything like the 1865 trip from Iowa to Marysville that had taken 6 months of hard going. He knew just how fast the times were changing; travel here, there, and back was becoming more common and faster. Western travelers with loads of goods to transport might still take the wagon train option, but Allen knew that the stagecoach's time of dominance had arrived. He could now think of the trip in terms of days not months. He knew perfectly well that making up to 110 miles on average a day (sometimes including nights) in a coach, would beat all that walking next to oxen and overloaded wagons making only 10 miles a day if lucky.

So, when Allen was ready and with more efficient modes of travel available, he sent Emeline a letter letting her know he would be coming "home". He left mid-September 1866 for Mitchell, home to his wife and three children and the place he was now sure would feel most like home to him. The trip took him less than a month. Though traveling long distances by stagecoach was much more efficient and comfortable than by wagon train, the new mode had difficulties and dangers of its own, as Allen well knew. He'd heard the stories about attacks from Native Americans and from robbers, attacks against a single stagecoach with much less protection than a whole train of wagons afforded. He'd heard that often coaches traveled at night when clear skies and moonlight allowed. He tried not to dwell on having to sleep sitting up all night, crammed in with others while traveling bumpy roads, or to imagine stops at the stations along the way with sub-par accommodations and food that he'd heard was generally not good.

But he was on his way. Then at one station Allen experienced a unique stagecoach travel danger. Two stagecoaches, Allen's and a competitor coach from a different company, arrived at a way station at about the same time, traveling to the same destination. Who would get there first? Reputations were at stake; the winner would be able to boast that his company had the best time. "Best time" became an advertising staple; the race was on.

Allen yelled at the driver, "You have passengers, slow down, someone is going to get hurt or worse."

Three of the others in his coach backed him, one yelling physical threats at the driver, but there was no response.

Allen became really angry then. "If anyone in this coach gets hurt, I will sue both you and your company. I'm a lawyer; you can count on it."

The passenger who had threatened the driver physically got more specific. "Slow down now or I'll blow your head off." He did have a gun, as did several other passengers, including Allen. Still no response from either the driver or from the conductor who rode up front with him and was technically his superior.

A few minutes later the rough race became even worse when the two wheels of Allen's coach, the ones nearest the edge of the trail, ran off into a ditch, as the driver attempted to pass the other coach on a stretch too narrow for the recklessly driven coaches. Allen didn't have time to yell as the driver over corrected and in mere moments struck the other coach sending it off the trail completely. Allen couldn't really see what happened; he had to wait several days to find out. Two wheels on the other coach were twisted out of shape and two of the four horses stumbled and broke their legs. Both had to be put down on the spot. Allen yelled at the conductor this time. "Slow that driver down, or I'll report you both to the director! I'll threaten the lawsuit unless he fires both of you." The other enraged passenger shouted a more immediate threat. "He won't have to fire dead men."

This time the threats caused the conductor to finally respond. He shouted at the driver, "Slow down now; you heard them."

The driver grumbled but obeyed. Allen did not carry out his threats at the next way station, knowing that he needed to wait until they reached a station that served as a director's headquarters before his complaints would have a chance of leading to action. It would take a director's level of authority to act in any way sufficient to satisfy him.

The skies began to cloud over, so with no moon to light the way, they stayed the night at the next station. Luckily there was an inn nearby, and the food was better than usual. The passengers ate, drank, and then fell asleep quickly, catching up on sleep missed when the moonlight allowed night travel. They got a new driver and conductor before they reached a station with a director. Maybe the race crazy driver had passed the message along; no more such reckless behavior occurred. Allen and even the threatening passenger seemed somewhat mollified, but that did not mean Allen wasn't going to let the director know his concerns.

The director greeted them as they arrived, and Allen took that opportunity to request a private meeting. The director didn't wait; he invited Allen into his office and offered the courtesy of using first names as they talked, giving his as Darius.

Darius went on, anticipating what he thought Allen might want to discuss by saying, "Allen, is that right? I hope that you realize we are here, I am here, to be sure that this coachline company does everything it can to make passengers as happy and as comfortable as possible. I'm guessing we may have fallen short of your expectations."

Allen replied, "Darius, then, well, yes, short of expectations, but that's not the point. The driver out of Deer Creek Station put our lives at risk. He seemed hell bent on beating another coach, racing recklessly. The climax, well, I suspect it would have scared even you as it did me and the other passengers. He tried to pass the other coach and ran it off the trail in doing so. I heard later that the other coach lost two horses and had damage done to the coach itself when they collided. Hope those passengers weren't injured."

Darius, managing a concerned expression, but one that looked a bit practiced, responded, voice deepening, "The driver was a young fellow, I believe, recently hired. The conductor should have handled this. I assure you I will."

Allen, not at all ready to let him off that easily, sharpened his tone a bit. "This is not just an incident requiring that you hand out discipline to a couple of your people. No, I believe, judging from some of your ads boasting about how your times beat other companies, that this is a company-wide problem. The more I see such ads the more likely, as a lawyer, that I'll seek out any possible lawsuits supporting injured clients. Can't you stop those ads? You must know that for the drivers they're incentives to recklessness?"

Darius paused. He knew he had no way to stop those ads; all the companies used them. He responded carefully, "I understand what you're saying, and I will pass along your concern to the owners. I do know that competition for drivers is fierce, and younger men apply often. They find the job exciting. We try to educate them about safety, but we have to trust them to listen."

Allen, recognizing a dead end when he'd reached one, simply dismissed Darius with a parting comment as he turned toward the door. "We seem to have circled back to disciplining a few drivers. Never found much use in going around in circles. At least, perhaps you might tell the next driver to avoid racing. I would like to live to see my family."

Darius managed to get out, "Yes, I will", before the door slammed behind Allen's exit.

Maybe Darius did talk to the next driver and even ask him to pass along warnings to avoid races for the rest of Allen's trip. Nothing like a race occurred again, and Allen arrived home in Mitchell unscathed.

Too Long Delayed - Mitchell Reunion

Meanwhile, back in Mitchell, Emeline prepared for her husband's return. While he was away, she guided the farming, stored food for winter, cooked, and raised her children along with all the other chores required of her. The Miner boys, Lemuel, Leander, and Henry, ranging in age from 12 to 18, were perfectly able to handle the physical farm work, as well as their home school studies, and did so. Her eldest son with her late husband, Edwin Caldwell, had remained in Mitchell, although her three younger Caldwell sons had moved to Washington state. Edwin moved there later, but in the meantime, living nearby with his wife, he helped oversee the farm and added his experience to the effort. Mary Amanda, Allen's last child with Sophina, and her husband Milton Rice Dudley lived nearby and could be relied on for any extra help that might be needed.

For Emeline, having Edwin around helped in even more important ways. He was a mature 33-year-old; she could talk to him openly, and she needed to talk. Although she was an active church member, and she could talk to other church members or the pastor, sitting down at home and talking to her son—to family, helped much more. One of those sit downs with Edwin took place a week before Allen was due to arrive home. The younger sons were never part of these discussions; they were always sent out to do farm chores, so the two could talk openly.

Emeline took the lead which came naturally to her, especially in delicate personal discussions. "I do wonder sometimes why my husband spends so much time away from his home here.

'Sometimes', well, let's say often. Think of it. The 6 months of hellish travel to Marysville by wagon train. Why? Then he stays there for months. OK, I can sort of understand waiting for Lucinda's arrival, a party too; I guess I'd have stayed for that. But why wait for months after that?"

Edwin had no good answer and was smart enough to redirect the conversation. "Well, he stayed there for a party. Why don't we match that with a welcome home party for him here? Would be a good start, anyway. Invite some of his favorite people from the church, even the pastor. Does he like the pastor? Not sure. Sit him down, put my son, little 3-year-old Grant, in his lap, let him tell stories about his—well, let's call them adventures. Adventure, right, only reason I can think of for that, as you put it, 'hellish' wagon train trip."

Emeline wanted to answer with enthusiasm but couldn't drop her frustration without comment first. "Men, 'adventures', translation— 'foolishness'. Over 60 years old and walking a couple thousand miles; just plain 'foolishness'. But a party, let him talk, brag, explain, he'd like that; I might even like that. He does like young ones. Grant in his lap; he'd love that. OK, so a party. Hard not to invite the pastor, whatever Allen thinks of him. I'll ask some of his close friends at church for some help. I'll make a list first, check off who can do what."

Edwin, smiling now, replied, "Great, I'll go hunting with Lemuel, Leander, and Henry. It'll draw them in. Prepare whatever we can get. Leander's getting to be a good shot these days. He'll enjoy hunting and preparing something for his dad. Think he misses him the most."

Emeline agreed but added, "Of course they all miss him, but, right, Leander in particular. OK, confession, I miss him too."

Edwin, "He might like to hear that at some point."

Emeline, "Um, well, hmm."

So, a party it was to be. Planning began the next day, and Emeline did her recruiting on Sunday, two days later. Allen was still popular at the church, and People were pleased to help, anxious to see him again. Some even talked enthusiastically about wanting to hear his adventures. Emeline had adopted the word, despite her private thoughts.

So, by the time Allen arrived, family and friends were ready to celebrate his return. Leander had been lucky and skillful enough to bring down a deer the day before. He did the field gutting again as Edwin had instructed a month earlier when they went out together and succeeded the first time. He had jerky prepared from the first successful hunt and freshly cooked venison from the recent one for his dad; he'd done the field work all by himself but allowed his brothers to help with preparation both times once they got home. He was more than pleased. By the time Allen arrived, all those contributing were ready with a feast that rivaled Lucinda's return party in Marysville. No oysters this time but home grown and prepared food aplenty.

Allen had thought he might arrive in the evening, and he did. The party took place the next day after he'd had the rest of the evening and the night to settle in, to reunite with his family he'd missed so much, and to catch up on his sleep. No one even tried to hide the plans, though, to make the party a surprise, as those who planned Lucinda's event had. Lemuel couldn't have contained himself anyway; he was the first to spring news of the party, even managing a few details like the fact that his own church friends would be there. Leander had warned his younger brother not to mention the deer. That was a surprise he was saving for the party, so he could bring some to his father personally and tell his own story.

Emeline greeted her husband with an enthusiasm that surprised her. She had meant to be affable, but on seeing his joy at the sight of her, she felt the joy rise within her. She had missed him; she cared, and that night she let him know.

Welcome Home - Mr. Adventure

Food and fun, and, yes, flasks with friends and family. Edwin knew his father-in-law Allen well enough to see to those flasks. A true home coming for Allen, and he was ready to enjoy. He was rested, pleased with his wife's love—he was all smiles. Then Edwin seated him, gave his 3-year-old son Grant a hug, and placed the child on Allen's knee. Mary Amanda, not to be outdone, added her 3-year-old daughter Ida to Allen's other knee. Well, that was all the welcome home he needed.

Friends gathered round and did what friends do; greeted him heartily and asked about his adventures. The pastor summed up the questions by simply asking in an appropriately gentle but humorous manner, "How did you do it? We have all heard that you made that wagon train trip, and we know you had to walk most of the way. I've got to say I've been known to stumble on the three church steps."

Allen, amused, chuckled, then replied. "Well, faith, pastor. I simply had to and prayed that I could. We're about the same age, and I suspect faith and prayer, coming from you, has helped others through even worse ordeals."

The pastor had a response. "Worse? I guess death is harder. We've lost friends, church members, here. Perhaps such losses qualify as harder; worse, well, that depends on the Lord. But here you are, looking healthy. It's time to make the day even better, here's a plate for you."

Leander, bubbling over, saw his chance and grabbed it. "I've got something special for you, Dad. We went hunting twice, and I got a deer both times. I field dressed them and when we got the one from the first hunt home, we smoked most of it, and we put the one from yesterday's hunt in the cold cellar and cooked it up this morning for your party. Here's some of both."

Edwin, wanting to let Allen know just how much his children had missed him, added, "Your three youngest and I had fine days hunting. We're all calling him 'one shot Leander'. All three shared in the preparation work, and work it is, as you well know. If anything remains it will make fine treats through the winter. Or maybe 'one shot Leander' will bring down another."

Edwin and Mary removed their young children from Allen's knees. They were just as happy on the rug with a couple of toys. Edwin added some other offerings to the venison on Allen's nearly full plate while others circled round the table filling theirs. Several close friends continued the conversation about his adventures.

Allen chose to respond by recalling Lucinda's letter to her husband James, comparing her trip around Cape Horn to his across the plains. He thought of that letter as about the best way he could think of to turn the hardship to humor, just what he wanted for his party. He began laughing himself as he shared Lucinda's line to her husband as they parted on their separate trips. "Enjoy bumping along the trails while I glide to California."

Emeline had shared a letter from Allen with the family about the buffalo hunt, and she brought it up again by comparing his efforts on the trail to Lucinda's sitting in a chair waiting for cooks to do all the work. Lemuel wanted to hear about the braves at the buffalo hunt. He jumped right in. "Were the Indians all dressed in war paint, feathers, and buffalo robes? I've seen pictures."

Allen, anxious to emphasize the positive, responded, "Pictures are often misleading, people want to show something exciting, crowd pleasing. Yes, buffalo robes, maybe some feathers; Cyrus didn't say. Not at all war like; no war paint. A peace sign was shared and then Cyrus worked with the tribal leader to divide the buffalo the braves had wounded first, but then James killed. Not a great picture, I guess, but maybe a lesson in how we should treat each other."

Lemuel simply nodded without indicating what he thought. Friends still gathered around Allen expressing support or not, but no one openly challenged Allen's feelings. It was a party for him, after all. They'd have time later, maybe after church in a week or so, to question his sentiments. Question them as naive, perhaps.

Maybe even bring up the slaughter of soldiers during the Platte River Bridge battle, too recent to be forgotten.

Henry then brought up what excited him; he'd seen stagecoach drivers arrive in Mitchell, read about their exploits, and admired them, like many of his friends. "Tell us about the stagecoach trip and the drivers. Was it as exciting as it sounds. Papers have lots of stories, Indian attacks, robbers. There's lots about how fast they go; times between destinations keep improving."

Of course, Allen understood his 18-year-old son's enthusiasm. He knew the drivers were admired, particularly by those of an age likely to consider such careers exciting, like his son. But he didn't want to go into his thoughts right now and especially not his recent experience. That discussion could wait for a private moment. For now, he just replied quite calmly, considering how he felt. "Yes, an adventurous life, no doubt. I'll give you a full account later. But now, where's that flask, Edwin?"

Friends and family took that question as a signal to give Allen a break, time to enjoy his food and drink. Emeline took the opportunity to move her chair next to her husband's and reached out to touch his hand. In good time Emeline struck up a conversation by asking how his family in Marysville were doing.

Allen again put off a full account, reaching out for her hand and holding it before responding. "Such busy folks, I'll tell you all about them when we get another chance to be alone."

Emeline chuckled, "Somehow I'm relatively sure we'll arrange that." Later that evening, after the guests had departed, they did manage that alone time, and Emeline repeated her question about the Marysville family.

Allen took her hand in his once again and prefaced his answer by smiling and repeating how pleased he was to be home with her and his Iowa family. Then he quite simply replied, "They are all healthy and seem happy, but they sure are restless. Elizabeth and Lewis moved to the Mattole Valley, California; it borders the Pacific; hard to go any further. Then Lucinda and James joined them. Cyrus and

Jacob remain in Marysville, but I seldom saw them; their freighting businesses keep them on the road mostly."

Emeline nodded as if understanding in some sense but couldn't help adding what had immediately occurred to her. "'Restless', restlessness must run in the family. I'm sure hoping you plan to stay with us for a while."

Allen was quick to respond. "I've no plans other than to enjoy being here. Family and friends; I like feeling I'm home. I'll get back into the church, become active again. Even given some thought to restarting my law practice. I didn't mention my stagecoach problems coming here. Didn't want to counter Henry's youthful feelings about stagecoach drivers during the party. But one of our early drivers was extremely reckless, raced a driver from a competing company and ended up risking our lives and knocking the other coach off the road. I threatened a lawsuit all the way up to the director in charge of the section. Guessing the threat got passed along, no racing or reckless driving for the rest of the way. If I read of a possible case, just might take it on."

Emeline's response came with an inner sigh of relief, "Well, I know how much the church has missed you. Members mention you often. Law? I know you've been a busy lawyer, one who took an interest in local government and politics, too. I suspect, given your strongly held views, you'll get back into all that."

Allen didn't disagree. "Might even help with the farming, too, though you and our sons seem perfectly capable without me."

Emeline, poking him playfully, joked, "No, we don't need you messing around with our smoothly running operation. We might allow you to tinker with, maybe even fix, equipment occasionally. But, only if you must."

Ground rules established, Allen did pretty much what he had layed out. Over the next year or so, he became again a crucial church member, helping with the practical matters of finance and operations but more significantly supporting the church's moral stances. Pastors in Iowa tended to lead the strong abolitionist movements in the state, and Allen's pastor was no exception, but his attitude toward native Americans was less accommodating, reflecting what many in the church felt.

Several weeks after Allen's return, after finishing a finance session with the pastor, Allen began one of the discussions he'd avoided at the party. "Remember when I brought up the buffalo hunt episode, you and others had reservations about my conclusion. You know, I suggested that the peaceful incident and the way the braves cooperated with Cyrus and the others with him seemed like a model for getting along together."

The pastor hunched forward in his chair looking a bit concerned, and responded carefully, "Our church members remember the Indian attack at Platte Bridge. You know, it's such a recent memory that it's hard to think about getting along, so soon."

Allen expressed understanding but added some of what he felt. "Yes, hard to forget Platte River Bridge. Hard also, for those who attacked, to forget previous attacks from soldiers, some unprovoked. It's a war, but wars must end somehow. I'm just trying to say that both sides need to see the humanity on the other side. It's an image, dividing a buffalo together. Think of what you and other pastors along with many church members have done for freed slaves. That movement, so morally right, started with understanding Black humanity, something slave owners, given generations of tradition, had such great difficulty understanding. Some slave owners eventually did come to understand and became abolitionist converts and like all converts generally ardent in their new beliefs."

The pastor understood but added a caution, "I understand what you are saying but you've got to give it some time."

Allen, ready to let it go at that, responded smiling, "Time, right; I'll check with you next week."

The pastor chuckled and then altered Allen's response a bit. "Right, next year it is." Over the next few weeks both the pastor and Allen had several conversations with church members and others who had heard about Allen's opinion, and both repeated the same sort of statements they had made when talking alone together.

Henry's enthusiastic vision of life as a stagecoach driver came up again when the family, including Emeline and Allen's other two younger sons, sat down to relax after an evening meal. Henry had waited as long as he could but gave up and simply mentioned Allen's earlier promise. "Dad, you were going to tell us about your stagecoach trip here. What was it like?"

Allen sat back considering just how he wanted to tell that story without upsetting his son or himself. "Well, I guess I'd have to say that the beginning was not without adventure. We had a young driver, found out later that in fact he was relatively new to the job. Maybe he wanted to make a name for himself; whatever the motive, he put our lives in danger. He got in one of those races you hear about with a driver from another company. We reached a bend as he was passing the other coach and he had to drive off the road slightly to make room. Then he came back but overdid it and knocked into the other coach sending it down an embankment and tipping it over. Horses were injured and had to be put down. Haven't read anything about passenger injuries, but I suspect there were some."

Henry had a better response than Allen might have expected. "Maybe we haven't read about it because it wouldn't be good for stagecoach business. Faster times make the news, not so much, the accidents, I guess."

Allen pleased and relieved, responded, "Right, son, and you can be sure that everyone up to the director heard about it from me. Not odd, in my opinion, that the rest of the trip went so smoothly. Word was passed along, I guess, and drivers drove safely. Word, as you said, that did not make the newspapers."

Emeline couldn't help noting that word she had focused on previously, "'Adventure' you called it. Thought you liked adventures?"

Allen as always admired his wife's ability to counter cleverly, smiled and responded as best he could. "Right, but I like to survive adventures, and this one, well, was a bit too close a call, I guess."

That ended the discussion; bedtime awaited them. It would be over a year before that word, adventurer, took on meaning for their lives once again. In the meantime, Allen continued his church work, did some legal work unrelated to stagecoaches, and once again became active in county affairs, eventually serving as an election judge for Mitchell County. Politically, Iowa became the sort of state that Allen proudly supported.

Chapter Twenty-Three

And then...

Again

After Allen's return to his family in Mitchell in the Fall of 1866 and on into 1868, Allen lived a comfortable though active life surrounded by family and friends. Toward the middle of January 1868, he did receive one of several letters sent over the year from his family in Marysville, CA., one containing a different idea than the others. Cyrus wrote that he and Jacob were thinking about visiting family already in the Mattole valley well north of San Francisco, on the Pacific Ocean. He wrote that, of course, the usual plan for such a visit would be to take the trails used by stagecoaches to Sacramento and then to San Francisco. From San Francisco land access by wagon to Petrolia in the Mattole Valley would be a bit difficult but possible.

But Jacob loved rivers having established his ice business near where the Feather and Yuba rivers emptied into the lake, or glacial spillway, in Marysville. He was fond of exploring along the rivers whenever he got the chance. On one of his hauling trips from Marysville he reached the Mattole River, which gave its name to the valley extending all the way to the Pacific Ocean. He took the time to fish there and enjoyed the break. He talked about that trip often and declared the river a favorite. One night, after recalling the trip once more, he blurted out a thought. "Why not make our way to the Mattole River and then just follow trails along the river on through the Mattole Valley all the way to the Pacific Ocean and to our families there?" Struck by the idea, Cyrus included it in the letter.

After reading the letter, Allen handed it to Emeline without comment, figuring no comment from him was the best way to introduce to her such an unusual escapade as the one Cyrus had suggested. He had been immediately intrigued, but there was no sense in revealing his interest so obviously. Emeline, knowing her husband too well for his lack of reaction to stand, responded as nonchalantly as she could manage, "Cyrus and Jacob would find a way to avoid the usual. Wonder what the trails are like along the river?"

Allen, attempting his own version of nonchalance, pleaded ignorance. "Don't know about the trails, never been there."

Both were quite willing to drop the matter at that and did. Then another letter arrived a few weeks later, a letter that clearly indicated how far the plan had evolved. Charles Johnston Sr., Jacob's father-in-law, had joined the conversation and changed the purpose of the trip from a visit to a move. He wanted to take along members of his family and doing so would involve using wagons to carry supplies for the trip and items they would need after they arrived. This time Allen and Emeline read the letter together out loud so that sons Henry, Leander, and Lemuel, who were in for the mid-day meal, could hear.

Henry broke through all previous reserve so carefully maintained by both Allen and Emeline blurting out, "You know, what do you think, we could take the stagecoach to Marysville and join them on the river trip. Sounds exciting."

"'We'?" Emeline responded. "Not me. And 'we' do have a farm to run here. Does that 'we' include just you and, of course, your dad, or Leander and Lemuel, too? Or would they stay behind doing the work while you two traipsed across the plains, oh and mountains and rivers?"

Allen tried to reassure Emeline by toning down any speculation about such a trip. "Henry, your mother brings up serious issues about any such change in life here. Besides, you know that your younger brothers would not want to be left with all the work. They'd want to go too." He left it at that not mentioning thoughts that were already percolating in the back of his mind. There would be time for more serious conversation when he could talk to Emeline alone.

That time came eventually, and somewhat surprisingly Emeline brought it up. She knew there was no hiding what was going through his mind from her. "You have been trying so hard not to show how excited you are about this Mattole adventure. I know you, and I do appreciate your attempts to hide your excitement, and that you don't want to worry me. But it's an adventure. You can't just let it go. Besides I'm betting you want your sons to experience challenges like you have. I do understand. But what do we do with this farm? Sell it? That would take some time and it seems like Cyrus and the others in Marysville mean to leave before we could sell at a good price and then get you all to Marysville. Besides, at age 63, are you really in shape to do this?"

All Allen could think to do was flex his biceps and then to acknowledge what his wife knew anyway about selling the property. He did add a solution she hadn't mentioned, or maybe even hadn't considered. "Well sure, you're right. Hard for me to pass this one up, even at my age. And, yes, I do want the boys to experience some of what I have done, something beyond the repetitious life of farm boys. Selling the farm, well, would be, as you say, hard in such a short time. Might work though. I did have another thought. Why not just hire a couple of young folks? Plenty around here looking for extra work and the money the jobs would provide."

Emeline replied, "Hiring, hadn't thought of that. Good idea. I do like this farm and my life here. Of course, if you and the boys go, I'll miss you all. Yes, even you. I do assume you'll all return, right?"

Allen, becoming more than comfortable with the discussion, decided to reassure his wife before solidifying the plan. "Of course, we'll be coming back. Let's first send a letter to Cyrus letting him know, and then if all is OK with him, we'll let the boys know."

Emeline responded, "OK but I think we can just let the boys know our plan now. They might even suggest a couple of their friends for hiring."

And so, that evening, Allen and Emeline revealed the plan to their boys, and Allen sent the letter off to Cyrus. Henry was overjoyed as were Leander and Lemuel. Henry spoke up first. "A stagecoach ride then going along with lots of family from Marysville. Down a river, too. We've got lots of friends who'd like to make a little extra doing farm work here. We'll check that out." His brothers were quick to agree and were quite obviously excited.

Assuming Cyrus would get back with a 'yes come along' invitation, Allen and his sons began preparations, setting aside items they felt they would need for the trip and that wouldn't be needed on the farm. By the time Cyrus' return letter arrived, toward the end of February, they were ready and eager. Two older neighbor boys, Henry's friends, were prepared to take over the farm work after a few days of learning where things were and what was expected of them. Stagecoach tickets were reserved from Mitchell to Marysville, and Allen had let stagecoach directors know that he would not tolerate any racing, emphasizing that three of his sons would be aboard with him. And then, in the middle of March 1868, Allen left his wife again for yet another adventure, this time taking their three sons with him.

For those three boys, the beginning of the 'adventure' was not what they had anticipated. Instead of an exciting and glamorous stagecoach wild west romp, they endured an extremely tiring and downright boring ride jolting along trails, often while trying to sleep through the jolts on moonlit nights. It crossed Lemuel's mind that farm life wasn't so bad; at least the food was good back home. Simply put, they all were glad to reach Marysville and leave that stagecoach behind.

On to the Mattole River
The Marysville Settlers

The newest travelers to Marysville were greeted heartily and invited to stay at Jacob and Cavy's place for the same reasons previous family visitors had been—their large, comfortable house in the center of town. Having arrived late in the afternoon, mid-April, well-worn from their stagecoach experience of sleepless nights and lousy meals, they happily accepted some good, home cooked food at last, along with a brief conversation, followed by a thoughtful suggestion from Cavy's father, Charles Johnston Sr., who happened to be visiting, that they might want to get a good night's sleep. And they did want and get just that, in the most comfortable beds they had slept in for over a month.

They spent days recovering and enjoying the hospitality Jacob and Cavy were so capable of providing before Cyrus, along with several members of the Johnston family, arrived to lay out plans and arrange for departure, somewhat loosely scheduled for the end of April or thereabouts. Cyrus explained, or more accurately began to sketch out, what they had discussed before realizing he'd forgotten introductions. "We'll have a number of wagons; wait, I'm not sure you know that several of the Johnston young folks will be along." Turning to his father-in-law he added, "Guess we should introduce the boys to them. Ladies first, though; here's Mary and her husband, William, and then our youngest traveler, Laura, about your age, Lemuel. How am I doing Charles?"

Charles, amused, responded, "Well with the ladies, as I'd expect. Some of my sons are coming along, too, you know. Here's Samuel, he'll be along, and Richard as well as Charles, both Richard and Charles are close to your age, Henry. Eldest son, William, will stay here and watch over our place. Guess that about does it." Then he quickly added while pointing to each one in turn; "You all meet Henry, Leander and Lemuel."

"Good", Cyrus added, "now where was I? Yes, wagons for passengers and supplies along the way and for whatever else we take with us that we'll need when we get there. We'll follow trails west to Briceland. Jacob and I have both been on them, they're not too bad. Then we pick up the Mattole River and follow trails along it to the Pacific; not sure about those trails—neither of us have used them."

Allen couldn't help a comment in a voice indicating some level of concern. "Guess we'll find out, for sure, when we get there." Nods of agreement from Cyrus and Jacob.

Well, it was a little more than a week, more like a couple of weeks in fact, before they left. Cyrus and Allen led in Cyrus' single wagon. The Johnstons followed with two wagons, and Jacob, along with his wife Cavy, trailed behind with their wagon, taking only what they would need for the trip and for basics once they arrived. They took a couple of spare oxen Cyrus had insisted on in case of any injuries to the others. Allen's sons were assigned to help Jacob and bring up the rear. Lemuel and Leander walked just behind Jacob and Cavy's wagon in front of the spare animals that wagons or riders might need along the way and the animals to stock their homesteads once they arrived. Henry followed the animals, herding them so they kept up with the wagons. By the time they left, Lemuel had sought out as many opportunities as he could to see and even talk to Laura. That interest continued as they traveled.

The first day out proved as easy-going as Cyrus and Jacob had promised. Some of the younger folks walked as westward bound travelers were accustomed to doing, leading the oxen that were pulling the wagons. Allen, older and a bit more sensible now than he had been on his 1865 trek (credit his wife), took Cyrus' advice and sat on the driver's seat of the lead wagon. Relatively comfortable, with no preceding wagons blocking the view ahead, he enjoyed himself, admiring the scenery, spotting birds and wild animals out in the fields.

Toward evening Allen called Cyrus over, after seeing deer, and suggested that maybe Henry and the Johnston boys might want to try their luck at hunting. Cyrus liked the idea and rounded up Henry, Richard, and Charles for the purpose. They rode horses quite far ahead but saw no deer within range, so they ended up with little for their efforts, just a couple of rabbits.

By the time they returned, the wagons had pulled over for the evening. With just rabbits as fresh meat, Allen suggested, and others approved a stew using some of the root vegetables they'd brought with them. Not at all strangely, Lemuel managed to be available to help Laura wash and cut up the vegetables, leaving the hunters to prepare the rabbits. All the young folks gathered wood adding to what they'd picked up along the way, and the older folks set up the fire and stew pot. The stew smelled good in the cooking and tasted just fine when eaten around the warmth of an enlarged fire, a fire much appreciated on a cold, early mid-Spring winter evening. Not a bit was left after they all dipped their bread into the pot and soaked up the last of the drippings. Cavy and Laura began cleaning up, and somehow Lemuel tore himself away from the guys and helped.

Over the next couple of weeks, they made good time without any serious incidents. The hunters brought down a buck and field dressed it, providing the evening meals for several days. The trail did narrow a bit, and Cyrus warned the others to be careful. They all listened until one forgot. Jacob had gone ahead to check with Cyrus, leaving young Lemuel in charge of leading the oxen for his wagon. While Jacob was up with Cyrus, they noted a particularly narrow section with a downhill drop on the right side. He headed back to warn Lemuel, but he was too late. Maybe Lemuel spotted deer or allowed himself a Laura daydream. Whatever took his attention away from the task at hand, a shout of "look out" from Cavy, who was riding in the wagon, brought him back quickly. The wagon slipped off the road into a tree that, quite fortunately, kept it from sliding down the hill even further and may well have saved Cavy from injury.

That tree stopped the wagon and saved the oxen from what might have been serious injury. Jacob took over from Lemuel and quickly tugged the reins so that the oxen angled back toward the trail. The Johnston boys saw what had happened, stopped their wagons, and signaled Cyrus. Cyrus and the Johnston boys left Allen and Charles Johnston in charge of the wagons that had made it through and hustled back to help Jacob. Allen's sons were anxious to help but had no idea how.

Cyrus and Jacob took charge, but even they were not sure what to do. Then Cyrus had an idea. "Jacob, why don't we get those two spare oxen and attach them to the side of the wagon. If we angle them forward some, we should be able to coordinate their pulling of the wagon with the ones pulling up front. All the ones pulling from the side need to do is get the wagon off that tree far enough to clear the rear wheels, and then the ones up front should be able to pull it forward and back on the road."

Jacob, ready to try anything that might work without damaging the wagon any further, agreed but added his own thought. "Right, let's give it a try. First, though, let's dig a bit around the wheels so that when we pull sideways, the wheels aren't pulled uphill but instead slide down into the holes we dug."

Cyrus agreed. He ordered those standing around to empty the wagon, reducing its weight, and then helped Jacob dig the slots for the wheels and attach the two oxen to the side of the wagon directly across from the tree. Cyrus took their leads and guided them forward, gauging the angle that would have them positioned so that, once the lead oxen pulled the wagon wheels forward enough to clear the tree, the side pullers would be properly placed. Getting that angle right meant that the side pullers would not become backward pullers. Fortunately, it was California's dry season, so their calculations didn't need to account for slipping and sliding in wet soil. On a slow count of three, they got those oxen all working together, no small feat. And—it worked. Cheers all around.

That "fortunate" dry spell became acute as it continued through June, eventually having its own consequences. Animals need water, and they had lots of animals; oxen, horses, sheep, pigs, and several dogs. They carried some fresh water from their wells back home for their own use as drinking water, but for other uses and for the animals, they needed to find sources along the way. They did pass rivers and streams, but they had less and less water as they proceeded and the drought continued. Even the drinking water from home became dangerously low.

They knew that soon they would have to stop at one of the few farms along the way and quite simply beg or barter for water. Finally, they spotted a farm that looked large and well run, just what they figured they would need. Cyrus brought the wagons to a stop and walked toward the farmhouse. Before he reached the door, a man, presumably the owner, appeared from the barn nearby. He walked over and introduced himself as William Lowden. William was an impressive 6' tall, slightly taller than Cyrus, and he had the build of a farmer accustomed to hard work. Travelers often stopped by, so he was used to company and always glad to greet them. Cyrus returned the greeting, but before he could even ask for the water they so badly needed, William anticipated his request. "Betting your animals could use water and maybe you, too. Got a good well here for your folks, and I was just about to take my horses down to the Trinity River, still flowing some despite this dry spell."

Cyrus smiled and thanked him, adding, "The animals do need that water. Once you show us the way, we'll get them all down there for a good drink. First, though, maybe I could have some of our young fellows come down to fill buckets at your well, if that's OK with you."

William replied, "Good, take care of the folks first, and then on to the river. Once I show you the way, you can come back and take the wagons, too; it's on your way."

The plan pleased Cyrus more than he could find a way to express, so he just smiled again and said, "be back with the young folks; they'll be pleased", and then he headed for the wagons. When he returned, he introduced Henry and Leander Miner and two of the Johnston boys, Richard and Charles. William greeted them and helped them fill the buckets they'd brought—two each, plenty of water for all until they could re-supply in Briceland, fortunately not too far away. The boys took the water back to the wagons, and Cyrus left for the river with William.

William strung several of his horses together for the trip to the river, and finally Cyrus was able return a small portion of the kindness they had received by taking a few more of William's horses along than William could on his own. Once they arrived, William showed Cyrus a deeper section of the stream where animals could drink clear water and then guided him along the path to a dry section where the wagon train trail crossed the river. They returned with the horses and then William spent a pleasant half hour just talking with Cyrus and his group. William was curious about where they were headed and why. Cyrus explained that they intended to visit family or actually join family members living in Humboldt County but failed to mention that they would then follow the Mattole River all the way to the Pacific, leaving William with the impression that they would be stopping somewhere near Briceland, also in Humboldt County.

On to the Mattole Valley Via the Mattole River

The rest of the trip to Briceland went well. There were dry roads with no narrow spots, the animals having been happily watered had plenty to eat along the way, no 'adventures' to overcome, just walking and riding along the trail.

When they reached Briceland, they stocked up at local farms as intended for the final leg of the journey, staying just long enough to do so. They were getting anxious to see their families living in the Mattole valley around Petrolia, so they hurried on to the Mattole River, driving their wagons over Elk Ridge and then descending another ridge through what became known as Crooked Prairie.

When they reached the Mattole River, they were surprised to find that no wagon trail followed along its route. They sent out Richard and Charles Johnston as scouts to look for a wagon trail somewhere nearby, but the boys found nothing. Nobody wanted to bring up the obvious; they had a chance to ask about trails along the way any number of times, but no one did. All they found along the river was what looked to them like an old native trail, wide enough for horseback, meandering along, and breaking off from time to time. One way forward remained; the riverbed was even dryer than the low sections of the Trinity. On they went down the Mattole riverbed with their oxen, wagons, horses, and all their other animals.

It was not so bad; all went well until, after several miles, they came upon a narrowing filled with water. They'd reached Sterrit Hole, named after Frank Sterrit, who drowned there. They sent out the scouts, Richard and Charles, again to see if the hole was just an anomaly or the beginning of a river filled with water. The scouts rode several miles before that native horse trail disappeared entirely; maybe it had been flooded out from winter rains. They saw water down river as far as they could see, so they returned and reported what they'd seen.

Given that information, Cyrus suggested building rafts and floating down the river the rest of the way. There were plenty of trees along the river, and they had all the equipment they needed for the project. Jacob, quite willing to follow Cyrus' advice after successes like the wagon rescue, agreed and sent Mary's husband, William, and all the younger folks off to harvest logs. Cyrus indicated the size he wanted by cupping his hands, with thumbs extended, and separating his hands the right distance. They were going to need a raft for each wagon, so they spent many days building four of them; time they regretted losing, time that included sending Jacob back to Briceland to buy more rope they needed.

Once the rafts were built, just logs tied together with the rope and with a rear paddle device for steering, they had to get the wagons on them. This time Jacob had an idea. He had noted that one side of 'Sterrit Hole' was quite shallow for about five feet out. "We can back one wagon into this shallow water, then attach the oxen to it with what's left of the rope. We'll push the raft in the water up to the wagon and then use the oxen to pull the wagon onto the raft. Again, we'll need to empty the wagons first to lighten the load. Also, I guess we should pound a couple of stakes in the stream bed against the raft to keep it steady." Cyrus and Jacob made a good pair. Cyrus thought up the main plan and Jacob made it work by adding necessary details.

They did this routine all four times successfully, re-loading each wagon and then tying the loaded raft far enough down river to allow room for the next. Then Cyrus insisted on guiding each raft himself through Sterrit Hole, in all about 100 yards long. They planned to take the animals along the horse trail where possible and up whatever ridge they needed to whenever the path disappeared. Some discussion followed over who would handle the rafts from there and who would take on the more onerous task of leading the animals along a path they knew would disappear all too soon. The only fair solution was to take turns when possible. They also decided that when the path disappeared, they'd tie up the rafts and have all the younger, more agile members trek up and over ridges with the animals.

All went as planned. Cyrus, Jacob, Allen, and Charles Johnston handled the steering paddles while the younger folks called or pointed out directions from the front of the rafts. They had paddles, too, in case needed for difficult steering situations. Lemuel was particularly active. He had managed to jump aboard the raft carrying Laura and did not miss an opportunity to impress her.

Meanwhile Mary's husband, William, along with Samuel Johnston and Henry, shepherded the animals, following the trail. The oxen, linked together by their reins, were led by William, followed by Samuel leading the horses, also tied together, with Henry herding the rest of the animals from behind.

All went well for the rafters until they reached a section of the river near Pringle Ridge where the river was narrow and filled with boulders. They could see that rafting through boulders with no room to maneuver would prove impossible, so they unloaded the wagons from the rafts and hitched up the oxen for hauling them over the ridge and then back to the river. They simply left the rafts behind.

Hauling the wagons, filled with belongings, along with the horses and animals, over ridges with no roads turned out to be even harder than they imagined. Almost any moment might result in a damaged wheel from hitting a rock or a rut just the wrong way or might result in an oxen injury from misstepping and falling. Cyrus and Jacob knew the dangers, and the others had learned to rely on their previous experience, so they all moved carefully and slowly.

Also, they all knew that other possible dangers might lie ahead. Plenty of wild animals ranged the area, and they had their farm animals, including pigs, sheep, and even lambs, as well as dogs to protect. They were careful but not careful enough. A lamb wandered off down a nearby gully just before they reached the end of their climb up Pringle Ridge. Lemuel saw the lamb enter the gully and immediately took off after it, shouting back to the others, "Lamb loose, got it." Cyrus yelled back, "Stop, it's dangerous." But, Lemuel, already out of hearing, plunged carelessly down into the gully. Moments later he faced a terror that caused him to turn and run. A giant grizzly had the lamb but raised full height when Lemuel came into view. It was an eight-foot tall, massive, and fearsome creature; fortunately, it was more interested in the lamb.

At least Lemuel had a story to tell that evening as they all rested after that hard day of climbing. He'd learned well from the others the art of elaboration, and that bear got bigger and brawnier in the retelling. "It was nine-feet tall at least with feet twelve inches or so long, claws that looked to be over two inches." Henry, Richard, Charles, and Samuel couldn't help laughing at those final details, Richard jokingly summing up their thoughts with, "Mighty calm of you to measure foot and claw length faced with that terror."

It was a pleasant evening to be followed the next morning by a sobering discovery. Scouts were sent out again. Could there be a road somewhere? No. But, also, there was no good route back to the river. The scouts came back with the news that the only route back seemed to require descending some and then climbing another ridge. It was called Abb Ridge, but of course they didn't know that; they just knew they would need to climb it and suffer more brutal and dangerous hauling. Cyrus and Jacob took a bit of good-hearted ribbing over this discovery. "'Just follow the Mattole River'", Allen said snickering a bit, "Isn't that what you said?" Others joined in. "That's what they said, 'no problem'. Just no road, the rapids, and mountains; they left all that out."

The slight descent down Pringle Ridge to reach a way up Abb Ridge certainly seemed best, though taking care to lead the oxen slowly and carefully downhill with the weight of the wagons pushing from behind had its challenges. They almost made it down before what they feared happened—a lead oxen tripped and fell, breaking a leg while also dragging several other oxen down. The lead ox had to be put down and replaced by one of the spares. They did take time to field dress that unfortunate ox, but they took only some, because it wasn't even close to being a favorite meal. Cyrus recovered a bit of credit for taking time to prepare it, though, and even more credit for having insisted on spare oxen. Fortunately, only one was needed, leaving one more. The other oxen that were pulled down escaped serious injury, just a few scrapes here and there.

The climb up Abb Ridge and the eventual return to the Mattole riverbed went well as did the next six miles down the riverbed to Pritchett Creek. Then deep water stopped them again; two miles of deep water. The pattern repeated itself, just different terrain. They were getting tired of the routine but also good at it. The wagons were taken out of the riverbed on the south side of the stream onto yet another ridge.

As they got closer to Petrolia, they found a few settlers who had built their homes in the wilderness. Before leaving Marysville, they'd received a description of the Mattole Valley from Allen's daughter, Elizabeth. She mentioned that most building in the area, at the time, hugged the coast where transportation by ships in the bay made both existence and business easier. She did write that a few settlers had headed inland, following the rivers like the Mattole and then clearing the land of forest to create their farms. She added that clearing the forest had turned into quite a business opportunity; the wood was needed back in Petrolia and elsewhere. The gold rush had accelerated the demand for timber. Gold miners used wood to build flumes that carried large amounts of water down to mining areas to wash out nuggets and to provide for their other water needs. Ship builders, and eventually railroads, along with all sorts of builders needed lumber as the area grew.

As the Miner/Johnston party made their way along the Mattole, they suspected that danger of a Native American attack still existed, like what some of them had experienced in earlier travels. They saw that the timber business caused reckless clearing and damage to the magnificent forest along the river where they knew Native Americans had lived, fished, and hunted for thousands of years. They took such damage to native territories to mean that retaliation would be likely.

They learned, once they reached Petrolia and spoke to their relatives there, that indeed the natives had attempted retaliation with the usual results. As early as 1864 only a small number of natives remained huddled in the last of several reservations, this one at the mouth of the Mattole River, most of the Mattole natives having been slaughtered in raids by locals and the army. By 1868, as their wagon train made its way down the river, the Mattole Native Americans barely survived and could not have posed any threat. In fact, that same year all but a few died of a measles epidemic.

The settlers along the Mattole River made it possible for the Miner/Johnston wagons to get through the forested sections along trails they had created. The wagons left the riverbed near the farm of one of the most successful settlers, W.E. Roscoe, and then halted one mile from the river south of the Krill farm. They then headed northward down a ridge called Hazel Prairie to Shinn Field, west of a hill called Kelsey Knob and then back to the riverbed. Just seven miles down that riverbed and they reached their destination, Petrolia.

They had pushed themselves hard those last seven miles, arriving late in the evening. It was time to set up their last encampment of the trip, eat whatever they had that required minimal preparation, and get down to sleep as soon as possible. In the morning they'd get in touch with Elizabeth and Lewis Cummings, and Elizabeth and Lewis could then contact Lucinda Miner Dudley and her husband James, along with their four children.

Morning came and, as if in welcome, the sun shone brightly. Finding anyone in Petrolia didn't present any problems given a small and declining population. The brief oil boom that gave the town its name had gone sour, and many left. They had an address; Lewis Cummings had solidified his preemption claim near the Mattole River by improving the land, creating the beginnings of a farm and erecting a residence of sorts, in line with the 1841 preemption law requirements.

It was quite a gathering, this meeting of so many of Allen's offspring along with their husbands, wives, and children as well as all the Johnston's who had traveled with him. There were now so many people that the already overwhelmed home couldn't possibly house them all. No problem, though, the new arrivals just set up camp one last time next to a barn under construction and enjoyed the best campsite of their event-filled trek down the Mattole.

Allen felt the warmth of his family gathered there as the days passed, felt it so strongly that he knew someday the Mattole Valley would be the home that would draw him west one last time. He could see that Henry, Leander, and Lemuel felt the draw, too, as they frolicked with the other young people there, made their way down to the river, and—once rains filled it again—swam and fished. Allen made sure they all got to see the bay and even took them on a trip further north where they could look out on a site of sites, the Pacific Ocean itself. Someday he felt sure he'd have his whole family here—his wife Emeline, for sure and maybe even some of their children by her previous marriage. Someday...

Epilogue

Someday Dreams Come True

This epilogue is designed to briefly fill in the history of Allen and his family up until Allen's dream, of bringing all of them together in the Mattole Valley, is fulfilled. Someday would turn into some year before Allen and the portions of his family living in Mitchell moved permanently. Two years after the historic trip down the Mattole River, the 1870 Mitchell, Iowa census lists Allen age 65, Emeline 60, Henry 23, Leander 19, and Lemuel 16. In 1875 both Allen and Emeline wrote letters from Mitchell to family in Mattole. Allen's letter confirms that he is aging, as he freely admits. Emeline's letter mentions that his sight is declining, making future letters unlikely and the one he wrote difficult, as he specifically stated himself.

Though Allen's writing has declined, his hopes for a grand family reunion remained. However, those feelings turned to pleading, and one might even say became almost pathetic. "...it has ben (sp.) a long time since I got a letter from you it seems you have almost forgotten me, I should be glad to here (sp.) from you often but I can't see to write very well I would be glad to see you all and have thought some times of trying to come out there but don't know how it will be." Seems like he had given up on punctuation. Emeline, in her letter, did forget punctuation occasionally but not always. And her penmanship and spelling were much better. See a portion of Allen's letter below.

Probably in August of 1875 they did move. The 1876 voter's registration for Humboldt County, CA has Allen listed. In November 1878 he purchased land from his son Jacob and remained there until his death on November 6, 1880. Two of Allen's sons, who had still been living in Mitchell, Iowa—Henry and Leander—moved to Mattole by 1875 or 1876, judging from the birth records of their children. A single line in the Mitchell County Press notes that Allen and Leander left for Petrolia in August 1875. By 1880 the Petrolia census has the last son from Mitchell, Lemuel, living with his mother, Emeline, in Petrolia. They may well have come earlier with his other brothers, but I can't find any documentary proof.

If we think back about moves from Mitchell to Marysville or to the Mattole Valley, we might think that the older folk at least would have one hard trip, even if they took a stagecoach all the way and left the youngsters to bring goods using wagons. But the times they were a changing. By the end of 1869 passengers and goods could take the new transcontinental railroad from Iowa (Council Bluffs, remember Council Bluffs of wagon train fame?) to San Francisco. Ship passage would have been convenient from San Francisco to the Mattole Valley, probably easiest on the oldsters. One wonders if Allen knew how easy it would be given at least one interpretation of the following line, "...have thought sometimes of trying to come out there but don't know how it will be." 'Will be' to travel or 'will be' to sell all or 'will be' to convince Emeline to leave?

Certainly, selling the farm wouldn't be a problem as Emeline makes clear in her letter, "...there's nothing at home to stay for as we have no farm only ten acres of meadow and a garden plot, no horse one cow..." Convincing Emeline? She seems to have convinced herself. She goes on to list all the friends and family that were there in Mitchell but aren't there now ending the list with, "I had much rather see you and talk with you than write..." And so, as they both now seemed to believe would be best, they would leave, giving Allen four or five years before his death to live that dream.

Mitchell S D March 14 75

Dear children I thought I would try and write you a few lines we are all well and hope you are enjoying the blessing we have had the coldest winter we ever had here since we come to this place it has begun to thaw a little now times is so harde here monney carce, wheat 60 cents a bushel and taxies high 5 cents on the dollar. the boys are in Osage in the boochier waile and ire ding well most of the old inhabitents is ded or moved away there are but few you would know it has ben a long time since I got a letter from you it seems you have almost forgot en me I should be glad to hear from you often but I cont see to write verry well I would be glad to see you all and have thought some times of trying to come out there but dont know how it will bee I would like to know how you are getting a long and all the rest of them yor folks is ill well as common now

March 15 snoweing to day I dont know of enny thing of intrest to write I wish you wold write to me and let now how you are getting a long and all the rest of the connection as to property we hold our one I would write more if I thought you cold make out what it is I should be

11.

Portion of a letter saved in the family genealogy by Leah Miner Kausen.

Afterword

Source Notes

This afterword is simply my way of giving credit to major sources. In the age of the internet, the notion of giving specific credit to every source I came across seemed to me to be outdated. Often, when I scanned the internet for some historical detail, I'd find many sources. An ibid or op cit or just a credit for everything I found seemed unnecessary, and I think doing so would have detracted from the major sources I wanted to credit and, in many cases, thank by highlighting. I met a number of local librarians, a couple in person and others through extensive email contact, who were more helpful than I had any right to expect. Also, the Miner family is blessed with several excellent genealogists. One provided my first exposure to Allen's adventures; others provided extensive detail not available anywhere else. Chapter by chapter credits follow.

Fields, Mistress Mary quite contrary

I relied heavily on several genealogies. There is a very thorough one entitled Miner Family History from George Buck Miner and put together by Elvie Burnell Thomas with Leah Miner Kausen as an acknowledged co-contributor. My interest in the genealogy began with Leah Miner Kausen's own work dated 1967 in which she credits Ruth A. French as particularly helpful.

A couple of facts that would be helpful in this chapter have remained sketchy despite all the research done. Reference to the birth of the main character, Allen Miner, is clear about the date but very general about the location. All references refer to the county, Steuben, NY, but not any location within the county. I ended up using a landowner map dated 1857 that showed ownership in Steuben

County by several Miner families and chose one in Greenwood that I considered most likely. I must admit another motive for the choice. The location I chose fit well with the story I wanted to tell. Allen's parents can't be traced accurately either. Not even DNA matches on Ancestry seem to help.

Used a couple of sources for sections on leather care and making oak barrels. The Reenactor's Guide to Leather Care in the 19th Century, By David Jarnagin & Ken R Knopp. Weis, Nat, PDF, How American Oak Barrels Are Made, Silver Oak Winery.

Headed for Painted Post, Watch Out for that Felloe

Couldn't help the pun, it just happened. Wheel construction and repair fascinated me, though I guess I could understand a reader finding it all just a bit much.

For background on Allen Miner Sr's friend, Nicholas Brotzman, see Genealogy Trails History Group, Stueben County, New York History and Genealogy, History of Jasper, NY, Canisteo Times 16 Aug. 1922, page 9, cols. 4-6.

For general information on wagon wheel repair the best source is Sandra and Tim, YouTube · WAY OUT WEST, Repairing A Carriage Wheel Without Dismantling It, with Sandra and Tim Jun 2, 2014.

Cider apple information comes from The Apple Hunter, by Fran McManus, photography by Miana Jun. The piece details the study of 19th century cider apples by Michael Clifford. It's fun to read if you really like detail—as much fun as the felloe.

Painted Post, Land of the Post

Local historical societies have been important sources again and again as I dug into local lore. Communicating with them and even visiting them has been one of the joys of research. For this chapter and the following one, I visited The Corning-Painted Post Historical Society and spoke with Monica Nix. She referred me to the Archivist Sheri Golder and through Sheri I reached Emily Simms, the Steuben County Historian. They provided particularly helpful information about bridges and rivers.

The primary source for citizens of Painted Post or Addison came from the Historical Gazetteer, Steuben County, New York, Part 1 and 2, Compiled by: Millard F. Roberts, John Single Paper Company, Ltd., Syracuse, N.Y., 1891. See Part 2 for the bear story. Further detail on individuals, once I had names and general information about them, came from Ancestry entries.

I used Erwin, Charles H., The History of Painted Post, Section 2 The Antiquity of Painted Post for details on Painted Post history, including information on the development of the lumber trade along the rivers.

The Buffalo Gazette June 29, 1813, page 3 has a good early description of Lundy's Lane and the activity around Buffalo. Allen Miner Sr. might well have brought this edition home from Addison.

Delivering the Goods, Take it easy

Information on rafts for transporting lumber is generally available. My primary source was the Historical Gazetteer of Steuben County, New York With Memoirs and Illustrations. Compiled and Edited By Millard F. Roberts, Publisher, Syracuse, N. Y. 1891. Transcribed by Jennifer Payne.

Home, Happy Trails

Allen, Sr. reads from the paper he brought home, The Buffalo Gazette dated June 29, 1813.

Militia, Off to Lundy's Lane

Information on the trails Allen Miner, Sr. and his son Allen might have taken are difficult to sort out. My best source turned out to be Family Search, Wiki Mohawk or Iroquois Trail, Migration routes for early European settlers to and from Steuben County, New York Genealogy.

Originally, I picked up local names near Greenwood and on up Bennetts Creek, like Stephens and Moore, from a map dated 1857 showing property ownership in Steuben County at that time. Lionel Pincus and Princess Firyal Map Division, The New York Public Library. "A topographical map of Steuben Co., New York" The New

York Public Library Digital Collections. 1857. It's an 1857 map, so I went from there to various genealogies for detail, especially one from The Painted Hills Genealogical Society. Canisteo, (From the History of Steuben County, New York by Clayton 1879), Submitted by PHGS member, Pam Davis.
https://www.paintedhills.org/STEUBEN/canisteo1.html

Decisions, Return

Information about Niagara and Buffalo supply trails as well as ideas about New England resistance to the war were taken from several sources. For instance, see Rochester History, Vol. 4, Oct. 1942 Vol. 4, War on Lake Ontario: 1812-1815, by Ruth Marsh and Dorothy S. Truedale.

I took information on Brigadier General Winfield Scott and his training routines from an American Battlefield Trust article, Winfield Scott in the War of 1812.

Off to Kentucky, Where?

For the relatives in Kentucky Allen leaves to visit, I used the 1820 census that lists John and Thomas Miner as residents of Shelby County and Shelby County tax lists from 1795 and 1797. The tax lists credit Thomas Miner with 100 acres near Gesses Creek.

The William Wombough trip to Philadelphia is mentioned in the Addison Gazetteer referenced above.

The Cumberland Gap, Allen Reaches Maturity and A Revelation, In the Dark of the Night

I used a detailed work as the basis for my description of the trails. History of Transportation in the United States before 1860, Carnegie Institution of Washington, Publication No. 215 c.

The whole story of what happened to Allen Miner Jr. on his way to visit his Kentucky relatives is my novelistic addition.

Kentucky, Home away from Home

For the Kentucky family names I used member entries, census data, and marriage records from Ancestry.

I took the description of the mouth bow from Wikipedia, 'Musical Bow'. As usual there are many references included in this Wiki entry. To hear the musical bow played, check out Buffy Sainte Marie "Cripple Creek".

The lyrics for the song about home are taken from Simpson, Alaba (2007) "Oral Tradition and the Slave Trade in Nigeria, Ghana, and Benin," African Diaspora Archaeology Newsletter: Vol. 10: Iss. 1, Article 9, p. 14.

Baptized Licking-Locust, What?

Took the name John Clynes and his property on Tick Creek from the 1795 tax list for Shelby County.

The Baptist History Homepage, Wright State University, CORE Scholar, Leland Baptist College, Georgetown, Kentucky has a search function I found particularly useful for issues related to The Baptist-Licking Locust Association as well as other names and places of interest in this chapter.

The Antislavery Movement in Clermont County, Bethany Marie Pollitt, Wright State University, p. 13-16 has a brief but useful description of the Kentucky Baptist Licking-Locust Associations origins and its connections to Claremont, Ohio.

Time to Leave, I'll Become a....

Picked up the A. L. Duncan name as a lawyer involved in Steamboat cases from Rolling on the River: Preserving America's Steamboats, by Claire Profilet Cothren, p. 15 and then used Ancestry for further information about the family.

For information on George Waller and his connections to the Bethel Church near Clay and to Louisville Baptists see William Cathcart, editor, The Baptist Encyclopedia, 1881; rpt. 1988, p. 1205.

The transition from the Baptized Licking Locust Association to the Kentucky Anti-slavery Society and the connection to Claremont, Ohio is mentioned in The Antislavery Movement in Clermont County referenced in the previous Chapter.

<u>Triumph at the Falls: The Louisville and Portland Canal</u>, Leland R. Johnson and Charles E. Parrish, Louisville District U.S. Army Corps of Engineers, Louisville, Kentucky has information on the falls and the canal.

Louisville, A New Life?

Took information on Pendleton County and the Baptist church there, as well as tales of David Barrow, from several sources including the dissertation referenced above, The Antislavery Movement in Clermont County, Bethany Marie Pollitt. The most concise account on Barrow came from Harper, K. (2015). "A Strange Kind of Christian": David Barrow and Involuntary, Unmerited, Perpetual, Absolute, Hereditary Slavery, Examined; on the Principles of Nature, Reason, Justice, Policy, and Scripture. Ohio Valley History 15(3), 68-77. https://www.muse.jhu.edu/article/597316.

See previous chapter entry, <u>Triumph at the Falls</u>, for information about James Guthrie.

"Free" Ohio, Lindale

Information on Tibbets and Coombs families is readily available on the Tibbets History Facebook page and on the related Tibbets Family Antislavery History site. Also, I used the online page Ball State University, Indiana Crosswords: Hoosier Civil Rights, John H. and Sarah Tibbets Home.

Martin Pease and reference to his naval capture and transport to NYC during the Revolutionary War can be found in <u>The Official roster of the soldiers of the American Revolution buried in the state of Ohio</u>, Vol. III., Roster listings.

The best information I found on Pease's friend Elijah Hayward came from <u>The Supreme Court of Ohio & The Ohio Judicial System</u>, accessed through The Thomas J. Moyer Ohio Judicial Center.

Cincinnati Docks, Down to the Docks

Hayward's pro-slavery views, referred to at the beginning of the chapter, can be inferred from his support of Andrew Jackson.

Cincinnati referred to as Porkopolis because of the hog slaughter houses down near the docks is well known, but see Donald Ralph MacKenzie, Painters In Ohio, 1788-1860 With a Biographical Index for one reference.

See Triumph at the Falls, above referenced for chapter "Time to Leave" for information on the Maysville, warping, and capstans.

A brief description of Daniel H. Vail's life and his time as captain of the General Clark can be found in the following genealogy— Genealogy of Some of the Vail Family Descended from Jeremiah Vail at Salem, Mass., 1639, pg. 146. Search for Page 151.

Cincinnati Hills, Up to the Hills

Information about the newspapers that Hayward eventually did edit can be found by searching for Elijah Hayward in The Supreme Court of Ohio & The Ohio Judicial System, accessed through The Thomas J. Moyer Ohio Judicial Center. Also mentions his law practice with David Wade.

I used The Cincinnati Directories for 1819, Published by Oliver Farnsworth, and 1825, by Harvey Hall to locate where lawyers mentioned in this chapter and the previous chapter lived. It's clear from the addresses that they lived up in the hills. Elijah Hayward and Daniel Wade did live in the same house.

References to potential land ownership legal cases can be found by Goggling "The Land Act of 1820". I used The Ohio History Connection, Ohio History Central, The Land Act of 1820.

Lindale, A New Home

For information on the Tibbets and Coombs families, including the Lindale Baptist Church founders, I again used the Tibbets History Facebook page and the related Tibbets Family Antislavery History site.

I found a description of the psychology behind the plantation owners view of overseers and by extension auctioneers and slave traders as the lowest of fellow Whites in Overseer Violence on Eighteenth Century Plantations, By Robert D. Bland, June 5, 2019,

African American History Society, Black Perspectives. Robert Bland references <u>Masters of Violence: The Plantation Overseers and Eighteenth-Century Virginia, South Carolina, and Georgia,</u> by Tristan Stubbs, as a source. Allen refers to this attitude in several chapters.

Note that the capitalization of White and Black is a subject of ongoing controversy. Generally, the current tendency is to capitalize Black but not White. I capitalize both when they refer to race.

Sophina, Life Moves On and Courting, Western Style

No references worth mentioning.

Changing Times, Pro-Slavery Backlash

I took information on the 1820 Land Act from the Wikipedia entry the 'Land Act of 1820'. Plenty of references for details. See: https://www.blackpast.org/african-american-history/1804-ohio-black-codes/ for the 1804 Black Slave Code. Took information on the 1807 revision from Wikipedia, 'Black Laws of 1804 and 1807'.

<u>The Antislavery Movement in Clermont County</u>, Bethany Marie Pollitt, Wright State University, p. 49 mentions the participation of Andrew Coombs, Jr. in the Underground Railroad.

Reference to the Rankins' beacon on the hill can be found simply by searching for it. The National Park Service refers to their home on the hill overlooking the Ohio River as part of the Underground Railroad.

Organize? How

For information on Clermont County anti-slavery societies in the 1830s see <u>The Antislavery Movement in Clermont County</u>, Bethany Marie Pollitt, Wright State University, p. 31.

The various attacks on Theodore Weld and his audiences when he spoke about the virtues of the anti-slavery cause are documented in <u>The Passionate Liberator, Theodore Weld & the Dilemma of Reform</u>, By Robert H. Abzug, Oxford University Press, 1980, pg. 125. This book also covers entries in The Liberator containing the Lane Students' "Statement of Reasons".

For a short description of the Hall of Free Discussion and the ex-Lane students' use of what was also called the Ludlow House see The Hamilton Avenue Road to Freedom, Hall of Free Discussion, pg. 283.

Information on James Bradley, one of the best sources is his own letter to the editor of The Oasis from Lane Seminary in June of 1834. https://www2.oberlin.edu/external/EOG/LaneDebates/BradleyLetter.htm

For Thome see the Debate at the Lane Seminary, Cincinnati: Speech of James A. Thome, of Kentucky, delivered at the annual meeting of the American Anti-Slavery Society, May 6, 1834.

Slavery, Timorous Cautionists or Not

For the Thome speech I used Debate at the Lane Seminary, Cincinnati: Speech of James A. Thome, of Kentucky, delivered at the annual meeting of the American Anti-Slavery Society, May 6, 1834. For Bradley's speech I used Bradley's own letter to the editor of The Oasis from Lane Seminary in June of 1834. I made slight edits to make it sound more like a speech and to clarify where my editor suggested.

Anti-Slavery Societies, Immediate Emancipation

For the Lane Anti-Slavery Society preamble and constitution see The Library of Congress, The Standard—Extra, Preamble and constitution of the anti-slavery society of Lane Seminary.

A Balm in Gilead, Lindale Baptists Heal Themselves

"There is a balm in Gilead to make the wounded whole", Nina Simone. The healing for all involved in slavery is critical to anti-slavery arguments. Scripture for a balm in Gilead Jeremiah 46:11.

The 1836 attacks and the two pro-slavery placards can be found in the Wikipedia entry 'Cincinnati Riots of 1836'. Also, see Ford below. Captain Perrin and the Moselle. See History of Cincinnati, Ohio, with illustrations and biographical sketches, by Henry A. Ford and Kate B. Ford, Scholar's Choice, pg. 88,89.

Images of the Clermont Gilead Anti-Slavery Society minutes were provided by Ohio History Connections, Selections, Gilead Anti-Slavery Society of Clermont County Minutes. Thanks to Lauren Kennedy and Jenni Salamon for arranging permission to use them.

Indiana Tour, Ripley, Believe It

Physical description of Otter Creek, Ripley, Indiana comes from photos like those that picture the Otter Creek bridge.

I took information about Ichabod Sheldon as the pastor from the Indiana Department of Natural Resources, Division of Historic Preservation & Archaeology, The Story of the Union Church in Ripley County. The document stated that Ichabod Sheldon was replaced by Elder John Courtney in 1845. I assumed that Pastor Sheldon might have been available when Allen and John visited the area. The church was well known for its Anti-Slavery views.

Indiana Historical Society, Early Black Settlements by County, Rush County has a description of the African American community of Beech, the Resident Willis Rogers, and the Quaker influence.

The National Park Service, National Road, America's First Federally Funded Highway has a simple map showing the route of the National Road through Indiana including the cities of Richmond and Indianapolis. For the history of the Michigan Road there is an ample summary provided by the online site The Historic Michigan Road, Explore Indiana's Pioneer Highway, under About the Road. It also contains a simple map.

Society Business, The Mundane

For the financial crash information, I relied on the Wikipedia article 'Panic of 1837'.

For Channing's letter and Birney's response I consulted the original paper 'The Liberator', 02 Jan 1837 using Newspapers.com.

Indiana, An Ally

The Wikipedia article 'Panic of 1837' mentions the change to gold specie for land purchases.

The macadamization of portions of the National Road is described in 'Touring Ohio, The Heart of America', under Ohio's Road, National Road.

Levi Coffin wrote his own story late in life, 'Reminiscences of Levi Coffin, the Reputed President of the Underground Railroad, Robert Clarke & Co., 1880. The stories I used came from the electronic version created by Academic Affairs Library, UNC-CH, University of North Carolina at Chapel Hill, 2001 with funding from The Institute for Museum and Library Services.

Indiana Plans, Jeffersonville Meeting

I found the actual land record for Allen Miner's purchase by searching Amazon Land Office Records. The Indiana purchase specifies Jeffersonville as the site of the land office and the date as August 10, 1838.

John Tibbets' purchase of 40 acres is confirmed by the land record from the US department of the Interior, Bureau of Land Management, General Land Office Records, dated August 15, 1838. Issac Jones on the same day purchased 40 acres at the same Jeffersonville land office. The township and range for both purchases are the same.

Risky Business, Ride through the Night

Stories in this chapter are based on 'Reminiscences of Slavery Times', written by John Tibbets in his 70th year (1888). A copy can be found on the Tibbets History Facebook page, dated August 5, 2011, last edited May 5, 2021.

On Their Way, New Friends

For a description of the modified farm wagons, I used National Oregon/California Trail Center, Historical Trails, Trail Basics-The Wagon.

Indianapolis, Dreams

Used an Ancestry entry created by Debra Hutchins Duncan for basic information on Hezekiah Hutchins. The entry included his residence in Perry Indiana north of Levi's place.

Information on horseshoes, nails, and the clincher can be found in the Wikipedia entry, Farrier. Best reference given is Cherry Hill's Horse Hoof Care under Finishing, by Richard Klimesh (2009).

Information on the Potawatomie Trail of Death comes from the Wikipedia entry with that title. This entry was remarkably complete and well written.

Indianapolis 2000, Cincinnati 40,000. Wikipedia, Timeline of Indianapolis, gives an 1840 population of 2692 referencing The Encyclopedia of Indianapolis, Edited by David J. Bodenhamer and Robert G. Barrows, Indiana University Press, 1994. Online under US Biggest Cities the 1840 census gives the population of Cincinnati as 46,338.

A description of the early Washington Street Market can be found in The Encyclopedia of Indianapolis, Downtown Indianapolis, The evolving heart of the city, By David G. Vanderstel, January 22, 2021.

Samuel Merrill and wife Lydia and house sharer Calvin Fletcher are well known in Indiana history. See Fletcher's own Wiki entry. Merrill has a Wiki entry too with references. For their joint ownership and the moves involved see the Blake Family Collection, ca. 1830–1977, Manuscript and Visual Collections Department, William Henry Smith Memorial Library, Indiana Historical Society.

Otter Creek Indiana, A New Life

The side road to Otter Creek may very well have been as bad as I described; many roads to remote farm communities were.

John Miller and Patsy Ruby were not childless. Altered history here to fit my narrative.

Madison Indiana, A Young Man's Dreaming

James and Lucy Nelson are mentioned as strong anti-slavery people in 'Reminiscences of Slavery Times', written by John Tibbets in his 70th year (1888) when he records his marriage to their daughter Sarah Ann Nelson.

The PDF Underground Railroad Network to Freedom, The Story of Georgetown District in Madison, Indiana contains information on

Elijah Anderson, the Black Underground Railroad leader from Georgetown as well as a description of the low water levels of the Ohio river at Madison. It also mentions Elijah Anderson's light skin allowing him to transport slaves to freedom by posing as a White master traveling with his slaves.

Farm Life, Community Effort

Took information for historical methods of clearing stumps from "For pioneers, farming started with stump clearing" by Marilyn Salzi Brinkman published in the Feb. 14, 2015 edition of the St. Cloud Times, Saint Cloud, Minnesota. Also, How Settlers Cleared Their Land by Gwen Tuinman.

Information about the Neil's Creek Anti-Slavery Society was taken from the Minute Book of the Neil's Creek Anti-Slavery Society 1839-1845 provided by the Jefferson County Historical Society. Thanks to Victoria Duncan, Rare Books & Manuscripts Division Supervisor, Indiana State Library for providing permission for including the related illustrations.

Information about the 1838 drought and the 1839 Spring weather came from Ball, Timothy H. 1900. Northwestern Indiana from 1800 to 1900 or A View of Our Region Through the Nineteenth Century. Chicago, Illinois: Donohue and Henneberry.

Neil's Creek Anti-Slavery Society, Developments

Members' names and what they decided to include in their society constitution are taken directly from the Minute Book of the Neil's Creek Anti-Slavery Society 1839-1845 provided by the Jefferson County Historical Society.

William Anderson's story comes from his own life narrative the Life and Narrative of William J. Anderson, Twenty-four Years a Slave; Sold Eight Times! In Jail Sixty Times!! Whipped Three Hundred Times!!! The electronic version was produced by UNC-CH digitization project, Documenting the American South, transcribed from a photocopy supplied by the University of Minnesota, Minneapolis.

Wikipedia covers the Pinckney Resolution under Gag rule (United States), an apt description. The Wiki reference is The Constitutional and Political History of the United States by Von Holst, H. (Hermann), digitized by Google from the library of the University of Michigan.

Wisconsin? Why?

1839 financial crisis reaches mid-west and farming. See "What Caused the Crisis of 1839? by John Joseph Wallis type in page 17 actual 15.

Details for this chapter like Samuel Lewis' home with as many as 24 occupants including the Johnson's, Native American trails, the friendly Winnebagos, Chief Little Thunder, early residents, and more come from the History of Union Township, by Ruth Ann Montgomery, Evansville Historian.

http://evansvillehistory.net/files/Union_Township_History.html

News from Wisconsin, Moving On

Details for this chapter (like Peter Aller's marriage to Ebenezer Temple's daughter Eleanor as the first recorded marriage in Union, the positions of Allen Miner and David Johnson in the first organization of Union, the position of Fence Viewer, and the difficulty of getting farm produce to market) come from the History of Union Township, by Ruth Ann Montgomery, Evansville Historian. See entry for previous chapter.

Calhoun and the importance to farmers of fences. Danhof, Clarence H. "The Fencing Problem in the Eighteen-Fifties." Agricultural History, vol. 18, no. 4, 1944, pp. 168–86. JSTOR. http://www.jstor.org/stable/3739332 Accessed 16 July 2023.

The town meeting as party time and the Jessie Aller fight is described in Pioneer Days of Evansville and Vicinity, by Byron Campbell, pg. 8.

For information on fences—rock, live Osage Orange, and split rail see History of Early American Landscape Design, Fence section, A Project of the Center for Advanced Study in the Visual Arts, National Gallery of Art.

Wisconsin Politics, What's Happening?

The interest of Allen Miner and Jacob West in the Whig Party is confirmed later in 1848. Both are listed as representatives from Union to the Whig Party nominating convention. Reported in the Janesville Gazette (Janesville, Wisconsin), 1848 October 12.

Getting Involved, Support

See Britannica article, "The Whig Party years and disappointment of Henry Clay" for the history of Henry Clay's Whig presidential candidate attempts.

The difference between eastern and western Wisconsin on the issue of slavery is fully explained in Wisconsin Magazine of History Archives, Wisconsin magazine of history: Volume 52, number 3, spring, 1969, pg. 253. Pg. 254 mentions the Racine Anti-Slavery Society meeting.

Reverend Edward Mathews is described as an ardent and courageous anti-slavery advocate in Wisconsin Magazine of History Archives, Wisconsin magazine of history: Volume 52, number 3, spring, 1969, pg. 248.

For Henry Crandall's house as place Seventh Day Baptists met see "Architectural and Historical Survey of Milton Wisconsin", by Carol Lohry, Cartwright, Milton Historic Preservation Commission: City of Milton, Wisconsin, 2013, pg. 6.

A brief synopsis of Joseph Goodrich's life and his academy can be found in the Historical Essay, Goodrich, Joseph 1800-1867, Wisconsin Historical Society.

The use of the ferry to transport runaway slaves across Lake Koshkonong operated by Joseph Goodrich's brother William is recorded in Welch, Doug, "The Milton House and the Underground Railroad." The Wisconsin Magazine of History, vol. 103, no. 1, 2019, pp. 19-20. JSTOR, https://www.jstor.org/stable/26864290. accessed 22 July 2023. Doug Welch exchanged emails with me giving me helpful information. Much appreciated.

Racine, Anti-Slavery Society Meeting

Milton, Henry Crandall's house "Architectural and Historical Survey of Milton Wisconsin", by Carol Lohry, Cartwright, Milton Historic Preservation Commission: City of Milton, Wisconsin, 2013, pg. 6.

Information about Edward Mathews, Wisconsin Anti-Slavery Society founder, comes from Edward Mathews. "An Abolitionist in Territorial Wisconsin: The Journal of Reverend Edward Mathews (Part IV)." The Wisconsin Magazine of History, vol. 52, no. 4, 1969, pp. 330–43. JSTOR. http://www.jstor.org/stable/4634462. accessed 26 July 2023.

Information about William Allan of the Illinois Anti-Slavery Society as well as quotations from his Lane Seminary speech come from "William T. Allan – Lane Rebel from the South", by Ron Gorman, Oberlin Heritage Center volunteer docent.

The Chespeake Steamship. After the Civil War, Dutton would reveal to the most well-known of Underground Railroad historians, Wilbur H. Siebert, that the Chespeake was indeed a go to ship for trips to Canada by run-aways. Dutton turned out to be the only Wisconsinite mentioned by the scrupulously inclusive Siebert, an indication of just how important this link became.

Time to Meet, Plans

The fear by Whigs that their opposition to the annexation of Texas cost Clay the election is documented in Morrison, Michael A., "Westward the Curse of Empire: Texas Annexation and the American Whig Party." Journal of the Early Republic, vol. 10, no. 2, 1990, pp. 221–49. JSTOR.

Allen Miner Jacob West, and S. B. Lewis are listed as Whig representatives from Union Township in the Janesville Gazette, October 12, 1848. Peter Aller's Whig affiliation was assumed.

Private Lives, Public Lives, Sad Days

For Clay's loss and the Texas annexation, see Morrison above.

For Conscience Whigs and Cotton Whigs see Britannica, History and Society, United States presidential election of 1848, Whig Party.

For the Albion Baptist Church see Welch above pg. 20.

For Jesse Saunders' part in the church see: https://freepages.rootsweb.com/~fitchett/genealogy/Person_Sheets/ps33/ps33_310.html accessed 02/25/2024.

A brief description of issues and conventions leading to Wisconsin statehood see Wisconsin State Constitutions of 1846 and 1848, Wisconsin Historical Society.

Wilmot Provision information comes from U.S. presidential election of 1848 Britannica, History and Society, United States presidential election of 1848, Candidates and issues.

For his marriage to Emeline Wolcott Caldwell see Allen Miner Wikitree.

For those representing Union Township at the 1848 Whig convention held in Janesville—Samuel Lewis, Jacob West, Alanson B. Vaughan, and Allen Miner—see the Janesville Gazette, October 12, 1848.

For information on the Free Soil Party and the Buffalo Convention Platform see Britannica, History and Society, United States presidential election of 1848, Campaign and results.

For the 1850 "Compromise" and its history as well as William Lloyd Garrison's rejection of politics and the union see "Garrison's Constitution, The Covenant with Death and How It Was Made", National Archives, Winter 2000, Vol. 32, No. 4, By Paul Finkelman.

California Ho, Gold—Yes. Ice?

Genealogical information comes from an exceptional genealogy by Elvie Burnell Thomas mentioned earlier in this afterword under **Fields, Mistress Mary quite contrary**. Her credits include Leah Miner Kausen as a primary collaborator and help with various branches of the family from Denis Edeline and Ruth Morehead French.

For information on the development of the ice industry I used a Wikipedia quotation from Cummings, Richard O. (1949). The American Ice Harvests: A Historical Study in Technology, 1800–1918.

Steamboat history came from Switzer, Ronald R., The Steamboat and Missouri River Commerce, University of Oklahoma Press. It was so helpful that I purchased the Kindle Edition.

See https://www.findagrave.com/memorial/45388162/jacob-miner for Jacob's success in the ice and teaming business and his marriage. See also the Elvie Burnell Thomas genealogy above.

For Placerville history including the quotation see City of Placerville California, Our City, Placerville City History.

Different Opportunities, Different Places

Careful readers may note that I have my characters recorded in a July 1856 census as residing in Mitchell, Iowa but then I have them in Linn, Kansas prior to that date. Census data would have to be collected well prior to the publication date.

The Elvie Burnell Thomas genealogy was used several times in this chapter.

Information about and quotations related to the Kansas/Missouri conflict prior to the Civil War came from several sources, listed below.

Ball, Durwood; Army Regulars on the Western Frontier, 1848–1861.

A History of Lawrence, by Rev. Richard Cordley, (Kansas Collection Books), chapter VII, Published by E. F. Caldwell, LAWRENCE, KANSAS, 1895, LAWRENCE JOURNAL PRESS. Provided the quotation from the Quaker volunteer and other information about the Fort Franklin battle. Rev. Cordley was an early settler and pastor in Lawrence.

US History, Bloody Kansas, Canefight! Preston Brooks and Charles Sumner, see O'Bryan, Tony, "Jayhawkers" Civil War on the Western Border: The Missouri-Kansas Conflict, 1854-1865. The Kansas City Public Library

O'Bryan, Tony, "Red Legs" Civil War on the Western Border: The Missouri-Kansas Conflict, 1854-1865.

Soodalter, Ron, The 1861 Jayhawker Raid in Osceola, under Missouri History, Missouri Life Magazine (March 31, 2020).

Moving On, Epic Journey to Walla Walla WA

Cecil S. G. Cummings, My Life in the Walla Walla Valley, 1978. The description of the trip with the details of places and happenings are from this account. Cecil Cummings in turn credits Gideon Cummings writing "I have taken the following accounts approximately as they appear in Gideon Cumming's diary." I have reworded the account instead of using quotations or crediting each instance. I've updated place names and descriptions as I find more accurate ones.

Cyrus Miner is not mentioned in the Cummings' account and probably not in the diary, but the Elvin Burnell Thomas genealogy makes clear that he took part. I have added the conversations and opinions whenever Cyrus or others speak or are credited with opinions. I try to imagine what they might have said or thought. Cecil Cummings does not use the word 'entrepreneur' as I do but does express the frustration felt about increasing prices as the trip progresses. The inclusion of General James Blunt in the telegraph message is my addition, though the Cecil Cummings account does mention the telegraph report of the bad war.

Other sources include the Kansas State Historical Society, Manuscript division, Samuel Lyle and Florella Brown Adair Family Collection and the Kansas Historical Society, Manuscript Div., John Ingalls, letter to his father, May 21, 1859.

Coming Together? Mitchell Iowa

Most of my information about Mitchell Iowa and what the Miners and other characters did there comes from a single source. Lori Mark scanned the records of the Mitchell County Iowa Historical Society using a list of names I provided for the purpose. The results were voluminous with relevant information from contemporary press reports, the "History of Mitchell and Worth Counties, Iowa" 1883-84 and 1917, and the Mitchell County Iowa History 1989, and a genealogy by Starla Cassman. The detail included marriage records, land sales, business enterprises, platting records, offices held, church membership, biographies, burial records, and so much more. Lori even included a wagon train trail map and a train schedule at my request, helping me to solve, at least to my satisfaction, an issue that has bothered a number of family genealogists. How did family members seem to be in Iowa and California at approximately the same time? All the Iowa related chapters use this information. Thank you, Lori Mark and Starla Cassmann.

Much of the source information on the Oglala Sioux comes from Crazy Horse The Strange Man of the Oglalas, Mari Sandoz.

Information on the Potawatomie Trail of Death comes from the Wikipedia entry with that title.

Mitchell Reunion 2, Not to Be

See Lori Mark for Iowa family information, as in the previous chapter.

Information on Mark Twain and on Cyrus Miner's trips to Nevada in part comes from the History of Humboldt County, California, by Leigh H. Irvine, published in 1915.

Even more information on Mark Twain and the stories he told came from the web site www.twainquotes.com, created by Barbara Schmidt, web site publisher, Virginia City Territorial Enterprise 1862-1868, newspaper articles.

Marysville? Mitchell?

The Black Hawk capture and release of Charles Johnston is taken from the History of Humboldt County referenced in the prior chapter. It's not the most reliable of sources, and the Charles Johnston mentioned may not be the same Charles Johnston I'm following here.

Information on Wyatt Earp's Iowa to California trip taken a year before the trip described here comes from Wyatt Earp: Facts, Vol. V, By Wagon Train From Iowa To California – 1864. It includes mileage information, horses vs. oxen, and other useful details. Also used the Encyclopedia Britannica Prairie Schooner article by William E. Hill, as well as many other online sources for trail information.

The Cape Horn trip discussed in this chapter was well known at the time. Details come from several sources. The Miner family History by Elvie Burnell Thomas mentions Lucinda (Miner} Dudley's trip with her three children.

Off to Marysville, Separate Ways

A fine description of the luxury Lucinda would have experienced on her steamboat trips can be found in A History of the Missouri River, by Philip E. Chappell.

Most of the Steamboat details such as those about the sinking of the Bertrand, the Herndon House stories, the location of the A. J. Majors at the time, etc. came from The Steamboat Bertrand and Missouri River Commerce, by Ronald R. Switzer. Note, Bob Wright was not the captain of the A. J. Majors. I just picked a captain's name because no one I could find mentions the captain of the A. J. Majors.

Most of the trail details including optimum departure times, food along the way, dangers, and much more came from the Backwoods Home Magazine article Oregon Trail preparedness: What supplies did the settlers carry? by Don Lewis, Issue #176 • April/May/June, 2019.

Children on the Mormon Trail, A thesis presented to the department of history Brigham Young University by Jill Jacobsen Andros, December 1997 gives actual accounts that I used to describe the children's activities. Also used in the next chapter.

Long Way to Go, Through Better or Worse

The elaborate description of the M. S. Mepham comes from the University of Wisconsin Libraries, M. S. Mepham (Packet 1864-1868). I added a guess about the gold mentioned and a couple of other changes to the quotation to clarify. Captain Thomasson is mentioned as the master.

Information about the horse buying and selling racket along the trails comes from Wyatt Earp: Facts, Vol. V, By Wagon Train From Iowa To California – 1864. The book also describes the conflicts among the settlers themselves.

The Wyoming Historical Society article, Crossing the North Platte River, provides information on the trail and the telegraph. For the Fort Laramie telegraph the easiest reference is The Historical Marker Database. The Fort Laramie marker had all I needed.

Easy Ways, Well...

There are many sources describing the conflicts between the Crow and Sioux and conflicts between settlers and natives often involving the army. I chose The Wyoming Historical Society articles The Battles of Platte Bridge Station and Red Buttes, and Connor's Powder River Expedition of 1865, both by Ellis Hein, as main sources.

Welcome to San Francisco, The Emperor

For the description of the emperor, I used the one I found in Norton I *Emperor of America and Protector of Mexico*, a 2 act play by Arthur W. Ritchie and Barbara J. Agins. Barbara Agins, a good friend, let me know about the emperor and her play.

Marysville, Long Awaited Family Reunion, sort of

Description of the stagecoach incident is based on Genealogy Trails. A Brief History of the Stagecoach Decorum, Capt. John Silas, Pioneer Stage and Rail Man.

Ideas for the homecoming meal were taken from Food Timeline FAQs: 19th century American foodways and Mary Randolph, The Virginia Housewife (1824).

The description of the turkey pin feathers comes from History. Because It's Here!!, Drive a Thanksgiving Turkey! powered by Weebly.

Home, Marysville, Mitchell, Mattole?

THE STAGE COMPANY HIERARCHY, By Mary A. Helmich, Interpretation and Education Division, California State Parks, 2008 was my source for stagecoach company organization.

Old Settlers Gazette, 2007, California State Parks, Lawsuit against the South-Western Stage Company, by John Bradbury provided information on conditions experienced by stagecoach passengers.

Deer Creek Station as a stagecoach stop can be found under the name by searching the Wyoming Historical Society.

Too Long Delayed, Mitchell Reunion

For church affiliations in Mitchell, I used Lori Mark's scanning of the records of the Mitchell County Iowa Historical Society referenced above under the chapter Coming Together? Mitchell Iowa.

Welcome Home, Mr. Adventure

I took information about Iowa's progressive history from The Fortnightly Review, The Historical Case for the Iowa Caucuses, By Jon Lauck. The article is thorough with extensive credits. Here's a sample, "AFTER THE CIVIL WAR, Iowa became known for its racial tolerance. In 1868, Iowans voted to extend full suffrage rights to Blacks, joining five New England states and Minnesota as the only states to do so. In the 1860s and 1870s, Iowa courts ruled that Black students should be allowed to attend school with White children and that racial segregation on steamboats and other common carriers was illegal, steps that preceded many other Northern states. In 1884 and 1892 the Iowa state legislature adopted a civil rights law and prohibited discrimination in hotels, public transportation, barber shops, theaters, restaurants, lunch counters, bathhouses, and other facilities." The article also mentions the active participation of pastors.

Facts about Allen Miner's legal work in Iowa come from the work done for me by Lori Mark mentioned several times in previous Afterword entries. Allen is listed as an election judge. His obituary in the Mitchell County Press mentions his active participation in the M. E. church from its founding.

And then…, Again, On to the Mattole River, The Marysville Settlers, and On to the Mattole Valley, via the Mattole River

These three final chapters have similar sources. A description of the bizarre trip down the Mattole River came to my attention when reading the first genealogy on the Miner family I came across, put together by Leah Miner Kausen with an acknowledgment of help from others, especially Mrs. Ruth A. French.

The Kausen genealogy contained an article from The Humboldt Times, March 1, 1953, by Andrew Genzoli. The article mentions that the Miners and the Johnstons were early settlers of the Mattole valley, though not among the first. But they did arrive there by making a memorable journey the article describes "as difficult and spectacular as any recorded in the annals of California history."

The article mentions lots of the details I've included, details I rather recently discovered were provided to Andrew Genzoli by George Buck Miner. George Buck Miner provided further detail in his book The Origin of Mattole Through the Eyes of a Salmon. George's own life story is "as difficult and spectacular" as any you are likely to find. Check out My Darkness under the Sun, his autobiography. Over the last several years we have been in touch trading stories and just talking over the phone—another friend this project has brought my way.

Epilogue

Information for the Epilogue comes primarily from the Elvie Burnell Thomas genealogy.

Illustrations

Fields, Mistress Mary Quite Contrary

Sketch, illustrating young Allen's garden game, provided by 11-year-old Eddie White, the author's grandson, close enough to Allen's age at the time recorded in the chapter.

A Balm in Gilead, Lindale Baptists Heal Themselves

Courtesy of the Ohio History Connection, image number Om_1156106_002. Special thanks to Lauren Kennedy and Jenni Salamon.

Society Business, The Mundane

Courtesy of the Ohio History Connection, image number Om_1156106_011.

Neil's Creek Anti-Slavery Society, Developments

Courtesy of the Indiana State Library, Rare Books & Manuscripts. Special thanks to staff members Victoria Duncan – Supervisor and A.J. Chrapliwy—Assistant.

Epilogue

Portion of a letter saved in the family genealogy by Leah Miner Kausen.

About the Author

I grew up in Chatham, NJ living an all too typical, comfortable, suburban life. I did act as the student leader of a very active Congregational Church student youth group. We took trips every year to various places unlike Chatham. Imagine our group visiting a Southern Black Church in the fifties, and you get the idea of just how unlike Chatham. We went to an Ohio farm community, and I remember seeing a bull; so large it was. Went off to college entirely paid for by my parents and passed everything I needed to enter Tufts Medical, but in my junior year I met interesting students studying English Literature; would be doctors, such a boring bunch. So, I switched majors, graduated with a degree in English Literature and entered a master's program at Rutgers.

At Rutgers I met more of those interesting literature majors including my friends Phil Rowe and Lee Parks. We lived together in various locales as we attended graduate school. We all completed course work and oral exams for our PhD's in English but never finished our dissertations. I wrote one, at least, and wrangled some about it with the professor in charge but had to drop it when our first child arrived. Seems I needed to work. That job led to a career in computer software ending with the title Senior Director of Global Services for a small but successful software company in NYC. I loved the city, the commute on NJ Transit, and the job itself, even though a short day was 10 hours.

My teaching career included a year at Western Michigan University and one at Monmouth College where I met my wife. She was the late 60's early 70's leader of the women's liberation movement on campus and she was a farmer's daughter. That bull I saw in Ohio? Well, as a child she would climb a tree, wait for a bull to come along, and drop on its back for a ride. How different from suburbia was that? And yet one date, then three weeks and we decided to marry. Three months later we did and then returned to spend that year at Monmouth. She still puts up with me.

At Western Michigan I became a faculty advisor for the Western Activist newspaper, started by progressive students advocating positions like integration and an end to the Vietnam war in a city and on a campus with newspapers solidly conservative. Recently I returned to campus to celebrate, along with those progressive students and others, the digitalization of the Activist, a project we worked on for several years. I got to speak to current students. My best received line? I advised the young men in the audience that, if they intended to choose a woman for a lifelong partner, choose one with a heart and head stronger than their own, like I had. The young women cheered; the young men had to be satisfied with a give away from me; those women will be smart enough to let you lay claim to the muscle chores.

I've been retired for years now. I spent some of my retirement gardening, splitting wood, sailing, and hiking. I took up blogging on My Space about Obama and the issues surrounding his first 4 years as president. The blogs morphed into a book, <u>Blogging through the Obama Years</u>, still out there on Amazon. We have not resolved any of the issues, so I like to think the book is still relevant. Note, if you buy the paperback, you will receive the improved 2nd edition.

Both my friends from Rutgers, Phil Rowe and Lee Parks, passed away, and since their death I have dug up their unpublished works and published them as a tribute and as a way of giving something to their children who have been part of our life since their birth.

More recently I've been working on this book that Janaway Publishing has been so helpful in publishing. Prior to sending a final copy to them, I needed an editor, so I turned to an editor of submissions to the FDA of Aids medications, my wife, the brains and the heart.

Richard and Blossom

www.ingramcontent.com/pod-product-compliance
Lightning Source LLC
Chambersburg PA
CBHW011719220426
43663CB00018B/2917